Business Culture in Putin's Russia

This book examines how Russia's entrepreneurs operate in a business environment beset with risk and uncertainty. The challenges they may encounter include an unreliable judicial system, insecure property rights, arbitrary interference from officials, as well as corruption, harassment, suspicion and violence. Based on extensive original research, including fieldwork within three businesses, this book explores how entrepreneurs survive and some thrive. It focuses on the kind of obstacles they face from day to day, details their motivations, rationale and methods, and describes the actual relationship between ordinary entrepreneurs and the state, providing new insights into business–state relations.

John Kennedy completed his doctorate at the University of Birmingham.

BASEES/Routledge Series on Russian and East European Studies

For a full list of available titles please visit: https://www.routledge.com/BASEES-Routledge-Series-on-Russian-and-East-European-Studies/book-series/BASEES

This series is published on behalf of BASEES (the British Association for Slavonic and East European Studies). The series comprises original, high-quality, research-level work by both new and established scholars on all aspects of Russian, Soviet, post-Soviet and East European Studies in humanities and social science subjects.

Governing the Soviet Union's National Republics
The second secretaries of the communist party
Saulius Grybkauskas

Putin's Fascists
Russkii Obraz and the politics of managed Nationalism in Russia
Robert Horvath

Building Communism and Policing Deviance in the Soviet Union
Residential childcare, 1958–1991
Mirjam Galley

Translating Great Russian Literature
The Penguin Russian classics
Cathy McAteer

Labour, Mobility and Informal Practices in Russia, Central Asia and Eastern Europe
Power, institutions and mobile actors in transnational space
Edited by Rano Turaeva and Rustamjon Urinboyev

Business Culture in Putin's Russia
John Kennedy

The Donbas Conflict in Ukraine
Elites, protest, and partition
Daria Platonova

Business Culture in Putin's Russia

John Kennedy

Routledge
Taylor & Francis Group
LONDON AND NEW YORK

First published 2022
by Routledge
2 Park Square, Milton Park, Abingdon, Oxon OX14 4RN

and by Routledge
605 Third Avenue, New York, NY 10158

Routledge is an imprint of the Taylor & Francis Group, an informa business

British Library Cataloguing-in-Publication Data
A catalogue record for this book is available from the British Library

Library of Congress Cataloging-in-Publication Data
A catalog record has been requested for this book

ISBN: 978-1-138-60308-0 (hbk)
ISBN: 978-1-032-10078-4 (pbk)
ISBN: 978-0-429-46917-6 (ebk)

DOI: 10.4324/9780429469176

Typeset in Times New Roman
by SPi Technologies India Pvt Ltd (Straive)

Contents

Preface

This book is about contemporary Russian business culture. In Russia, where the state has been the 'dominant force' in the economy throughout history (Connolly 2020: 6), conditions for private enterprise have always been challenging and property rights weak, while in the popular imagination *biznes* (business) is still as much associated with crime and corruption as it is with legitimate enterprise. To an extent, the story of contemporary Russian business is the story of post-Soviet Russia itself: those with political connections have done well while the rest find their way by hook or by crook. In my encounters, Russian entrepreneurs frequently reverted to humour or an ironic expression when I raised the subject of *Russkii biznes* (Russian business): 'Haven't you heard about our police?' replied one with a wry smile; another had personalised his car registration plate to combine the word 'thief' (*vor*) with the phone number of the local police department. While such responses are ironic, they are also grounded in hard fact: although President Putin's governments have spent 20 years talking up the need for business development and entrepreneurs' rights, he himself has often contradicted that message, most recently drawing associations between business people and swindlers (2020: online). These remarks reveal the basic fact that, despite a number of formal initiatives to support business, in practical terms the Kremlin has created a specific form of capitalism characterised by a predatory, interventionist state. Under these conditions, why would any Russian become an entrepreneur, and how would they survive in business? These are the questions I explore in this book.

In my view, study of the relationship between the strong state and weak private sector (save for a set of state-affiliated enterprises and their patrons) is an essential tool for interpreting the Kremlin's decision making in domestic and international affairs. However, this is not a book about whether government policy could be improved to support business development better, because it is evident in research, press coverage and popular culture (and Putin's remark above) that independent businesses operate in a commercial environment beset with risk and uncertainty. Indeed, I will argue that a weak business class is a feature of the political economy President Putin's government has created rather than a problem it is working actively to solve. Instead, I focus on how entrepreneurs respond to these conditions, what it is like to be an entrepreneur under these circumstances and why they bother in the first place. In sum, I aim to offer a sense of contemporary Russian business culture among entrepreneurs operating in the real economy.

I approach these questions through an investigation of business practice based on observation of commercial life within three Siberian companies. As I reason, doing business in Moscow and St Petersburg is not the same as that undertaken in the majority of the country, while too few Western studies have focused on life in Russia's regions. While I draw in evidence from across Russia as a whole, I hope this study offers specialists and general readers a greater sense of contemporary life in the country's regions. As I find, all my informants resent the risks, challenges and vulnerabilities they encounter and which I describe in detail, but they have also developed capabilities to survive or thrive in spite of these obstacles. In my interpretation, their capacity to survive is less a result of their commercial acumen than their understanding of what can be achieved in their particular circumstances; their knowledge that business–state relations take an informal, personalised form; and their preparedness to resist predatory outsiders.

In setting out these findings, I claim that Russian entrepreneurship has peculiar features resulting from a political economic context in which the state and its officials can wield formal and informal power over the private sector. However, my informants' experiences also present a challenge to the idea in predominant political economic theories that the Russian state dominates the private sector altogether. As such, a theoretical framework must be found that can accommodate the considerable agency displayed by my informants as well, and I draw on Douglass C. North et al.'s limited access order theory to do so. Overall, my intention is that this book makes two contributions to knowledge of the Russian political economy. First, through detailed observation of everyday life in three business, I offer a sense of what entrepreneurship is like in the now well-established conditions of Putin's political economy, how businesspeople fare, and why they bother. Second, I use this to develop a theoretical framework that accepts both the dominant role of the state and the agency displayed by entrepreneurs.

The book is set out in a traditional research format, beginning with literature review and methodology chapters, before proceeding to the empirical research, theoretical matters and a conclusion. Chapter 1 provides an overview of what is already known about Russian business culture, and I make the case for studying it more closely in practice. In Chapter 2, I set out my research design and chosen method, arguing that ethnography offers an effective way to understand business practices in detail, within the theoretical framework of North et al.'s limited access order (2007; 2013a; 2013b). In Chapters 3 to 5, I present three ethnographic case studies of business practice, each in a different business and Russian city. In each chapter, the systemic and acute challenges facing entrepreneurs are clear, but the unique capabilities and motivations of each entrepreneur to survive and, in two of the three cases, thrive is described. In Chapter 6, I consider how to position my findings in existing literature and, in doing so, offer a novel perspective, which challenges received wisdom about the relationship between the dominant state and independent business. I draw this together in Chapter 7, where I offer four specific conclusions, of which the most important is that Russian entrepreneurs I study are in it not just for commercial prospects but the type of life it represents – one that is autonomous and necessarily resistant to a predatory state. Businesses do not expect change; they understand that the system, in the words of Putin himself, regards them with contempt, but they choose an entrepreneurial path in spite of and because of that.

Finally, it is my intention that this book is also useful for the casual reader, so each chapter is (in theory) accessible in its own right, offering insight relating to, respectively, what is known about the characteristics of the Russian political economy and business practice already (Chapter 1); methodological concerns prescient to foreign researchers considering their options in Russia and the merits of ethnography for studying matters normally studied at a distance (Chapter 2); descriptive details relevant to both the political and real economies, as well as everyday life in Russia in general (Chapters 3–5); while the remainder offers analysis and conclusions relating to the interaction between state and business, which are useful for those interested in how Russia works and in whose interests, especially in Russia's regions.

Acknowledgements

This book develops on my PhD (Kennedy 2017), which was a study of Russian business culture and entrepreneurship in the language-based Area Studies tradition, combining ethnography, political economy, institutional theory and a small dose of Kremlinology. I am very grateful to Peter Sowden at Routledge for the opportunity to bring this research up to date and for his kind advice, patience and guidance in preparing it for the BASEES/Routledge Series on Russian and East European Studies.

Ethnography relies on the good will and trust of many people, and I extend my gratitude to those who supported me. I am grateful to the staff of the Centre for Russian, European and Eurasian Studies at the University of Birmingham, where I was a doctoral researcher when I completed the majority of this work. I thank Dr Richard Connolly for suggesting that I turn my research into a book and for his advice since then; my supervisors, Dr Jeremy Morris and Dr Derek Averre, who offered support, guidance and inspiration as I developed the skills required for Area Studies research: Russian language, methodological training and learning on the job in the field.

This research was possible thanks primarily to the extraordinary generosity, kindness and hospitality of my informants and hosts in Russia, who allowed me to observe them freely, continually and openly, answering innumerable questions over many months with only good humour. I remain sincerely grateful to them. One of the benefits of completing this book four years after the PhD has been the opportunity to consider whether my conclusions stood the test of time as the Kremlin responded to the pressure of sanctions, as Putin passed 20 years in power, and as Russia entered another economic crisis in 2019 as result of another oil price drop and the spread of COVID-19. In my view, these events have hardly improved the structural and institutional conditions facing the majority of Russia's entrepreneurs. Although this book reveals only elements of time with my informants, I hope it reflects their remarkable efforts to improve their lives despite the profound challenges they continue to face.

I am indebted to Professor Larisa V. Deriglazova, Dr Irina G. Popravko, Dr Vitaly V. Kashpur and Elena M. Karageorgiy of Tomsk State University, who were enormously hospitable and offered great personal support to my research, both academically and by helping me to develop my personal network in Siberia. I also thank Dr Larisa V. Kosygina, formerly of CREES and now at Novosibirsk State University, for welcoming me to Akademgorodok and introducing me to her colleagues in the Institute of Economics. I am grateful to Professor Yurii G. Chernyshov and his colleagues at the School of Political Research at Altai State University for inviting me to speak to their students about my fieldwork in Siberia and for their great enthusiasm and ideas for developing my research.

I wish to extend my thanks to the staff of Exlinguo immersion school in Novosibirsk, where I spent several months between 2013 and 2014.

Upon completing my PhD, I worked at the UK's Department for International Trade in roles focused on the UK's economic and business relations in the former Soviet Union. In the course of that work, it was necessary to put my personal communications with friends and acquaintances in Russia on hold, and I lost contact with many of the people who had supported my work in Russia. I remain very grateful to them even so.

I am grateful to the Economic and Social Research Council (ESRC) for the +3 scholarship in Area Studies that it granted me through the University of Birmingham Doctoral Research Centre (DTC) and the additional funding and support for fieldwork I received through a European Union Marie Curie Action International Research Staff Exchange Scheme entitled 'EUinDepth – European Identity, Cultural Diversity and Political Change'. Without the support of these bodies, this research would not have been possible.

Finally, my wife, Hermione, has offered enormous support with this research and offered constant encouragement along the way. I thank her and our children, William and Agnes, for their patience and kindness in my frequent absence as I have been finishing this book.

Note on transliteration

In this book, I have transliterated from Russian into the Roman alphabet using the CREES Transliteration Table. I have accepted alternative transliterations for the names of authors or public figures when they have transliterated them differently themselves or when another convention for their name is more commonly used.

1 Introduction

Business Conditions in Putin's Russia

The development of Russia's private sector has remained an important feature in Putin's economic policy over his 20 years in power, but as I show in this introductory chapter, successive market-oriented policies and government-led incentives have not really transformed conditions for ordinary businesses operating under hard budget constraints. This is especially the case for individual entrepreneurs and small and medium-sized enterprises (SMEs), who still face many of the challenges of the 1990s, although state officials rather than criminals are often the main threat to independent businesses today (for example, Connolly 2020: 67). At the same time, even the most begrudging of my informants would acknowledge that Putin's governments have delivered greater economic stability to the benefit of the country as a whole, and some have developed ways of working that enable them to work profitably despite the risks.

What explains the difference between declared policy intent and actual outcomes with respect to private-sector development? First, a dynamic growth model based on the development of the private sector and diversification of the economy has been less important than macroeconomic stability and financial security (Connolly 2020: 88). The beneficiaries of this approach have been the country's leading and still-dominant state-controlled and state-affiliated enterprises, principally in the energy and metals industries. This can be seen clearly in Russia's GDP performance over the Putin period: while GDP grew at an annual average rate of over 5 per cent between 1999 and 2013, this was attributable to high prices for the most important exports – oil, gas and metals – rather than market reforms (Connolly 2015: 13). Russia's reliance on its strategic industries was revealed in 2015 when the 'dual shock' of Western sanctions and a collapse in oil prices triggered a recession, and GDP fell by 3 per cent. Growth returned in 2017 but at a slower rate than before and below the global rate (Connolly 2020: 82). According to Alexei Kudrin, finance minister under Putin until 2011, GDP averaged less than 1 per cent overall between 2013 and 2019. He predicted that, given the oil price crisis of early 2020 and ongoing global COVID-19 pandemic, it would decline between 4 and 5 per cent by the end of the year (TASS 2020: online). Thus, Russia's independent businesses have continued to play a marginal role

DOI: 10.4324/9780429469176-1

in the country's economic performance overall, even while the case for the development of conditions for business and growth-oriented reforms looks as clear today as it did at the start of Putin's presidency.

Second, while the government talked about economic stability and largely delivered, it also promoted private-sector development but did not achieve a great deal. In this book, I argue that institutional theory can help explain why. According to North, institutions provide 'the framework within which human activity takes place' (1990: 4), and in Russia informal institutions, comprised of cultural norms, values and codes of conduct, undermine the formal institutional rules and laws introduced to support business development. This has been called 'institutional asymmetry' (Williams and Vorley 2014: 843). This means that the government's policies and laws in support of business are undermined by behaviour determined by informal codes of conduct. To put it another way, institutional theory enables us to understand how formal policies have been insufficient to deliver domestic business reform and diversification. This leaves entrepreneurs vulnerable to predation, not least from state officials.

Considering both factors, it is clear that a specific type of capitalism has emerged in which the state has a steering role in the macro economy, but it is largely absent from the development of the real economy. Thus, for the purposes of this book, the dominant role of the state per se is not as important as the weakness of the private sector over 20 years of Putin rule despite the importance of economic modernisation and development to his economic messaging and policy. Conditions for entrepreneurs have remained, by some internationally recognised measures, the most challenging of any large world economy. This leaves them to deal with a high degree of everyday uncertainty and risk, but they are not without agency, even if they are relatively weak compared to state officials.

While officials may act according to their personal will, it frequently goes against the interests of entrepreneurs or the law. In turn, entrepreneurs tend not to rely on the government, law or policy but help themselves or turn to trusted acquaintances for support and have developed their own philosophical and practical responses. This is also explained by institutional theory: when individuals meet institutional constraints, they change their behaviour, which means, logically, that entrepreneurs will not accept their vulnerability to the state but seek to avoid it. As North puts it, 'if institutions are the rules of the game, organisations and their entrepreneurs are the players' (1993: 345).

In this chapter, I discuss these conditions further, detailing how a form of business–state relations has developed in the Putin era in which the weakness (rather than development) of business is inherent, but entrepreneurs retain a degree of control over their circumstances even so. I also show that, although much research has been undertaken showing that business is difficult, there has been little on specifically how entrepreneurs are reacting to these difficulties, which would require observation of business in practice. This allows me to move, in the following chapters, to discuss what these conditions are and why entrepreneurs bother with commerce if the odds of survival and profit are stacked against them.

Support for Business in Policy and Reality since 2000

At the outset of Putin's presidency, the prospects for the improvement of conditions for private business were uncertain at best. They were not highlighted in the economic aspects of his 'millennium manifesto', in which he first set out his key ideas (Putin 1999, online). He sought to strengthen the rule of law and the state's control over the economy (particularly its leading industries, exemplified by the so-called *shashlik agreement*, which set the terms and balance of relations between the state and Russia's post-Soviet business elite) and create the conditions for a stable economy. As Connolly has shown at length, the goals of the millennium manifesto were in large part met, and the state had regained both power and control over the economy. At the same time, the prospects for the development of new economic sectors decreased, and property rights remained weak (2020: 54–70). As Connolly wittily concludes, 'Putin had largely succeeded in stopping people from killing each other [but] failed to stop them from stealing from each other' (2020: 70). This is not to say that business development was absent from the Kremlin's agenda altogether. Rather, of the numerous decrees, resolutions and programmes for small business in the years before the 2008–9 economic crisis, the 'vast majority' were simply not implemented (Aidis et al. 2008a: 3). According to Puffer et al., the SME sector did develop during the first Putin presidency, but did so without significant government support (Puffer et al. 2009: 446).

In 2008, the prospects for the development of the private sector had improved. Macroeconomic conditions were better than in 2000, and the new president, Dmitry Medvedev, arrived with a modernising vision, which he set out in his 2009 article, 'Go Russia!'. In this, he stated that 'twenty years of tumultuous change has not spared our country from its humiliating dependence on raw materials' and called for an 'intelligent economy' based on knowledge, new technologies and innovative products (2009: online). Nevertheless, the global financial crisis, which caused a recession in Russia when oil prices fell, and Putin's relative (informal) hold on power held back progress. Putin's preference was for 'state-led solutions to economic policy [which] continued to prevail regardless of Medvedev's liberal rhetoric' (Connolly 2020: 73). Following that crisis, which indeed underlined Russia's acute dependency on oil and gas prices, the government sought to reinvigorate its support for business again. The 2007 law, 'On Developing Small and Medium Scale Entrepreneurship' (Ministry of Economic Development of the Russian Federation 2016a: online), which set out the 'basic goals and principles' of state policy towards entrepreneurs, gained new relevance.[1] Further initiatives to support entrepreneurs followed. A presidential decree in May 2008, 'On Urgent Measures for the Liquidation of Administrative Limitations Upon the Execution of Business Activity', tasked the government with taking steps to practically improve conditions for business activity in the country (Rossiyskaya Gazeta 2008: online). Under Medvedev, a new regulatory impact assessment was unveiled in 2010, and the Agency for Strategic Initiatives was created in 2011 with the purpose of providing support and removing barriers in the way of viable entrepreneurial projects.

The policy momentum of the Medvedev period continued on Putin's return to the presidency. His so-called May Decrees demanded 'a radical improvement in the investment climate and a major scaling back of the state's presence in the economy' (Guriev 2019: online). He also introduced the *100 Steps Programme* in 2012, with the aim of improving the country's position on the World Bank's Doing Business rating from 120 to 20, and installed a presidential commissioner to protect the rights of entrepreneurs (Yakovlev 2015: 59). Federal budget support for SME and entrepreneurship programmes was increased significantly from 3.9 billion roubles in 2008 to 23 billion in 2014 (Organisation for Economic Co-operation and Development [OECD] 2015: 15–16). In 2015, Putin introduced a law freeing small businesses from regular inspections until the end of 2018 as a way to stimulate growth in the sector, which, he said, contributed to only 21 per cent of GDP in Russia compared to over 50 per cent in developed economies (*The Moscow Times* 2015). This figure was indeed lower than in comparable developing countries as well (European Investment Bank 2013: 8; also OECD 2015: 20).

Despite the intensification of government attention on modernisation of the economy and improvement of business conditions following the crisis (Buckley and Weaver 2013), including after geopolitical and economic crises struck in 2014, in the end they did not make a significant difference to the everyday conditions encountered by entrepreneurs. Economic growth recommenced at a lower rate than before the crisis (OECD 2015: 26): in 2013, growth was 1.3 per cent, compared to an average of 7 per cent in the decade to 2008 (Connolly 2020: 79), and the persistent weakness of the private sector became more obvious. In 2014, Russia's Public Chamber found that only 3.4 per cent of SMEs lasted more than three years (reported in *The Moscow Times* 2014: 5), and the development of small business overall showed a 'declining tendency' (Kreidenko and Mironova 2012: 352) rather than growth. A 2013 OECD report described Russia's business climate as a 'persistent handicap' and stated that 'a range of indicators suggest that doing business in Russia is perceived as difficult and risky' (2013: 10). In 2014 a further OECD report remarked on the fact that while the authorities seemed to have become 'more energetic on fighting corruption and strengthening the legal protection of businesses … capital outflows and the low market valuation of Russian companies suggest that business is not yet fully convinced' (2014: 2). The key 'long term challenge', that report found, was still to 'reduce dependence on the volatile revenues from exhaustible natural resources, and strengthen sustainable, productivity-driven, regionally balanced and broad-based growth', which above all required structural improvement to the business climate, strengthening the rule of law and fighting corruption (OECD 2014: 4). Evidently, formal policies did not translate into substantive improvements in the business climate.

It is true that Russia improved its rating on the international Doing Business scale over this period, reaching No 51 by 2015 (World Bank 2016: 229).[2] However, this measure has limitations: it reflects the way regulation applies to business on paper rather than compliance with it; it is based only on the experiences of businesspeople in Moscow, and it does not acknowledge the informal economy (World Bank 2016: 19–22). In any case, any tangible effort to implement the May Decrees was 'sidelined by the need to respond to sanctions and the fall in oil prices' (Connolly 2020: 82). I will not detail Russia's responses here because these are covered elsewhere in detail (Connolly: 2018, 2020), but true to form, the Kremlin's economic focus remained on macroeconomic stability (with some success considering the low rates of growth and reduced foreign investment) rather than the development and diversification of the independent business sector.

Furthermore, in a second iteration of his May Decrees in 2018, Putin turned the government's attention away from private-sector development and towards public spending to stimulate growth through a series of 'national projects'. Accordingly, the weight of expert opinion has tended towards greater scepticism about the Kremlin's intentions for the development of independent business since the 2014–15 crisis. Whereas in 2015 the OECD still considered that 'positive momentum is being built up by public policy on the road to a more entrepreneurial Russian Federation' (2015: 15), today that might be seen less as momentum and more as rhetoric with few tangible results after two decades. Moreover, according to experts, the national projects are unlikely to stimulate growth more than any previous initiatives. Sergey Guriev, Chief Economist at the European Bank for Reconstruction and Development (EBRD) and former advisor to Medvedev, has noted that the ambitions in the first May Decrees never materialised (2019: online) and is sceptical about the Kremlin's turn towards growth through public spending and the national projects:

> It is not surprising that experts and investors have little faith in the effectiveness of large-scale public investment in a country notorious for corruption. The solution to Russia's problems lies in precisely the opposite direction – in implementing the long-promised reforms: protecting property rights, respecting the rule of law and competition, reducing the state's role in the economy, fighting corruption, reintegrating Russia into the world economy, and investing in human capital.
>
> (2019: online)

To this point I have argued that despite successive initiatives to support the development of the private sector over 20 years, substantial difficulties continue to face businesses. What are these difficulties specifically? Three stand out. First, state-owned enterprises (SOEs) have privileged access to finance, which 'complicates market entry and suffocates competition, while preserving pockets of inefficiency' (OECD 2014: 12; also Connolly 2015: 16–17). SOEs account for around half of GDP and hold a 'dominant position' in sectors including banking, energy and transport (Radziwill and Vaziakova 2015: 12), for instance, leaving the potential for independent businesses structurally limited. Second, there is a range of obstacles in the business environment in the way of prospective entrepreneurs. For instance, according to the European Investment Bank, 'tax legislation fluctuates wildly and tax administration is unduly difficult', while access to finance is limited and costly for SMEs, particularly new businesses (2013: 14). In the regions this can be intensified. As Razomasova found in a survey of entrepreneurs in Novosibirsk, for example, the burden of finding collateral to secure a start-up loan for new entrepreneurs is too high, especially for young first-timers without substantial assets, and that despite government promises, actual support for entrepreneurs was weak, insufficient and over-bureaucratised (2010: 131–4).

The third and most significant factor is that the state rhetorically supports the private sector but simultaneously allows it to be undermined: the largest and most longstanding problem entrepreneurs face is malign pressure from government officials. This means that the government's 'goodwill' towards business has rung hollow over time. As Aidis et al. stated after the introduction of the 2007 law, government policy has been 'declarative in nature', while a 'legacy of corruption and favouritism' means that many businesses accept 'the lack of a level playing field as the norm' (2008a: 8). When President Medvedev called for 'modernisation' of the economy in 2009, Guriev said that Russia's elites profited from a rent system and would prevent any modernisation that threatened it (quoted by *The Economist* 2009: online). In 2011, a literature review by Arto Ojala and Hannakaisa Isomäki on entrepreneurship and small business between 1991 and 2009 concluded that 'the same factors fostering and hindering entrepreneurship and small business can be found in the studies regardless of the year of publication … there have been few changes in Russia's business environment since the collapse of the Soviet Union' (2011: 16–17). This remains the case today. In Transparency International's Corruption Index, Russia has retained a score of between 27 and 29 out of 100 in every year from 2012 to 2019 and scores 137th out of 198 countries overall (Transparency International 2019: online). According to the World Justice Project's 2015 Rule of Law Index, Russia scored 0.47 (with 1 being 'strongest adherence to the rule of law'), placing it in 75th position out of 102 countries included, which makes it by far the worst performer among the 'high income' countries listed (2016: online). In 2019, its score was also 0.47, which placed it 98th out of 128 ranked countries that year (2020: online). A plain-speaking entrepreneur at the Moscow Economic Forum of 2015 put this in everyday terms and gained notoriety on the *Runet* (Russian-language internet) when he likened relations between the authorities and business to that of a butcher with a knife to the neck of a cow, asking 'What do we have today, beef or milk?' (Filipenok and Shtykina 2015; Gazeta.ru 2015; Schreck and Shakirov 2015).

According to some, the situation for business has been worsening rather than improving. Bovt claims that the distance between Russian law and its effective implementation is growing: the Duma decreasingly issues laws that are 'fit for enforcement' because they do not recognise the actual needs of the business sector and have no understanding of how they can be implemented. As a result, entrepreneurs cannot follow new laws but have to wait until authorities begin to interpret them (Bovt 2015: online). Lipman has argued that 'Putin has advocated freedom of entrepreneurship in a tightly controlled political environment, where there is no rule of law or independent judiciary, and with a legislature that has been entirely stripped of its representative function' (2014: online). This situation makes business vulnerable, and numerous examples can be easily found. In February 2016, for example, the Moscow city government destroyed 100 single buildings in a single night – dubbed the 'Night of the Long Scoops' – after the mayor, Sergei Sobyanin, decided to 'cleanse the city of street vendors' (*The Economist* 2016b: online). According to *The Economist*, he said that 'one cannot hide behind property papers' and claimed that the owners had acquired their title deeds illegally. The article concluded: 'On paper, Russia's business climate has improved recently. But when paper rights meet steel scoopers, the paper tends to tear' (*The Economist* 2016b: online). Indeed, the malign role of state officials in defrauding, raiding or simply destroying private enterprises is well known and a common theme in reportage on contemporary Russia (see, for example, Pomerantsev 2015: 93–123).[3]

Unsurprisingly, the judicial system offers entrepreneurs little protection. According to one Russian advocacy group for entrepreneurs' rights, every third prisoner in Russia may be a businessperson (Biznes Solidarnost' 2015: online), although this figure is unverified. Valerii Fedotov argues that as the economic situation in Russia has worsened since 2014, the number of acquittals in Russian courts has decreased by two-thirds, while the average bribe paid to officials has doubled (according to the Attorney General's office) to 208,000 roubles, or tripled (according to non-governmental organizations). He concludes that the government's formal support for entrepreneurs is undermined by its own officials and 'untouchable' security forces (2015: online), who use their position to extract personal gains in the private sector. This is the key problem for entrepreneurs resulting from Russia's institutional asymmetry.

Similarly, informality has become the pattern of governance in Russia. Among elites, the connection between business and politics has remained blurred. According to Inozemtsev, the families of the ruling elite have 'infiltrated government service', and successful businesses are being steadily converted into 'quasi-family enterprises'. This means that prized corporate assets and political positions are acquired and distributed patrimonially (2011: online), even though, according to an OECD report, civil servants are meant to vacate their roles every three to five years to prevent them from becoming too attached to the entities they supervise (Radziwill and Vaziakova 2015: 7). Russian officials have been obliged to declare their income since 2008, to close their foreign bank accounts since 2012 (and those of family members) and to repatriate financial assets to Russia or lose their positions since 2013

(Radziwill and Vaziakova 2015: 7). However, the existence of these laws is not a good indication of their effectiveness: some of Russia's most influential officials hold property abroad (*The Economist* 2016a: online; Harding 2016: online). Even Boris Titov, Russia's presidential commissioner for entrepreneurs' rights, and head of the country's business ombudsman, whose job is to support and protect entrepreneurs (OmbudsmanBiz, 2021: online), owns a property in London (*Private Eye* 2016: online). According to *The Economist's* 'crony-capitalism index', which measures the wealth of billionaires active in rent-seeking sectors as a percentage of GDP, Russia scored worst of the world's largest economies (*The Economist* 2014: online). The disparity between the formal and informal institutions explains why, considering the literature overall, the situation for the development of independent business continues to look bleak.[4]

Maxim Trudolyubov's conception of a 'two-tier property regime' in Russia serves to explain the connection between elite behaviour and the bureaucracy, which impedes the development of legitimate entrepreneurship. He points out that within this system powerful business owners are permitted to hold assets and money abroad in order to prevent them pressuring the government for property rights at home. Abroad they benefit from formal guarantees for their assets, whereas inside Russia their rights are dependent upon their loyalty (2014: online; also Inozemtsev 2011). Trudolyubov considers that in Russia, big business and politics are not separate but the same thing. Likewise, Inozemtsev argues that the bureaucracy writes laws not for the development of the country but 'its own comfort' (2016: online). As a result, independent entrepreneurs inside Russia are inherently vulnerable to the law while the country's most powerful figures function outside it. In this context, entrepreneurs tend to rely upon themselves rather than government initiatives. Indeed, although the government has placed much emphasis on establishing associations to support entrepreneurs,[5] Courtney Bain has found that many have rejected them on the grounds that their leaders prefer to lobby the government than to provide the practical support and advice they require (2007: 212–13). Overall, without political, legal or practical support, entrepreneurs have long turned to their own personal networks (Bain 2007: 213; also Aidis et al. 2008a: 13; Puffer et al. 2007; 9). As I explain in the case study chapters, self-reliance and rejection of the state are also important factors in the way my informants behave.

Overall, as Andrei Yakovlev has suggested, the major impediments to the advancement of independent business in recent years have been both bureaucrats in 'the middle and lower tiers of the state machine' focused on 'receiving rent from informal control over flows of financial resources' (2014: 11), and elites that 'deny … the interests of business and, on the contrary, insist on toughening of regulations and on firmer control and supervision' (Yakovlev 2014: 17). The latter group is made up of the law enforcement agencies, the *siloviki*, including the Investigative Committee, Office of the Prosecutor General, Federal Security Service, Federal Customs Service, Federal Tax Service and others, as well as top SOE managers such as Igor Sechin of

Rosneft and Vladimir Yakunin, formerly of Russian Railways (Yakovlev 2014: 17). The strength of this group has grown since the 2008–09 crisis as a result of the failure of anti-corruption measures, government pressure on entrepreneurs in response to the capital outflow and tax avoidance that followed the crisis, and because the political protests of 2011 and 2012 served to strengthen the position of the siloviki (Yakovlev 2014: 17). Yakovlev concludes that there are both simultaneous moves towards and away from business, with the effect that the difficult conditions facing businesses have not changed substantially over time (Yakovlev 2014: 17–18). Considering the preceding evidence, I argue that entrepreneurs must work in a business climate in which they are the recipients of verbal support but remain prone to malicious interference from outsiders and officials, in addition to the continuing challenges of the business environment itself.

The Role of Institutions in the Business Environment

How can the difference between Russia's nominal support for business and the reality of doing business be explained conceptually? In his Nobel Prize–winning work, North draws attention to the importance of formal and informal institutions in the process of economic development. He defines institutions as 'the rules of a game in a society … the humanly devised constraints that shape human interaction' (1990: 3). Formal institutions are 'the rules human beings devise', and informal institutions include 'conventions and codes of behaviour' (North 1990: 4). According to North, 'the major role of institutions in a society is to reduce uncertainty by establishing a stable (but not necessarily efficient) structure to human interaction. But the stability of institutions in no way gainsays the fact that they are changing' (North 1990: 6). North argues that the process of institutional change is 'never completely discontinuous', even in the context of revolution, but results from the 'imbeddedness of informal constraints in societies' (North 1990: 6). Thus, formal institutions may change quickly in line with political or judicial decisions, but informal institutions 'are much more impervious to deliberate policies' (North 1990: 6). From this perspective, it is clear that Russia's transformation during the post-communist period was never going to be a matter of policy alone. To understand the political economy that has emerged, and the place of entrepreneurs within it, analysis of *both* formal and informal institutions is required.

Drawing on North, several scholars have taken on this task. Williams and Vorley argue that a country's 'entrepreneurial capacity' is related to the institutional context in which it occurs (Williams and Vorley 2014: 840; also Estrin et al. 2007: 4). Sheila Puffer et al. argue that among post-communist countries, or most transition countries, there are 'formal institutional voids' (Puffer et al. 2009: 441). In Russia, these voids are such that laws are ineffective, the judiciary lacks independence from the executive and private property rights are 'frail', enabling officials to pressurise businesses unconstrained (Puffer et al. 2009: 447–8), and pushing entrepreneurs to depend on the 'personalised trust' they develop through their own networks (Puffer et al. 2009: 459; also McMillan and Woodruff 2002: 159). Ojala and Isomäki argue that the institutional environment in Russia 'creates barriers for business and entrepreneurship', leaving them prone to *reiderstvo* (or corporate raiding) (2011: 16; also Hanson 2014). Aidis et al. argue that

> the weakness of formal institution enforcement ... combined with the informal norms and values (negative attitudes towards entrepreneurship) ... create an atmosphere that is relatively less conducive to the development of new entrepreneurial firms, even than in countries of comparable levels of development.
>
> (2008b: 658)

As Chadee and Roxas concluded, Russia's 'formal institutional environment is yet to reach a stage of maturity that is capable of supporting an open, liberal and market-based economy free of corruption and crime' (2013: 33).

The relative influence of informal over formal institutions in Russia has led to a particular mode of post-communist capitalism in which personal networks, rather than regulations, have a determinant effect in the political economy. Puffer et al. argue that a form of 'state- managed network capitalism' has emerged in which three sectors – the market, the *siloviki* and the oligarchy – operate primarily according to 'cognitive' or informal norms rather than 'rule-based' regulations (Puffer et al. 2007: 3–9). This system, they argue, is embedded in Russian culture, with officials playing an important role, and the state able to act arbitrarily, within each sector (Puffer et al. 2007: 3–4). Similarly, Aidis et al. conclude that 'as formal structures in Russia fail, they are complemented by informal networks' that constitute 'intangible assets' enabling some entrepreneurs to overcome obstacles (2008a: 15–16). Ledeneva (2009) argues that personal networks (or *blat*) are integral to overcoming the travails associated with doing business in Russia, and they play a critical role at all levels of the political economy (also Castells and Kiselyova 1998; Hass 2012: 103–7). She argues that in Russia 'informality *is* the pattern of governance, even if hidden behind the formal discourses. It is rarely acknowledged as such but is often referred to in a commonly used euphemism "sistema"' (2009: 268; also 2013). Indeed, it is important to recognise the relevance and extent of informality in everyday life in Russia in general, not simply in business. As Morris and Polese state, reflecting North's institutional analysis, informality is still 'embedded in social life' in much of post-socialist Eurasia (2014: 8).

Before concluding, I wish to touch on the connection between institutional asymmetry and the capacity of the Russian state. It is clear that the vulnerability of entrepreneurs is not the result of a 'strong' state as such. On the contrary, the vulnerability of entrepreneurs comes from the weakness of formal institutions, which creates a situation whereby state officials, acting on their own initiative but with the authority of the state, can manipulate and take advantage of businesses. This will be described in the case study chapters that follow. Thus, when I refer to the vulnerability of business in the face of a 'strong' state in this book, I am referring to the malign potential of officials acting informally against entrepreneurs. In this way, the strength of the state is therefore relative to the longstanding weakness of entrepreneurs, which I have described. As Vadim Volkov stated nearly 20 years ago:

> The source of risk and insecurity in Russian business is not criminal groups (the so-called mafia), as it used to be in the past, but the arbitrary and commercially driven actions of poorly controlled segments of the state. Accordingly, the success of certain business groups depends on the availability of administrative and coercive resources of the state. This situation continues to produce incentives for enrichment by means of redistributing economic assets and accumulating rents rather than by the productive employment of these assets.
>
> (2002: 3–4)

Brian D. Taylor has drawn attention to the difference between state capacity and state quality. He defines state capacity as 'the ability of a state to ensure the reliable implementation of its decisions by its own personnel' (Taylor 2011: 89), while state quality refers to 'whether the state and its officials serve the interests of the population in a fair manner that promotes the general welfare' (Taylor 2011: 17). As he states:

> In ideal-typical high-quality states, bureaucrats see themselves as 'public servants,' bound by the rule of law and resistant to the temptations of corruption. The concept of state quality shifts the perspective from that of the rulers and their goals to the citizens and their needs, and from what states do to how they do it.
>
> (Taylor 2011: 17)

Bearing in mind these criteria, Taylor concludes that the Russian state is weak and questions whether Putin has been 'interested in rebuilding the Russian state at all, despite abundant rhetoric to the contrary … [or] more interested in looting' it (Taylor 2011: 310–11). Taylor's question remains important. This book pays attention to the actual relationship between the Russian state (and elites) and ordinary people. As I show, my informants also view the state as deficient, but they remain vulnerable to predatory officials who may act freely from a relative position of strength. Because this study seeks to understand entrepreneurs' perspectives in the political economy, it is important to bear this relative strength in mind, even if from a structural position the state is weak. It follows that Russia's institutional asymmetry and the weak state reinforce one another. It also follows that under these conditions, state quality and the specific conditions of institutional asymmetry will vary regionally according to administrative conditions, and that power is exercised by elites and businesspeople to different extents. These are questions I tackle with respect to case selection in the next chapter and draw out in my empirical findings.

Taken together, the literature I have cited makes entrepreneurship seem like a rather pointless and risky business, yet it continues, albeit at a lower level than in comparably large economies. Why? As Samuel Greene has written, scholars have 'broadly categorised the elite as powerful and the state as disenfranchised' but the state does not get what it wants all the time and 'significant power' can be exerted by the country's 'powerless masses' (2018: 333–4). And as North stated in his Nobel Prize–winning lecture, 'if institutions are the rules of the game, organisations and their entrepreneurs are the players', which means that a society's organisations, including businesses, 'reflect the opportunities provided by the institutional matrix' (1993, reprinted 1996: 345). Moreover, institutional change occurs when individuals and organisations 'perceive that they could do better by restructuring political or economic exchanges' (North 1996: 346), which means that entrepreneurs modify institutions as they respond to the institutional framework. Consequently, it cannot be the case that Russian entrepreneurs have no control over their destiny or that their vulnerability is structurally determined.

Summary

In this chapter I described conditions for entrepreneurs in contemporary Russia based on recent empirical literature. First, I showed that the government has given continual and considerable support to the advancement of entrepreneurship in declarations, policies and initiatives but business conditions remain challenging. As will be seen in subsequent chapters, entrepreneurs face significant start-up costs, widespread corruption, unreliable property rights, a politicised judiciary and the possibility that officials or rivals may freely intervene in their affairs. Indeed, even though GDP has grown, living standards have risen and a sense of order has been restored during the Putin years (Connolly 2015: 13–14), several entrepreneurs I spoke with claimed that the 1990s were a 'golden period' for business compared to the present. I therefore find that entrepreneurs operate under conditions in which they are simultaneously supported and undermined by the government. Second, I sought to explain this situation in terms of institutional theory, and I drew on several scholars who concur that Russia's formal institutions are insufficient to allow the development of entrepreneurship. Instead, a form of capitalism has developed in which personal networks have an organising function. In this system, elites, officials and ordinary entrepreneurs all participate, but the latter are weakest because they are vulnerable to the former. Nevertheless, as I concluded drawing on North, entrepreneurs have the capacity to challenge their institutional constraints, but little academic attention has been given to observing this. In the next chapter, I set out a methodology for doing so.

Notes

1 In this chapter I define entrepreneurship, simply and logically, in line with that law, specifically: entrepreneurs have established micro- (employing up to 15 people), small- (employing up to 100 people) or medium- (employing up to 250 people) sized non-subsidiary, independent firms in Russia (Ministry of Economic Development of the Russian Federation 2016b: online). This definition is sufficient here for providing an understanding of Russian entrepreneurship in the formal sense. In Chapter 2, however, I find this insufficient for my research, because Russian entrepreneurship is better understood not by how it is formally defined, but by what it informally involves. As I will show, commercial objectives and activities represent only one dimension in Russian entrepreneurs' everyday priorities. The basic goals of the law are, to paraphrase: develop SMEs in order to create a competitive environment; foster favourable conditions for the development of SMEs; ensure SMEs' competitiveness; assist SMEs in the promotion of their goods in Russia and abroad; increase the number of SMEs; and so on. Of additional interest are the 'Normative-Legal' regulations to assist the development of SMEs, which include: a special tax regime for SMEs; measures for safeguarding the rights and lawful interests of SMEs when state supervision is performed; measures for the provision of financial support to SMEs; and measures for the development of an infrastructure for supporting SMEs. In these ways the Law is uncontroversial and emphasises the assistance that the government will provide promoting SME development and ensuring a legally reliable environment.

2 Russia has continued to 'improve' on this measure, reaching 31st in 2019 (World Bank 2019: online), which raises questions about its effectiveness.

3 It is indicative of this subject that although much is colloquially known in Russia about the connivance of the state and its officials in the persecution of business, relatively little scholarly observation of this has been undertaken. Thus, most insight into the persecution of businesses and the corruption of officials comes from journalists rather than academics.

4 It is alleged, though widely accepted, that Russia's political elite use their official status for personal gain. Aleksei Naval'nyi and his team have offered the most high-profile examples in Russia over the years based on private investigations. For instance, they alleged that Yurii Chaika, former Prosecutor General, organised crime, murder, expropriation of private property and fraud (Naval'nyi 2015a: online). They also alleged that former Deputy Prime Minister Shuvalov, who was the senior Cabinet member responsible for economic policies until 2018 (Naval'nyi 2015b: online), Defence Minister Shoigu (Alburov 2015: online), and Presidential Press Secretary Peskov (Naval'nyi 2015c: online) have created financial schemes involving their family members for the acquisition of property in Russia and abroad far out of proportion with their public salaries. Indeed, the 'Panama Papers' (The International Consortium of Investigative Journalists 2016: online) alleged President Putin himself was involved in patrimonial activities of this kind too.

5 Russia's most important and state-approved business associations are the Agency for Strategic Initiatives, OPORA Rossii, the Business Ombudsman for the Protection of the Rights of Entrepreneurs and Delovaya Rossiya.

2 Methodology

In this chapter, I set out my approach to studying how businesspeople 'get by' under conditions of institutional asymmetry. I argue that ethnography has particular value compared to more frequently used research methods because it aims to reveal the differences between informants' attitudes and behaviour. I start by recalling that ethnographers made a significant contribution to understanding market adaptation during the post-communist period but, oddly, ethnography has been used far less to study the specific predicament of business through the Putin years. I then set out my specific methodological approach, which is a multi-sited ethnography, and introduce my three key informants. In doing so, I provide a hint about my key finding, which is that despite their differences my informants are primarily motivated to be in business to secure their independence while commercial goals come second. Finally, I introduce my theoretical framework, which builds on the ideas of 'entrepreneurial governmentality' (Yurchak 2002) to explain the agency of my informants despite the challenges they face, and North's 'limited access order' (2009) to explain their relationship with the state as they encounter it.

The Case for an Ethnographic Study of Business Practice

In the first post-Soviet decade ethnography was frequently used to investigate how Russians were adapting to the introduction of market conditions (for example Bridger et al. 1996; Burawoy and Verdery 1999; Humphrey 2002; Humphrey and Mandel 2002; Pine and Bridger 1998; Ries 2002). Anthropologists in particular were drawn to Russia by the prospect of studying a large, diverse and previously inaccessible country living through an unprecedented historical period and economic crisis (discussed by Tomlinson 2002: 12–15). These scholars sought to grasp how individuals came to reconcile the 'social and philosophical legacies of socialism' with new market pressures and possibilities (Patico 2009: 205). In this sense, the research effort was concentrated upon what the 'situation of post-Sovietness' (Patico 2009: 206) meant for the attitudes and behaviours of individuals encountering the market, rather than focusing on 'entrepreneurship' as an emerging formal profession. However, the myriad ways that their informants perceived, adapted to and coped with the momentous changes that occurred during that period

DOI: 10.4324/9780429469176-2

were by their nature 'entrepreneurial' in the absence of state support (Bonnell and Gold 2002: xv). As such, entrepreneurship was not simply a new vocation in business chosen by particularly enterprising people, but the various activities required for local survival in the face of material scarcity, economic uncertainty, violence, lawlessness, interference by officials and the other travails of the period. In this context, everyday life was

> [d]efined by the notions of crisis and the drive for autonomy, and how these new social forms could be innovative (in terms of formulating ingenious solutions to post-socialist dilemmas) and socially reproductive (by enabling individuals to function amid these dilemmas instead of addressing them) at the same time.
>
> (Shevchenko 2009: 176)

Overall, the anthropological approach underlined the importance of self-help as a reaction to the all-pervasive disorder that was the salient feature of everyday life. As I make clear in this chapter, I find the 'drive for autonomy' remains a defining feature in the contemporary experiences of my informants, in spite of an improvement in macroeconomic conditions during the Putin period.

In taking this approach, anthropologists in particular unveiled the dichotomy between policy and reality in the everyday context. Most significantly, this raised a challenge to the prevailing notion of economic 'transition' that framed the rhetorical priorities of the Yeltsin government's reform agenda and the international advisers supporting them (see, for example, Freeland 2000: 58–66; Nellis 2002). As Olga Shevchenko put it, the transition had two problems: it was implemented top down without public discussion, which made it socially illegitimate, and it was too technical, in that 'it failed to translate into a larger strategic vision of the transformation that could give meaning and coherence to a protracted process of social, economic and political change' (2009: 24). The anthropological work therefore underlined the 'institutional asymmetry' that I have described in post-socialist Russia.

Jeffrey Hass summarises the case for an ethnographic approach to Russia's post-socialist experience plainly. He argues that the demise of the Soviet Union meant more than the end of 'a set of institutions', but 'a set of categories reified through those institutions' (2012: 226). As a result, post-Soviet reform became more than an economic process, but an attempt to determine what the new Russia should be, in legal, social and normative terms (Hass 2012: 226). In this way, Hass contends that markets are 'learned' and 'arise imperfectly through trial, error and contention' (2005: 7). As a result, in his view, 'only with culture can we make sense of the unfolding of Russia's post-Soviet economic change, when practices changed more slowly than policies' to address 'what actors were thinking (categories, understandings) and the process of "learning the market" (even imperfectly)' (Hass 2005: 4). The Russian economy has a '"Russian" flavour', he contends, 'because of the cultural dynamics of learning and resistance', which must be examined with attention on culture, investigating 'previous institutions and cultural legacies' and considering 'how actors coded and addressed shocks and experiences' (Hass 2005: 7). Hass's argument underlines the appropriateness of an ethnographic approach to the study of everyday experience under institutional constraints.

However, despite the relevance of ethnography in the study of post-socialist experience, very few ethnographies of entrepreneurship have been undertaken during the Putin period. The exact cause of this diminished interest is not clear. It is plausible that when the economy started to recover, the novelty of studying post-communism fell, but this is speculation. More likely, the climate for extended research worsened as the Russian government became more antagonistic towards foreign interest in its political and economic affairs, culminating in the 2012 Law on Foreign Agents, which threatens to politicise and increase the risks associated with fieldwork. In recent years, the Russian authorities have increased their scrutiny of Western researchers travelling in the country (Schreck 2015: online). Most importantly however, independent business remained an insignificant part of Russia's political economy: small- and medium-sized businesses (SMEs) operating competitively in sectors such as retail, transport and business services account for only one-fifth of Russian GDP and employment today (Connolly 2015: 13). That said, there is a dearth of data on what a significant proportion of SMEs are doing: microbusinesses, those employing up to 15 people, represent by far the most common type of SME, according to Goskomstat, the Federal State Statistical Service (Goskomstat 2010), but this group was omitted from a recent analysis of the SME sector by that organisation (Goskomstat 2015).

Overall, there is currently insufficient empirical evidence about business practice, while the emergence of the market continues to present normative and practical dilemmas across Russian society. For instance, Nancy Ries has argued that any stability and growth associated with the Putin era is a tribute to the government's effective public relations, which has free rein while independent media is suppressed (2009: 188), rather than a substantive advancement in quality of life. Indeed, she argues that *dacha* subsistence (fruit and vegetable gardening) remains important in Russian society because people still seek to hedge against the possibility that the economy will fall apart (Ries 2009: 188). Jeremy Morris has emphasised how poor working Russians valorise self-resourcing and provisioning in communities that remain normatively and materially reliant upon the informal economy (2012a; 2012b). In her study of how middle-class teachers negotiated the changes wrought by marketisation on their moral and material status, Jennifer Patico argued that individuals apply moral legitimacy and social validation to different activities in different contexts, such that their meaning is continually reassessed in the post-socialist context (2009: 218–19). In Serguei Oushakine's study of how the remote Altai region was 'searching for its way in a market economy' without significant investment, he finds that the arrival of capital and commercial institutions was a 'culturally alien, geographically and historically distant event' that appeared as a 'physical rupture in the established social fabric' (2009: 77).

In attempting to reconcile themselves to these changes, a 'dizzying array' of social groups and tendencies emerged. In time, these coalesced around an 'organising plot' in which many people felt manipulated by external forces that linked money with lies and capital with corruption. This, he finds, led people to attempt to rekindle the past and reformulate a 'lost sense of unifying collectivity' or 'true Russian path' (Oushakine 2009: 77–78). If such studies demonstrate the continuing complexity of Russians' experience of post-socialism, it seems appropriate to examine the contemporary experience of entrepreneurs in more detail, particularly in light of their paradoxical status as both supported and undermined by the state.

Research Design: A Multi-sited Ethnography in Three Regional Businesses

I now set out my approach to studying business ethnographically. I draw particularly on Jan Kubik to set out my ethnographic approach. He has argued that the best research in post-communist studies accords with four principles, which he has drawn together in a research programme grounded in ethnography called 'contextual holism' (2015b: online). The first principle, relationism, demands that attention is given to historical relations, dependencies and entanglements such that individuals are considered to be 'embedded' between agency and structure. This is a reminder not to focus on 'the extremes' of agency or structure, but to work with them both. The second, historicism, underlines that history matters, so legacies, path dependencies, critical junctures and so on must be taken seriously. The third, constructivism, recognises that the way informants see the world has an impact upon what they do. The fourth, formal–informal hybrids, demands that researchers acknowledge that in the post-communist era much activity takes place between official structures and informal networks (Kubik 2015b: online). Combining these principles, 'contextual holism' 'privileges the local dimension of the post-communist transformations and attempts to generate analyses of the macro phenomena' (Kubik 2013: 63).

'Contextual holism' is also an attempt to reinvigorate Area Studies, which, according to Kubik, once provided interdisciplinary conversation between the humanities and social sciences about particular cultures, but has long been in crisis (Kubik 2015b: online). Today, he argues, 'Area' is better defined as 'a situation' determined by the factors categorised by contextual holism. Thus, in this study *relationism* refers to the informal networks that create and maintain the local situation for entrepreneurs, as well as the external networks between them and the centre; *historicism* refers to the legacies that define and legitimate the situation and the critical junctures that changed it; *constructivism* refers to the common interpretations or sensibility shared by entrepreneurs; *hybridity* refers to the tendency in post-communist societies (and therefore among entrepreneurs) to rely on informal social capital and formal institutions (adapted from Kubik 2013: 60; 2015b: online).

The other aspect of 'contextual holism' that suits my research objectives is its emphasis on ethnography. Kubik argues that ethnographers view agents as capable of 'fixing themselves' and 'adjusting their strategies in order to cope with the changing environment' according to behaviours emerging from their '*historically evolved* social and cultural environments' (2013: 66), which provide templates that can make their apparently contingent existence predictable. As he puts it,

> Many such templates are formed and reformed in institutions that are often informal-formal hybrids and as such are best investigated through case studies designed to generate richly textured knowledge. Ethnographic participant observation is particularly suited to this task … [which makes it] possible to observe and reconstruct actors' strategic creativity and thus serve as a welcome corrective to approaches that treat postcommunist transformations as phenomena of the macroscale.
>
> (2013: 66)

In these respects, contextual holism offers a methodological and analytical framework grounded in post-communist studies that is appropriate for the requirements of this research: it represents a shift in post-communist studies towards the actions of individuals within structures rather than elites (Daniel 2015: 55). As Kubik puts it,

> Thoughtful scholars of post-communism have come to realize that the seemingly intractable duality of structure and agency cannot be sidestepped but must be unpacked and theorized – even if unperfectly [sic] – if we hope to improve our understanding of … regime change and transformations.
>
> (Kubik 2015a: 355)

Bearing Kubik's approach in mind, I resist the convention to adhere to a formal definition of entrepreneurship. According to the definitions set out in Russian law (see Chapter 1) my three informants all run SMEs. The first, Anna, is an 'individual entrepreneur' and the others, Oleg and Aleksandr, run 'micro-businesses'. However, these definitions are rather meaningless because, as the case studies reveal (Chapters 3–5), what they portray their business to be formally, and what it actually is (or will be) are not the same thing. Instead, the point of this study is to describe what entrepreneurs are doing in order to define entrepreneurship more effectively. This approach is supported by the fact that, as I have already written, there is very little empirical information available about Russian business in practice.

That said, my informants do own 'legitimate' registered businesses, which they established themselves, so for the sake of convention Victoria Bonnell and Thomas Gold's definition, taken from their editorial chapter on business development in post-communist Europe and Asia, is sufficiently broad to encompass the commercial activities I observed. According to them, entrepreneurs

> Organise and direct businesses, assuming risk for the sake of profit … carry out certain necessary tasks, including perception of economic opportunities, assembling the financial and material resources and inputs for innovation, recruiting personnel, and dealing with suppliers, purchasers, and the government.
>
> (2002: xv)

Nevertheless, due to its contested status, I maintain that 'entrepreneurship' in Russia is better defined according to inductive study. As I will show, my informants' entrepreneurial activities were not limited to commercial ('conventional') business activities but a range of formal and informal everyday actions aimed at securing their status as entrepreneurs. Indeed, I will show that my informants' activities are revealed more accurately by examining what Yurchak has defined as their 'entrepreneurial governmentality'. This, as I will show, is to know 'what an entrepreneurial act is, who can act entrepreneurially, and what or who can be acted upon in an entrepreneurial way' in the context of a state which has been partly privatised by officials about whose power they can do very little (2002: 310–313).

The breadth of definition I demand at this stage does not mean that the case studies have little in common. The businesses are located in one of three neighbouring *oblasts* and united by their shared location in a single federal district, Western Siberia. The choice of these Siberian regions for the research requires careful justification, however. Russia is the world's largest country, which endows it by definition with significant regional diversity. In particular, as Baranov et al. state,

> The institutional environment in Russia is highly uneven across its vast territory, and Russian regions exhibit significant differences in investment attractiveness, business climate, and regional government effectiveness … As a result, Russia-wide measures of institutional quality could be at best accurate on the average and remote from the actual conditions on the ground in a particular region. Therefore, there is a strong need to measure institutional performance regionally.
>
> (Baranov et al. 2015: 155–56, 161)

In spite of these differences, Russia's regions also have significant factors in common, not least of which include a shared historical legacy, national institutions, policies and laws (Baranov et al. 2015: 156; Sharafutdinova and Kisunko 2014: 2). Moreover, institutional asymmetry is a general feature in Russia, even if its particular characteristics and quality vary from region to region; this is a point that my case study materials will underline. For example, according to Baranov et al., between the first and second half of the 2000s, 'the groups of regions with the greatest danger of doing business (variously measured) have changed their compositions by more than 50 per cent' (Baranov et al. 2015: 174). This suggests considerable institutional instability, and therefore state quality, facing private enterprise across the country. It is therefore not entirely useful to choose a region based on its relative institutional characteristics because those characteristics are in significant flux countrywide. The importance of regional specificity to business conditions is reinforced by Sharafutidinova and Steinbuks (2017), who drew on survey data on Russia's business environment to conclude that Russia's firms hold a 'strong preference for a more stable and predictable environment and intense dislike of political change' at the regional level, and a 'strong preference for locally embedded authorities', which indicates the value of 'local social capital and pre-existing inter-elite connections for state-business relations in the regions' (2017: 16). Besides, as Baranov et al. also argue, 'one should still expect that regional indicators of economic, legal and political institutions broadly follow overall Russian trends – if for no other reason than because national indices are aggregates of regional ones' (Baranov et al. 2015: 175).

Nevertheless, Zubarevich has pointed out that studies of Russia tend to focus too much on geographic variations. Researchers often position their work in the context of the Volga, the Urals, Siberia and so on (2012: online). These regions are themselves very large, so the significant variation within them is missed. Zubarevich argues that researchers should instead re-examine the country through the lens of four different 'Russias' (Zubarevich 2012: online) according to population and quality of life indicators rather than geographical boundaries. The first Russia is that of the post-industrial cities of 500,000 to 1 million people, which amounts to thirty per cent of the population (or forty per cent if it includes towns of over 250,000 people, although the differences between these towns increases greatly with this categorisation). The second Russia is that of the blue-collar workers, including industrial towns that retain 'a strong Soviet ethos and way of life'. These towns have populations between 25,000 and 250,000 inhabitants, and together amount to 25 per cent of the population. The third Russia is that of the rural and semi-urban populations who live 'off the land' and are 'indifferent to politics'. According to Zubarevich, these three Russias are defined 'using the centre-periphery model, which explains social variations by geographic factors, that is to say their position in a hierarchy of settlement from the most modernised large cities to the patriarchal rural periphery' (Zubarevich 2012: online). This model does not work for the fourth Russia, however, which is constituted by the less developed republics of the northern Caucasus and Southern Siberia (the Tyva and Altai areas), home to less than 6 per cent of the population, and where there are towns but 'none of them have any industry' (Zubarevich 2012: online).

Given the significant territorial and socio-economic differences I have described, drawing on Baranov et al. and Zubarevich, the question of choosing a case remains. It appears that no oblast or city can be adequately representative of Russia. Every location offers characteristics that make it both distinctive and typical of the country: state capacity, quality and institutional conditions vary. For example, Roberto Stefan Foa and Anna Nemirovskaya have found that 'frontier zones' such as Siberia, as in other parts of the world, are characterized by a deficiency of state capacity and lower rule of law (Foa and Nemirovskaya 2016: 429). Nevertheless, because this is an ethnographic study, I do not seek to make general claims about Russia as a whole by inferring from a particular region. Rather, my objective is to examine institutional asymmetry from the perspective of the entrepreneur rather than their region or with respect to state quality. This does not, however, detract from the utility of the approach. As a recent World Bank report on Russia stated,

> Only small … in depth ethnographic studies are usually able to capture the variety of particular rules, norms and agreements that structure social relationships, including the interactions among state and business actors. Still, their significance in state–business relations is critical. The prevailing informal rules and agreements explain not only how these relations actually function; their understanding is crucially important for designing realistic pro-growth policies.
>
> (Sharafutdinova and Kisunko 2014: 4)

In this way I argue that what my study may lose in 'representativeness' it gains with in-depth material describing business–state relations under conditions of institutional asymmetry from the viewpoint of my informants. The findings offer an indication of how entrepreneurs can get by in Russia, even if they cannot be called representative of Russia as a whole. This leaves the question: why have I chosen Siberia? Most significantly, as Oushakine has argued, Siberia offers above all an unusual field site simply because it is away from Moscow and St. Petersburg (or Zubarevich's 'first Russia'), which are the most common locations for scholarly research (Oushakine 2009: 7–8). This in itself offers something distinctive to the field of Russian studies. Some, like Hill and Gaddy, argue that Russia's particular geography presents a unique challenge to the development of the market because the population is distributed in cities that are relatively small and distant from one another across its entire territory, which is a characteristic not shared by other market economies (2003: 17–25). This challenge, they contend, is most pronounced in Siberia, where the cost of transportation, the establishment of trust between market actors and 'the creation and functioning of shared institutions' are all hindered by the region's enormity (Hill and Gaddy 2003: 25). This represents a challenge to my choice. However, I argue that their analysis is correct only if one accepts that Russian capitalism is developing in a fashion that resembles the Western market. Yet it becomes clear in the course of this book, if it is not already, that while there are certainly geographical limits on the profitability of business in Siberia, Russia is not really becoming a Western-type market economy at present. Besides, the idea that Siberia is poorly endowed for the market economy is debatable. Inozemtsev argues that by late 2012 (as my fieldwork began) Siberia provided the materials to make the products that constitute up to 75 per cent of Russia's exports and, more fundamentally, a majority of the subsurface mineral extraction tax and export duties for oil and natural gas that make up over 50 per cent of Russia's federal revenues (Inozemtsev 2013: online). Thus, Leonid Khotin has argued that Siberia is less a victim of geography than plundering by Moscow (2007: 48), and this, I contend, makes Siberia an integral part of Russia's contemporary political economy.

More to the point, if Siberia does present some of the most challenging conditions for business, it seems appropriate to study them over the more 'conventional' conditions found elsewhere in Western Russia. That is, Siberia presents unique factors that others do not. For example, as I will show, especially in Chapter 3, Siberia does present geographical limits on the market available to small businesses, however that this led my informants to trade in the social, rather than purely economic, interest. Even so, I have considered my case study choice with national, regional and institutional factors in mind. The three cities in which this research was undertaken are in neighbouring oblast in Western Siberia, which offers a comparable element within a large federal district in the middle of the country. Despite the common idea that Siberia is exceptional, these cities actually have large populations sufficient to place them within Zubarevich's 'first Russia'. As a consequence, my informants operate their businesses in by far the largest settlements in their respective oblasts. This means they are subjected both to Siberia's unique geographical challenges (see particularly Chapter 3) but that they also habitually interact and trade with populations from Zubarevich's other 'Russias'.

What else makes my Siberian cases representative of Russian entrepreneurs' experiences and comparable? First, my informants all came of age in the late communist period, which meant they were among the first generation of Russian entrepreneurs. Second, they did not inherit or assume the leadership of former state enterprises but established *de novo* businesses according to their own initiatives between 1989 and 2000 in their home cities. Third, although their businesses have changed over time, they have all managed to stay in business in spite of a variety of difficulties, which I will describe. The most fundamental characteristic uniting them, however, is the very different approaches they have each taken to negotiating the institutional environment that they encounter. It is this factor that, I argue, justifies my reluctance to define entrepreneurship too rigidly or become too preoccupied with the regional aspects of their experience: from the outset, these entrepreneurs could not follow an established entrepreneurial formula but learnt how to do business *by doing it* (see also Hass 2005: 10), with varied approaches and results. This, I will argue, is the most significant influence of Russia's institutional asymmetry upon entrepreneurship.

Introduction to the Case Studies

In a region as large as Siberia (one that inherits the Soviet Union's peculiar spatial industrial character, with distinct geographical, economic and social characteristics), each oblast is somewhat unique – and potentially identifiable when described in detail. Thus, while the three cities I describe have distinct historical, socio-economic, geographic and post-socialist experiences, I have also changed the names of my informants, with their permission, as well as the names of their businesses, cities and regions to protect their anonymity.

The first case study describes the entrepreneurship of Oleg and his directors, Irina and Dmitrii. He established *Sibtekhnika* in 1991 in *Priyatnyi*, the administrative centre (regional capital) of *Priyatnaya* oblast, which has become a successful group of companies (*gruppa kompanii*) offering design and fitting services to the retail sector, and industrial equipment and furniture to the commercial, education and construction sectors in several Siberian cities. Oleg's entrepreneurial success derives from his desire for independence from the state and his ability to bring this about by working pragmatically with the full range of actors in Russian business, whether they are entrepreneurs, state officials or criminals. In spite of his success, however, he is an opponent of the political economic status quo and has established a private community centre to quietly advance values he supports and, in a small but determined way, undermine the state.

The second case study describes the entrepreneurship of Anna, who established her company, the Centre for Small Business Growth (CSBG) in 2000 in *Oblomov*, the administrative centre of *Oblomovskaya* oblast. Anna studied in Europe before securing financial support to establish CSBG with the objective of supporting the development of entrepreneurship in *Oblomov*. However, despite her connections in the West, her knowledge of how Western business works and her commitment to Russia's transformation into a market economy, these advantages have not translated into business success in Russia; her company has been in a state of crisis for over three years as a result of a poorly judged business deal and a series of malicious interventions by officials and former clients. Nevertheless, Anna has managed to survive in business even as the demise of CSBG appeared inevitable. Her survival results less from her business acumen than the necessity of working between the formal and shadow economies, and by assiduously invoking the state's formal institutional support to entrepreneurs against her attackers. In this way, Anna works between Russia's formal and informal institutions to create the conditions for her survival, which necessarily involves undermining the state.

The third case study describes the entrepreneurship of Aleksandr and his son Yurii. Aleksandr established a construction company in 1991 in *Normalnyi*, the administrative centre of *Normalnaya* oblast, which became one of the most successful businesses in the region over the course of the next decade, but which was then acquired by officials in a case of reiderstvo in the mid-2000s. This led to his imprisonment for several months. Unusually, and with the significant financial resources he held at the time, Aleksandr fought successfully for his release. Since then, he has re-established himself as an entrepreneur and started a new company, *Promploshchad*, which is a commercial site with light industrial units let to other small enterprises. With his experience of both the great potential of independent business and the predatory capacity of the state, Aleksandr's entrepreneurial approach is characterised above all by a wariness of the state, whose representatives he seeks to avoid unless completely necessary. Although he is sufficiently well connected and experienced to succeed in expanding his business, his plans are nowadays tempered by the desire to combine a steady profit with a low profile.

Preview of Key Finding: The Prospect of an Independent Life Outweighs the Risks of Business

Considering only these brief descriptions of my informants' experiences together, a clear factor uniting them is that the arbitrary and malign potential of the state has had a determinant effect on the trajectories of their businesses and, therefore, their approach to relations with officialdom. Their survival or success has depended on their abilities to use their own resources to respond to a state that does more to undermine than support them. Although they are opposed to working this way, they have to do so because of Russia's 'institutional asymmetry' and, accordingly, the precariousness of their situation. To therefore state the obvious, working between informal and formal institutions is not an indication of the 'corruption' of Russian entrepreneurs, but of the pragmatism that is a consequence of a political economy in which there are no alternatives. To be in business between formal and informal institutions is to operate in a precarious legal limbo that resembles the 'suspended punishment' common in the Soviet period and defined by Alena Ledeneva:

> [Freedom was] predicated upon following the unwritten rules and a subtle understanding of what was possible and what was not, and to what extent one could pursue one's interests… the availability of unwritten codes alongside the written ones, and the usual practice for authorities to switch to the written code only 'where necessary' created certain freedom and flexibility. On the other hand such leniency could be restricted at every moment. This arrangement is based on the idea of suspended punishment.
>
> (1998: 77)

These blurred lines between public and private affairs and the constant risk of falling victim to predation appear to be alive and well in contemporary Russia. Consequently, defining my informants' businesses according to their profitability, number of employees or size is not a useful guide to either their experiences or, as I show, ambitions: their companies have grown and contracted as they faced conditions beyond their control, so their priorities are continuity and independence, whereas commercial growth is an aspiration.

However, while institutional theorists may welcome the empirical evidence in these case studies, I do not find 'informal activity' alone a persuasive explanation for how my informants 'get by'. For example 'social capital', the linkages between individuals that 'give the collectivity cohesiveness and thereby facilitate the pursuit of collective goals' (Adleft and Kwon 2002: 21), is often described as a substitute for formal institutions (for example Puffer and McCarthy 2007: 9), but it does not give my informants safe passage, so I argue that it cannot be used with such certainty. The state can still do whatever it wants: to take a famous example, the jailing of Mikhail Khodorkovsky, an extremely influential man, and the re-nationalisation of his company *Yukos*, the largest in the country, demonstrates this very clearly (on this case see Sakwa 2014: 91). Oleg has excellent social capital and is the most 'successful' of my three informants, but knows that he could suffer a similar fate at any time, just as Anna and Aleksandr also did. As such, further explanation is needed of whether he has simply been lucky and what has motivated him to carry on in spite of this risk. Likewise, Aleksandr has experienced first-hand how a successful business can be consumed by the state but still decided to start again. Moreover, Anna failed in legitimate business but retreated to the shadow economy in order to avoid giving it up altogether, even with the odds stacked against her. Hence, a conceptualisation of entrepreneurship is required that accounts for how entrepreneurs work amid institutional asymmetry *and* why they become, and continue to be, entrepreneurs in such a risky environment.

Entrepreneurial Governmentality

In order to achieve this in my case studies, I draw on Yurchak's concept of 'entrepreneurial governmentality', which reconsiders what it means to be 'entrepreneurial' in the Russian context. Yurchak bases entrepreneurial governmentality on the concept of governmentality conceived by Foucault, which meant the 'art of government', the 'rationality of government' (Foucault in Yurchak 2002: 279), or the

> Way or system of thinking about the practice of government (who can govern; what governing is; what or who can be governed), capable of making some form of that activity thinkable and practicable both to its practitioners and to those upon whom it was practiced.
>
> (Gordon in Yurchak 2002: 279)

Taking this conceptual approach, Yurchak seeks to conceive of entrepreneurship as 'a form of governmentality' (Yurchak 2002: 279). That is, Yurchak is concerned with the *art or rationality of entrepreneurship* in relation to the state and other features in society:

> In Foucauldian terms, then, to be an entrepreneur is to have entrepreneurial governmentality that makes it 'thinkable and practicable' to relate to different aspects of the world – people, relations, institutions, the state, laws – in terms of symbolic commodities, risks, capital, profits, costs, needs, demands and so on. It is a way of knowing what an entrepreneurial act is, who can act entrepreneurially, and what or whom can be acted upon in an entrepreneurial way. The category of entrepreneurial

> governmentality will allow me to speak about entrepreneurship in a context in which there was no private market or business.
>
> (Yurchak 2002: 279)

Additionally, Yurchak argues that 'no relationship between the individual and the state is marked only by official codes. The state's institutions, laws, and ideologies everywhere are related to a mixture of terms that allow individuals to "officialize" or "personalize" them depending on the context' (Yurchak 2002: 279). Yurchak argues, moreover, that the 'mixture' of personalised and officialised terms was most pronounced in the period of late socialism (Yurchak 2002: 279), which resulted in a hybrid state and had profound implications for the entrepreneurial patterns which have emerged in Russia today. In this respect, Yurchak calls for analysis of entrepreneurship that focuses on both structural constraints upon agents and how agents act in their relations with official structures.

In Yurchak's view, the features of post-communist entrepreneurship have roots in the late 1970s when Soviet society began to view Soviet state ideology more pragmatically and less idealistically (2002: 282). As a consequence of this shift the public sphere was reorganised into a hybrid form in which social activity took place within 'officialised-public' and 'personalised-public' spheres (Yurchak 2002: 287). For Yurchak, conceiving of the Soviet state as a hybrid challenges the Western scholarly construction of state–society relations in which 'dichotomies as public vs. private, legal vs. illegal and state vs. civil society' delineate between two forms of behaviour. Instead, the two spheres of practice 'coexist and overlap in the same space and context' (Yurchak 2002: 287). This means that relations between the Soviet citizen and state took on a 'dialogical or hybrid cultural dynamic' in which official meanings were reconceived in personal terms. Citizens completed their official work in a way that 'took advantage of the distinctions between the hybrid spheres' (Yurchak 2002: 288) so that state plans were officially fulfilled but results were reinterpreted such that their 'fulfilment' acquired a meaning quite distinct from the original (Yurchak 2002: 288). To put this plainly, citizens began to consider that the state, including its laws, documents and representatives, should be obeyed only in the officialised-public sphere (Yurchak 2002: 301), which allowed them to work in between the two spheres and their personal interests at other times.

How did this change affect the emergence of post-communist business? Yurchak argues that during the post-communist period the officialised-public sphere, constituted by old communist ideologies, laws and institutions, entered a period of crisis that meant the personalised-public sphere, constituted by relations and practices, grew in everyday significance. This meant that as new businesses emerged, entrepreneurs drew on the 'understandings of that sphere' (Yurchak 2002: 311). At the same time, Yurchak argues, the state's personalised-public sphere 'did not collapse but rather readapted to the new situation much better than was obvious at the time' (Yurchak 2002: 311), meaning that it was state officials who were open to acting entrepreneurially within their role as circumstances changed, which ensured that they secured access to resources and power in the post-Soviet period. As Yurchak states,

> Because of the crisis of the officialised-public sphere, the process of constructing new institutions, laws, relations, and ideologies of the state became informed within personalised relations and understandings on all levels. The hybridity of the relations between the individual and the state became perhaps even more omnipresent than was ever the case during socialism.
> (Yurchak 2002: 311)

Consequently, most entrepreneurs still 'turn to the hybrid model when they interpret the rationale behind the rules, laws and actions of the state and its representatives (Yurchak 2002: 311), while most state representatives 'also expect their relations with businessmen to be based on the hybrid model' (Yurchak 2002: 311). In this way, entrepreneurs have continued to see the state 'as being partly privatised by state officials' (Yurchak 2002: 312) and are confident that all forms of power in the country have been redistributed already so their vulnerable position vis-à-vis the state is fixed and cannot be changed (Yurchak 2002: 313). As a result, they must 'rely only on their own ingenuity for the success or even survival of their family or business' (Yurchak 2002: 313), based on their ability to engage with the 'relations, practices and meanings of personalised-public spheres' (Yurchak 2002: 313). As I show, Oleg and Aleksandr share this perception while Anna now faces that reality even if she had been unable to see it before her crisis. Under these circumstances it is a mistake to consider Russian entrepreneurship in flux or through the paradigm of modernisation as the state would imply. The overall point, however, is that both entrepreneurs and officials recognise that the political economy is highly unpredictable because its officials tend to act in unofficial ways.

Entrepreneurial governmentality de-emphasises the commercial element that is at the heart of conventional definitions of entrepreneurship and replaces it with an emphasis on knowledge, skills and ways of thinking that developed in the late socialist era (Yurchak 2005: 297). The specific objective of this entrepreneurialism, moreover, is to ensure one's autonomy from the state or 'suspended punishment'. Thus, Yurchak finds that entrepreneurs

> … represent a group of active and creative agents who consciously try to stay relatively independent from the state and to insure themselves against its unpredictability. They engage in this entrepreneurial practice not simply to enrich themselves at any cost but to build a meaningful, independent, and 'civilised' reality for themselves, at least partly in spite of the state. It is among this group of people that a version of civil society may develop.
> (Yurchak 2002: 313)

In the case study chapters, I find 'entrepreneurial governmentality' a persuasive concept for explaining my informants' attitudes and behaviours. I argue that their shared attitude to entrepreneurship is based on a drive for their own 'civilised reality'. It can also serve to explain the various business outcomes of my informants without relying on social capital alone: Oleg's relative 'success', for example, is explained by his constant dedication to asserting control in the local market, working and negotiating pragmatically with the full gamut of personalities he encounters in the course of commercial life and limiting the arbitrary potential of local officials. By contrast, Anna and Aleksandr's recognition of the personalisation of the state has been reactive, responding to the respective crises in which they lost control of their businesses. Accordingly, the case studies show that relations between officials and entrepreneurs are not necessarily antagonistic but based on mutual interests decided in the personalised-public sphere.

'Entrepreneurial governmentality' can help to explain my informants' agency effectively, but I find it does not provide a wholly adequate answer to why my informants become entrepreneurs in the first place. That is, it cannot clearly determine why entrepreneurs deem 'civilised reality' to be worth the risks they have to take trying to get there. I therefore move beyond Yurchak conceptually to argue that my informants' entrepreneurship also displays a determined resistance to the state. Entrepreneurship, after all, is a chosen vocation that, in the Russian context, contains numerous difficulties and dangers. Although Yurchak does mention that entrepreneurs represent a potential bloc of opposition to the status quo (2002: 315), he does not explore it empirically. It has also been mentioned that the potential for opposition among entrepreneurs is one of the factors explaining the government's rhetorical support for business (Kesby 2012: online), but little is known about this empirically. What is clear is that SMEs, in contrast to larger firms, are not attracted to business associations that could represent their interests (Golikova 2009: 278), seeking instead, as I show, to solve their own problems autonomously. Thus, the specific ways in which entrepreneurs oppose the state are poorly understood. In my case studies, however, it is clear that my informants seek not only autonomy but, to various extents, work to change the material conditions of the political economy as they encounter it. This evokes North's point (Chapter 1) that entrepreneurs seek to change their institutional constraints when they encounter them. Thus, I find entrepreneurship is undertaken not only for the type of independent life it represents, but also because of the possibility it gives to surreptitiously undermine and challenge the status quo that my informants reject.

Theoretical Implications

To reiterate, the purpose of this research is to describe and explain what doing business in Russia is actually like in a political economy in which the state 'supports and undermines' entrepreneurs, at a time when there is a shortage of recent studies based on observation of entrepreneurship. However, ethnography is an inductive methodology 'generative of its own analytical categories' (Morris 2012b: 219). Thus, in the course of fieldwork it became clear that my informants' everyday activities and relations with officials could not easily be reconciled with prevailing theory about the structure of Russia's political economy. I find that the role and influence of business is under-represented in these theories, which assume the dominance of the state with a negligible role for other actors. Leon Aron, for example, conceives of the 'Putin doctrine', in which the state has reclaimed control of the 'commanding heights' of the economy, primarily the oil and natural gas industries (2013a: online) to become again 'the only sovereign political and economic actor in Russia, with the private sector, civil society, and its institutions mere objects' (Aron 2013b: online). In Aron's account, the Putin doctrine was created based on an assessment that the country needed to achieve economic growth of 4 to 6 per cent a year in order to keep up with developed countries, which meant that primary resources would 'be central to the country's economic development, security and modernisation' for at least the first half of the 21st century (Aron 2013b: online). At the same time, by controlling the 'rents' generated from hydrocarbon exports, the government can ensure the loyalty of the low-income and elite segments of the country that present, apparently, the greatest challenge to the stability of the state. As a result, the institutions required to develop business have never been a priority for the government.

Aron's account of a 'petro-gas state' (Aron 2013b: online) is but one of multiple conceptualisations of the political economy in which the state has a leading, arbitrarily dominant position and the private sector is powerless and vulnerable to interference. Other examples include Ian Bremmer's 'state capitalism' (2009: 41), Clifford Gaddy and Barry Ickes's 'rent management system' (RMS) (2015), Neil Robinson's 'political' or 'state' capitalism (2013a: 3–4) and 'patrimonial capitalism' (2013b: 137), Peter Rutland's 'petrostate' (2015: 67) and Pekka Sutela's 'dual economy' (1999: 10; 2012: 64). I term these theories 'hybrid' in the sense that the two sectors have essential roles in the economy, but an ontological delineation is made in which the state sector is strong and the private sector weak. Thus, the relationship between the two sectors in these theories is considered, to borrow Connolly's phrase, 'generally one-way' (2009: 186). It is true that not all analyses focus on two sectors alone. In Sheila Puffer and Daniel McCarthy's conception of state-managed network capitalism, for example, the division goes three ways – between market, siloviki and oligarchic sectors – but the role of the state is still central (2007: 8). Therefore, I do not claim that these theories are indistinguishable from one another, but that they do share the conception that independent businesses are dependent variables, reliant on the support of the state for the amelioration of business conditions and without the capacity to exert change on their everyday circumstances. In other words, entrepreneurs are perceived to lack agency. To an extent, this claim is unfair, because some of these theories do not really consider the role of independent business in any significant way at all; however, this absence only serves my general argument further, which is that the role of business in the political economy requires further empirical and theoretical attention.

A short glance at my case studies offers sufficient evidence to substantiate this point. Oleg is unambiguously negative about business conditions but has created a successful business. Moreover, he has developed amiable, pragmatic relations with local state-affiliated elites. More complicated still, Oleg has used his own resources to build and staff a local community centre that directly (if surreptitiously) challenges the prevailing political system. Hybrid theories cannot adequately account for why his business has thrived (or indeed any successful business), for his cordial relations with local elites, or for his ability to get away with challenging the state. Anna, in stark contrast, is unambiguously hopeful about the prospects for the Westernisation of Russian business conditions but has faced a major business crisis in which she must continually defend herself against adversaries and officials who wish to see her fail. Hybrid theories cannot account for her optimism, the survival of her business or her determination to fight the state. Moreover, Aleksandr was a victim of the predatory state and spent time in prison but managed to survive and rebuild a new business. Again, hybrid theories cannot account for the nuances of his survival or his re-emergence as a businessman. Therefore, the basis of my empirical critique is that hybrid theories can shed light on the relative *power relations* between the state and private sectors, but they do not reveal the *actual relations* between them. Their ontological delineation between a leading state and subordinate private sector misrepresents the way in which the two sectors are integrated, objectifying the business sphere as a dependent variable.

Thus, my case studies will show that although these entrepreneurs are relatively weak compared to the state as they encounter it, and there are significant differences in their relative experiences, they each wield considerably more influence than predominant theories would suggest. Several factors bear this out. For one, it will be clear that although my informants share a disdain for a political economic system in which they are vulnerable, they also share a determination to build their businesses regardless. Moreover, this motivation is not subdued by their negative experiences of the state but *enhanced* by them: they are unwilling to give up their status as entrepreneurs easily. The case studies will show, for example, that Anna refused to give up what seemed to be a hopeless set of circumstances, while Aleksandr returned to entrepreneurship in spite of losing his successful business. This makes their entrepreneurship more than a commercial decision: it is a normative choice to work in private business in spite of the risks. Second, their motivation to endure in business is supported by their knowledge of how to do so between the formal and informal spheres whether, as in Anna's case, they are enduring a crisis or, as in Oleg's case, overseeing a profitable company. Thus, it seems businesses can survive and thrive in spite of their vulnerability. Third, it is clear that 'entrepreneurs' are not the only people involved in 'business'. For example, Oleg's case demonstrates the continuing importance of the mafiya in the Russian commercial scene and the personal role of regional elites and their families in commerce and economic development in their territories. Anna's case shows how local officials became personally involved in the destruction of her business on behalf of their personal acquaintances in the private sector. Aleksandr's case illustrates the manner in which senior local officials devoted considerable personal attention and resources to the illicit acquisition of his company's assets. It is therefore not particularly meaningful to delineate between 'the state' and 'private business', as predominant theories do, because the distinction breaks down in the real economy. Fourth, I find that entrepreneurs are not necessarily subordinate to officials or elites all the time. I will show, for example, that when Oleg conducted a business deal with members of his region's elite, he was in a stronger relative position than them even though they held vastly more power. In fact, this business deal shows that relations between the private sector (represented by Oleg) and the state sector (represented by the elites) can be civil, productive and based on mutual interests. To put this another way, I show that while Anna and Aleksandr's antagonistic relations with officialdom may be more common, Oleg's relations with regional elites proves that the private sector is not necessarily at the mercy of the state. Fifth, and most interestingly, I find that each of my informants is able to resist and undermine the state and its representatives in their own way. Indeed, the case studies show that resistance appears to be an important part of my informants' entrepreneurship: it is the consequence of, and reaction to, the risky and informal context in which they are obliged to work. Overall, I will show that hybridity interpreted according to predominant theories does not represent business in the way I observed it in the field. My informants wield a kind of agency that allows them to endure and resist oppression in 'suspended punishment' so as to survive or even thrive. A better account of this agency, which is a response to institutional asymmetry, is required.

In order to account for the actual relationship between the state and private sector as I observed it, I will argue that a theoretical framework is required that puts institutions at the centre of analysis and draw on North et al.'s social orders theory to achieve this. This theory has been developed to explain the underlying logic of two patterns of social organisation or 'orders' and how societies can move from one type of order to another (North et al. 2009: 1). Specifically, social orders are

> Characterized by the way societies craft institutions that support the existence of specific forms of human organization, the way societies limit or open access to those organizations, and through the incentives created by the pattern of organization. These characteristics of social orders are also intimately related to how societies limit and control violence. Because social orders engender different patterns of behavior, individuals in different social orders form different beliefs about how the people around them behave.
>
> (North et al. 2009: 1–2)

Based on this definition, North et al. have developed a spectrum of three social order types. The first, the 'foraging order', is one of the 'small social groups' resembling hunter–gatherer societies' (North et al. 2009: 2). The second order, which emerged in the first social revolution, is the 'limited access order' (LAOs) or 'natural state' (North et al. 2009: 2). In LAOs,

> Personal relationships, who one is and who one knows, form the basis for social organization and constitute the arena for individual interaction, particularly personal relationships among powerful individuals. Natural states limit the ability of individuals to form organizations.
>
> (North et al. 2009: 2)

The third type, open access orders (OAOs), emerged with the second social revolution or rise of modernity. According to North et al., in OAOs,

> Personal relations still matter, but impersonal categories of individuals, often called citizens, interact over wide areas of social behavior with no need to be cognizant of the individual identity of their partners. Identity, which in natural states is inherently personal, becomes defined as a set of impersonal characteristics … Both social orders [LAO and OAO] have public and private organizations, but natural states limit access to those organizations whereas open access societies do not.
>
> (North et al. 2009: 2)

According to North et al., today all low- and middle-income countries are LAOs despite wide differences in their per capita incomes and quality of institutions (North et al. 2013b: 10). To differentiate them, they distinguish between fragile, basic and mature LAOs, which are 'differentiated by the structure of their organizations' (North et al. 2013b: 11), although the chief characteristic of all LAOs is that leaders limit access to opportunities for organisation (North et al. 2013b: 4). That is, a 'dominant coalition' forms that manipulates the political economy to create rents, which incentivises powerful groups to limit violence (North et al. 2009: 3; 2013b: 3). The dominant coalition includes a number of elite specialists in political, economic, religious and military activities who hold privileged access to vital functions like production, justice, trade, education and so on (North et al. 2009: 18–20). Because their positions depend upon 'the limited entry enforced by the continued existence of the regime', they are incentivised to help support and maintain it, or face violence, disorder and loss of rents (North et al. 2009: 19–20). A critical result of this arrangement is that the dominant coalition is able to control how organisations develop, who develops them and how rents are distributed. This induces discipline among elites because they rely on the support of the coalition, which receives rents from the organisation of productive resources under its auspices (North et al. 2013b: 20). This mutual interest between elites creates what North et al. describe as a 'double balance', meaning that peace is dependent upon the satisfactory balance of interests created by the 'rent-creation process' (North et al. 2013b: 20). Jong-Sung puts this most simply: 'Sustaining fundamental changes in either the economic or political system cannot occur without fundamental changes in the other' (Jong-Sung 2013: 313–14). In practice, this means that an LAO has to mature on its own terms: 'When the institutional forms of an OAO are transplanted to an LAO, the logic of the LAO bends them to the purpose of rent creation to sustain the existing dominant coalition' (Jong-Sung 2013: 314). The dichotomy between Russia's Western-style policies for the development of the business sector and their ineffectiveness in practice may be seen as an example of this.

Due to the fact that peace depends on the balance created by the 'rent-creation process', violence is always a possibility in an LAO, so different groups maintain their strength as a check on one other's power. As a consequence, the dominant coalition cannot last forever, while external shocks such as changes in relative prices or technology can also induce a shock (North et al. 2009: 21). For an LAO to mature, three processes are required. First, rent-generating activities are arranged such that more of the organisations with the capacity for violence are incentivised to reduce actual violence. Second, the rule of law is expanded over a greater number of activities but in a way that is consistent with the incentives that prevent organisations from using violence. Third, the government becomes more reliable in securing support for organisations and enforcing agreements among them (North et al. 2013b: 15–16). Thereafter, it is possible for LAOs to 'transition' to OAOs if institutional arrangements are settled that enable impersonal exchange among elites, and when members of the dominant coalition find it in their interest to expand impersonal exchange, incrementally increasing access. Under these conditions, 'the system changes from the logic of limited access rent creation to open access entry' (North et al. 2013b: 17). Nevertheless, as North et al. make clear, 'the dynamism of social order is a dynamic of change, not a dynamic of progress', and the natural state is the historical norm (North et al. 2009: 12–13).

To date, LAO theory has been applied convincingly to a number of empirical cases (see North et al. 2013b), including Russia (Connolly 2009: 199; North et al. 2007: 9). Indeed, limited access is characterised by the following factors and Russia is a clear fit:

> 1. Slow-growing economies vulnerable to shocks.
> 2. Policies without generalized consent of the governed.
> 3. Relatively small numbers of organizations.
> 4. Smaller and more centralized governments.
> 5. A predominance of social relationships organized along personal lines, including privileges, social hierarchies, laws that are enforced unequally, insecure property rights, and a perverse sense that not all individuals were created or are equal.
>
> (North et al. 2009: 12)

For my purpose of moving beyond hybrid theory, LAO theory therefore offers three significant advantages. First, it was not conceived to account for the Russian case alone, so presents the prospect of situating Russia's characteristics in comparative studies. Second, it can accommodate the most important and indisputable aspect of hybrid theories, which is the overwhelming power of Russia's state and its ruling elites to interfere arbitrarily in the political economy: North et al. argue that many LAOs have 'dualistic economies'

(North et al. 2007: 39–40) in which the governing 'dominant coalition' manipulates the economy to create rents that ensure powerful actors refrain from violence and prevent outsiders from establishing rival organisations (North et al. 2013b: 4). Third, unlike hybrid theories, LAO theory does not consider the private sector to be a dependent variable, although business is typically difficult, especially for new start-ups (North et al. 2007: 9). In fact, North et al. specifically call attention to the need to determine the role of the private sector and the reasons why ruling elites sustain and respect private organisations (North et al. 2007: 44). Moreover, although North et al. and Connolly have both described Russia as an LAO by examining its structural political economic features, no empirical work has yet been completed describing the specific characteristics of Russia's private sector in this context: it is a theoretical framework still under development (Connolly 2013: 4). Altogether, therefore, my case study material presents an opportunity to move beyond hybrid theories within a recognised theoretical framework.

North's emphasis on studying institutions provides direction for achieving this task. Tracing the ways my informants adapt 'their activities and strategies' to the 'opportunities and limitations in the formal and informal institutions' (Aidis 2015: 78–9) is required. This, in any case, is the original purpose of my research. Therefore, my case study material has both empirical and theoretical relevance: first, it offers evidence on how my informants practically overcome the difficulties they encounter in business, and second, it serves to reveal more detail about the specific characteristics of business–state relations. To put it specifically, it reveals how entrepreneurs deal with state representatives in Russia's LAO. As I will show, the personalisation of the state is again the key factor in these relations. The emphasis is on individuals as state representatives or entrepreneurs to personally make the best of their situation, which means that relations are not necessarily antagonistic, despite the power of the former over the latter. The motivation of these agents is a function of limited access and 'entrepreneurial governmentality': individuals act according to their perception of what is possible to limit violence, uphold their independence and secure access to resources.

Summary

In this chapter, I argued that ethnography offers an effective methodology for observing entrepreneurship under conditions of institutional asymmetry, which is necessary to show how entrepreneurs actually deal with the difficulties they face. Scholarly attention on the 'actually existing' political economy in Russia has also receded, so this study represents a chance to reinvigorate ethnographic study of business. I then outlined a multi-sited ethnographic approach away from Russia's two major cities, which draws specifically on the framework of 'contextual holism' and emphasises that agency and perception is situated in place, meaning that particular history, culture and institutional contexts create the framework for action. As Linch puts it, 'contextual holism' 'confronts the challenge of achieving the analytical clarity to generalize … without sacrificing contextual details vital to explanation' (Linch 2013: 12). This makes it appropriate for my work, which is necessarily focused on both agency and structure in the form of business–state relations. I then introduced my three key informants, whose experiences in business are varied but, as becomes clearer in the following case studies, all use their businesses as a means to achieve independence and resistance as much as commercial gain. Moreover, they have each been able to achieve this despite the challenges facing them. As I stated, this represents the most significant observation of my ethnographic research and one that could not have been made using a study gathering attitudinal data. Finally, I highlighted that this raises a significant question for predominant theories of Russian political economy about how to accommodate entrepreneurs' agency (which I defined using Yurchak's concept of 'entrepreneurial governmentality'). I argued that North's LAO theory offers a more appropriate theoretical framework to describe Russia's political economy, accommodating both the arbitrary potential of Russia's ruling elites and officials and the specific factors governing business–state relations that I observed. LAO theory is still under development to the extent that little is known about how private organisations survive within them. My empirical material can therefore contribute to its development. As I discuss in more detail in Chapter 6, LAO theory can account for the negative attitudes held by my informants towards the political economic structure in which they are inherently vulnerable *and* for my observation that relations with the state tend to be pragmatic, as opposed to governed by the power of the state. My informants seek to minimise their involvement with the state as much as possible and broker personal deals or find mutual interests when they must according to their local and personal situations. Their ability to achieve this accounts for their varied experiences far more than their structural vulnerability to the state as such. These empirical and theoretical findings are possible only with an ethnographic methodology.

In Chapters 3, 4 and 5, I present my three case studies. Each study offers a distinctive narrative because my informants' experiences in business vary considerably. However, they share the view that the state and its representatives have a malign influence on Russian business, and they are determined to avoid them. This means that they spend a significant amount of time not on business matters but trying to reduce their vulnerability to predatory outsiders and officials. This leads me to argue, drawing on Yurchak, that their entrepreneurship should not be judged according to conventional business measures alone, such as profitability, company size or longevity, but in terms of their ability to respond to an unpredictable state and secure their independence. I then go further to make the case that their entrepreneurship is also a form of resistance to the state. In these ways, entrepreneurship takes the form of a life project or mission. These observations, which underline the considerable agency of my informants vis-à-vis the state, represent my major empirical findings and lay the foundation for my key conceptual contribution, which follows in Chapter 6.

3 Case Study

Oleg

This case study is based on participant observation within Sibtekhnika, a business established by Oleg in 1991 in the city I call Priyatnyi. Oleg has built Sibtekhnika into a successful group of companies offering design and fitting services to the retail sector and industrial equipment to the commercial, education and construction sectors. The case study has four sections. First, I concentrate on Oleg's specific attitudes to business conditions and describe how this determines his everyday business practices. In his view, Russia is ruled by an 'imperialistic' government that centralises power, leaving regions dependent upon the Kremlin but rewarding the most loyal with funds earned chiefly from strategic industries and the extortion of private businesses. According to him, this system is well established, and entrepreneurs must work within it as found, accepting that the government does not support business development but rather the interests of the political elite. In response, he has developed an entrepreneurial approach based on strict pragmatism. His everyday effort is focused on maintaining the market advantage he has established by working in collaboration with his competitors to maintain their joint dominance of the regional market. I describe this arrangement by drawing on the concept of limited access to argue that Oleg has built a 'minor coalition' that functions according to the same logic as a 'dominant coalition' in an LAO. That is, the minor coalition enables Oleg and his partners to work according to informal behavioural norms to deter would-be extorters.

In the following section, I turn to the specific entrepreneurial activities of Oleg and his directors. I find that despite Sibtekhnika's prominent position in the local market, they work continually to minimise the uncertainty they perceive in the business sphere, assert control wherever possible over their business relations and contractual affairs through regular practical activities and strive every day to work diligently to a high level of quality. At the same time, I also find that the emphasis on asserting control is partially for display, signalling their entrepreneurial ability and competence in defiance of the difficulty posed to clients and staff. I therefore argue that pragmatism, together with rhetorical and actual control and competence, are the most important aspects in the entrepreneurial behaviour of Sibtekhnika's directors.

DOI: 10.4324/9780429469176-3

In the next section, I provide greater insight into the place of Sibtekhnika in the wider political economy by describing its transactions with three different types of clients, which offers greater understanding of the specific role played by private businesses in Russia. I first consider its work with a small rural company in the interior of the oblast, which provides an insight into the conditions for business in remote Siberia, away from the regional capital. I find that, in the small regional communities, there are limits to the extent to which Sibtekhnika can supply goods profitably, on account of the distances involved and low demand, but despite this the company makes a significant effort to supply them. Next, I consider Sibtekhnika's dealings with two state-affiliated companies. The first, *Promstroi*, is a large business constructing a pipeline though the territory; the second is a family-run enterprise that profits from its political affiliations to dominate commercial opportunities in a rural town. I show that although these clients derive their profits from the 'imperialist' political economy Oleg bemoans, they also offer highly profitable business opportunities to Sibtekhnika, which, according to Oleg's pragmatic approach, he cannot ignore. Conversely, I also show that these clients require access to resources that only private businesses such as Sibtekhnika can supply, which suggests that the private sector has a vital role in the economy despite the dominance of the state. Moreover, I find that despite the clear differences between these businesses and Sibtekhnika, the success of the latter appears to replicate the business model of the former. That is, Sibtekhnika derives profit from its shared domination of local trade in the city just as the state-affiliated companies derive rent from political domination over assets or territories. This, I argue, is most effectively conceptualised using the limited access order (LAO) framework.

Finally, I seek to explain how Oleg reconciles his distaste for Russia's political economic model with his pragmatic approach of dealing with business conditions as he finds them. After all, this approach has enabled him to become a successful businessman. However, Oleg's pragmatism is not an implicit endorsement of the status quo. In fact, he has also established the Cooperative, a social entrepreneurial initiative, to counter what he considers to be propagandistic and uninspiring state education and to encourage independent thinking instead. His intention is to broaden the horizons of local youth by offering high-quality, low-cost extracurricular activities. Because, in his view, nobody takes responsibility for the betterment of society, he wants the Cooperative to support the identification and development of youngsters who might become free-thinking entrepreneurs, potentially within Sibtekhnika. Thus, below the surface of Oleg's tough pragmatism, he is also concerned with challenging and changing political and economic conditions surreptitiously, both for society and for the longevity of his business.

In concluding, I aim to account for the difference between Oleg's successful business practices, which are characterised by caution, competence and control in an uncertain business environment – as well as a willingness to work with the full range of legitimate and illegitimate actors in the Russian market – with his desire to bring about an improvement in the local political economy through the Cooperative. I find this is first based on his belief that only by taking personal responsibility for his affairs, rather than relying on the government to improve political, economic and social conditions, will he be able to achieve anything. More importantly, however, I argue that Oleg displays 'entrepreneurial governmentality': by defining Oleg's entrepreneurial approach in this way, I can account for his activities that work with the grain of the political economy and his simultaneous resistance to it. I return to this in more detail in Chapter 6.

Oleg's Theory of Business

Prior to establishing Sibtekhnika, Oleg worked as an academic at the local university, which made him a keen student of social theory. This formative early career was instrumental in shaping his view of the Russian political economy and how entrepreneurs can 'get by'. That said, nowadays Oleg is semi-retired, and the majority of the company's day-to-day business is conducted by his two directors. However, as I will show, Sibtekhnika continues to operate as a model of his thinking within the Sibtekhnika group of companies. Dmitrii, his son, directs *Ofistekh*, which sells retail and office equipment and technologies. Irina, his long-time protégé and a former prosecution service official, directs three businesses: the first, *Magazinstroi*, provides design services for retail companies, such as shops, supermarkets, restaurants and beauty salons, then the materials and equipment needed to fit them out. The second, *Dyetskiisad Apparat*, sells playground apparatus and educational hardware such as blackboards and furniture to children's nurseries, as well as the appliances and other equipment needed for their kitchens and utility rooms. Third, Irina recently joined a production association (*proizvodstvennoe ob'edinenie*) called *Uchebresheniya*, which manufactures educational hardware, equipment and technology, to become its sole regional representative. Each of these businesses is on the Sibtekhnika site, and for all intents and purposes they are the same company; the different brands simply allow for a clear division of labour between the directors. Oleg himself has a roaming role in which he moves in and out of the office to talk things over and check up as the mood takes him. However, he dedicates most of his time to the development of the Cooperative, which is housed in an adjacent building.

Priyatnyi itself is the regional capital of Priyatnaya oblast, a region comparable in size to Poland or Italy, and therefore subject to particular social-geographic factors that affect the way in which business is undertaken. Approximately 30 per cent of the region's population work in the oil and gas sectors alone, while just over half the population live in Priyatnyi itself. Outside the capital, the population is widely dispersed. The next largest settlement, *Lesnoigorodok*, is not far and contains a further 10 per cent of the population. However, it is a closed city (*Zakrytoe Administrativno-Territorial'noe Obrazovanie [ZATO]* or 'closed administrative-territorial formation'), meaning that special permission is required for outsiders to enter, and business opportunities are therefore limited. Throughout the remainder of the oblast, the remaining population is distributed in far smaller regional towns and villages. The interior is also inhospitable all year-round, whether due to the cold for over half the year or the sticky heat and swarms of insects encountered the rest of the time. The paved or concrete roads are dilapidated and limited mostly to the south, while northern settlements are accessible only by boat along the river that bisects the oblast (when weather permits) or by aeroplane.

The importance of Siberia's natural resources to the regional economy and the state's emphasis on controlling their exploitation is at the centre of Oleg's notion of 'imperialism'. To him, Russia's regions have been shorn of their economic potential by an imperialistic central government, and Priyatnaya oblast is representative. Like Khotin, he therefore argues that Siberia need not retreat from Russia but should be granted greater economic freedom, stronger banking and financial services, the improvement of the protection of property rights, the enhancement of state regulation and the reduction of corruption (2007: 48). A particularly negative consequence of the state's involvement in regional economies, in his opinion, is that employment in state organisations is considered to be more attractive than in private enterprises. Most people see that the state still favours quasi-private national champions such as *Gazprom*, Russian Railways, and organisations within the military-industrial complex, whereas entrepreneurship is prone to multiple obstacles and suspicion. 'Many rely on the state and do not want to fight it', he says, and he uses his own family to make the point:

> My wife works in a local university, so receives her money from the state. My second son works in Lesnoigorodok. Even my sister who runs a business in the Far East supports the state because it wants good relations with China, where her suppliers are, and her region receives a lot of money from Moscow.

He concludes: 'The businessmen you have met who say they are against the system are not representative. People like me are only 1 per cent of the population'. Thus, Oleg considers his negative attitude to state primacy in the economy to be the exception rather than the rule.

In Oleg's view, private enterprise is unimportant to the state, which does not effectively regulate business or uphold the law, so entrepreneurs have to work in specific ways to regulate the business sphere themselves. Consequently, as he puts it, entrepreneurs must learn to 'get by' drawing on their own network of personal acquaintances:

> I work with my own resources, the contacts I have available. Maybe there are better people in the market but for me it is hard to have transactions with them, it is hard to negotiate with them. Even if better specialists are available, I will work with the people I have. And that's it! I rely on my own social network, because it is more effective. We deal with bonding capital. In our country, it has been this way for a century. We work with our circle, where our connections are free.

In this way, Oleg has, rather unusually, drawn on social theory to emphasise the importance of 'bonded social capital' and has used this as a basis upon which to develop his business. Paul Adleft and Seok-Woo Kwon define bonded social capital as 'the linkages among individuals or groups within [a] collectivity and, specifically, in those features that give the collectivity cohesiveness and thereby facilitate the pursuit of collective goals' (2002: 21). Thus, drawing on bonded social capital is a rational response to the vulnerability of private business. Deepa Narayan states that 'when societies are characterised by social groups with abundant cross-cutting ties and poorly functioning governments … the informal networks become substitutes for the failed state and form the basis for coping strategies (1999: 17; see also Woolcock 2001: 16). As I wrote in Chapter 2, social capital has been central in research on post-socialist Russia, ranging from studies of survival of the poor (for example, Burawoy et al. 2000: 60; Rose 1994: 47; Round and Williams 2010: 188; Williams et al. 2013: 68) to how Russia is governed (Ledeneva 2013). It is therefore no surprise that social capital should be integral to Oleg's successful entrepreneurship too. As two Russian specialists have written, 'A specific feature of post-Soviet, perestroika and post- perestroika economy was a dramatic increase in the economic role of kinship and family and friendship ties, the active use of these bonds for private solutions to economic problems' (Pokrovsky and Nikolaeva 2014: 478). Ledeneva described this phenomenon in her work on blat. Drawing on Richard Rose, she states that 'kin and social networks in Russia function in a pre- or anti-modern way to enforce loyalty and compliance with the informal ways of getting things done' (2009: 278). Schrader has also argued that post-socialist countries had transitioned to market economies, but they had not become market societies of which people 'felt' part. This requires not only institutions but 'institutional trust, system trust, and society-inherent social capital, so that people can choose between the market (faceless transactions) and networks (more personal relations) according to the criterion of transaction costs' (2004: 401). Oleg's reliance on personal networks and lack of trust in Russia's institutions or system of economic governance reiterates Schrader's analysis. Drawing on his social capital is the logical response to institutional asymmetry.

What is the utility of Oleg's social capital in practical terms? He is not merely concerned to work with his allies in order to meet his clients' demands, as one might expect a conventional business to do in the absence of state support. Rather, his priority is to ensure that he is known personally to his competitors and suppliers and that their joint interests are acknowledged. His objective is not to reduce regulation and outdo his competitors, but to work with competitors to self-regulate their joint dominance over supply to the market. Therefore, a key aspect in his entrepreneurial survival and success is that he can communicate with them about their mutual interests. 'It's similar to the mafiya',[1] Oleg explains, by which he means that he and his partners strive to achieve a degree of exclusivity over the supply of goods in his market.[2] Although this approach resembles a protection racket because it prevents outsiders from entering their market, violence is, unlike the mafiya, a rare rather than defining feature. Sibtekhnika may buy in protection occasionally (as I describe later), but it is cooperation rather than coercion that is the basis of their security in the market'. Plainly, violence no longer overshadows everyday economic transactions or governance in Russia (Gans-Morse 2012), but it remains an option in Sibtekhnika's modus operandi.

The way in which Oleg's social capital works has profound implications for understanding how Russian entrepreneurs can survive or even become successful. This arrangement, in which he works with competitors to secure mutual advantage over supply in their market, represents a system for injecting some control into and reducing some risk in the unregulated but notionally free market in Priyatnyi. I argue that this is an effective reaction to working in the context of a limited access order. According to North et al., in an LAO, members of the dominant coalition 'agree to respect each other's privileges, including property rights and access to resources and activities. By limiting access to these privileges to members of the dominant coalition, elites create credible incentives to cooperate rather than fight among themselves' (North et al. 2009: 18). Connolly was the first to describe Russia as an LAO (2015: 20) in which 'competition is suppressed to ensure that rent flows are managed to suit the interests of the political elite' (Connolly 2015: 12). Likewise, Oleg's arrangement constitutes a 'minor coalition' in the real economy: it replicates locally the dominant coalition that has structural predominance in the country as a whole. Thus, although Oleg's minor coalition is vulnerable because it does not have authority, it still serves the requirement to create order and security among his competitors, prevent the entry of outsiders and stabilise access to profits (as opposed to rents).

A question arises over how the minor coalition divides its interests in the market. However, because there is enough business to go around, the most pressing question is how the minor coalition protects its market from outsiders. Oleg was non-committal when I asked him, saying that 'together we would try to price them out'. I replied by asking what would happen if this was insufficient. 'We would watch closely and see', he rebuffed. This response has to suffice, because I did not observe such a situation during my fieldwork. Nevertheless, it is important to consider what Oleg and his partners could do if push came to shove. Unlike in the 1990s when Oleg had a '*krysha*' or 'roof', like many businesses (for example, Humphrey 2002; Ries 2002; Varese 1994) he no longer has such protection, so another form of security is required. Dmitrii offered some indication during a conversation about how business debts can be recovered. He stated that Sibtekhnika could not allow other businessmen to take advantage of them and said that when his girlfriend, a graphic designer, was not paid for several months by a client, his reputation alone ensured she got her money. Pushing the discussion further, I ask what would happen if a client had not paid a large debt. He replies that people come down from a town in the north and indicated where the knife would go in my gut. 'It's normal', he said, sincerely. This example shows that developing a business with one's own network and without the state as arbiter creates corporate cliques and rivalries that have to be underpinned by meaningful deterrence in order to be effective. The potential for violence would provide this. As North et al. put it in their definition of an LAO, 'the threat of violence becomes part of the arrangement that controls the actual use of violence' (2009: 20). Oleg's minor coalition provides this just as the Russian elites' dominant coalition serves the same function.

Even so, throughout my fieldwork, negotiation was the primary means through which deals were struck. For example, during my fieldwork Irina received a visit from a man who had recently introduced her to someone who became a new client. He had returned to intimidate her into a cut of the profit from the business with that client and, because his demand was based on intimidation, it could not be overlooked. Oleg lamented that the man was a 'most simple person', but both he and Irina agreed that a peaceful solution would have to be found. Violence was not justified; the man had helped their business in a small way, after all. They agreed to draw up some paperwork acknowledging his introduction to the client and setting a fee, then to feed the cost through the business. Afterwards, Oleg said that this sort of demand for *otkat* (a kickback) occasionally happens (*byvaet*), while Irina expressed her conviction that 'corruption is everywhere'. Otkat is an important feature in the construction industry in particular, she said, 'because officials ask "where's mine?"' and require payment before projects can begin. However, there is a difference between corruption (*korruptsiya*) and otkat. Simon Kordonskii has shown that corruption tends to lack specificity, whereas otkat refers to a widely accepted practice: 'I have never heard the people themselves, without irony, defined as corrupt. Rather, you can hear "he, she, they steal, they take everything"' (2012: online). This explains Irina's unspecific remark that corruption is ubiquitous. Otkat, on the other hand, is the consequence of the redistribution of assets upwards through the hierarchy that is a central aspect in Russia's post-socialist capitalism. Once assets have been allocated, entitlement to a cut is granted according to social perception (based on intuition and experience) of rank (Kordonskii 2012: online). Therefore, if officialdom is involved in a project, as it frequently is in Sibtekhnika's work, otkat is a given. Nevertheless, otkat is the norm in private-sector deals too, as Irina's experience in this case shows. As a result, states Kordonskii, the rhetorical fight against corruption is nonsense because it is a fight against the system itself. He notes that corruption itself only becomes formally illegitimate when one is perceived to have overstepped their entitled cut (2012: online). Thus, while otkat is common, entitlement is based on perception. The man who demanded a payment from Irina took advantage of this situation aggressively: he knew he was entitled to a cut but also knew he was low in the hierarchy and would have to go and get it rather than expect it to be given. This type of risk, in which any financial transaction can be perceived as worthy of personal reward, is precisely what Oleg has to be ready to deter; he must have a limit at which he is unprepared to be extorted, otherwise business would become unviable. This explains most persuasively the need for a minor coalition: instances such as this are infrequent as a result.

By working cooperatively through the minor coalition, he has established behavioural expectations among suppliers and partners. On this occasion, however, Oleg and Irina decided to cut their losses.

The necessity for both open communication and self-protection was illustrated on another occasion when we travelled to meet Vladimir, a man Oleg described as 'construction mafiya', in his office above a derelict yard. Vladimir owed Oleg two million roubles but, apparently, did not have it. All the same, Oleg wanted to remind him about his debt and did so by proposing a joint enterprise. Vladimir's appearance was caricature: over six feet tall, huge in every dimension, with several gold teeth, a shaved head and grey goatee. He swore several times each sentence in a gruff voice between draws on his cigarettes. His government contracts had dried up lately because staff there had changed, and his future in construction looked bleak. He had remortgaged the yard, but he needed more income to settle his debts. Oleg suggested to him that they jointly build a café on the university campus, where he had contacts. Oleg knew that Vladimir wanted to build himself a country house (*kottedzh*), but if he did and his creditors bankrupted him, Oleg would only receive a small part of his dues. Vladimir said he would think about the suggestion. Over lunch Oleg described Vladimir as dangerous, something I had naturally grasped, but also that he had been a great Soviet soldier, honoured for his service in Afghanistan. For Oleg, this was important: just because Vladimir turned to crime in the 1990s did not mean he was not reliable or a potential business partner. Therefore, it is clear that Oleg is, above all, pragmatic about his contacts and takes the view that it is important to work and negotiate with them all.

In summary, I have shown that Oleg and his staff perceive uncertainty and danger in the business sphere and have responded by developing a system that enables them to be prepared for aggression or the unexpected, to deter would-be extorters and which offers mutual assistance to partners. I have described this as a minor coalition that works in the same way as Russia's dominant coalition, which is to say according to the logic of limited access order, with its emphasis on cooperation to reduce the potential for violence. At the same time, it is also clear that when a threat arises, they can usually cut their losses or, more probably, cut a deal, even with unlikely figures, because mutual interests can often be found. Negotiation and deal-making is therefore more critical to Sibtekhnika's continued success than anything nefarious. Indeed, in this chapter Oleg and Irina are presented working with a large number of diverse characters with the key point being that they are in regular dialogue with these contacts and stay in a position to influence them. Thus, under conditions of institutional asymmetry, the importance of acknowledging others' interests grows, and this reinforces the importance of maintaining social capital. Accordingly, Oleg's social capital is extensive and includes the full range of actors involved in Russian business over the post-Soviet period, including criminals. Business conditions may have 'stabilised' since the 1990s, but business still involves such actors. This is at the core of the 'bonded social capital' Oleg described: the necessity of getting by with and making the most of one's contacts pragmatically, creating stable business conditions collectively through negotiation. Although moments of unpredictability or hostility in their business relations occasionally arise, this reinforces in Oleg and his directors a determination to bring about order and stability into everyday business. Thus, Oleg's theory of business reinforces itself, with stability and order as the main priorities for action.

Oleg's Entrepreneurship in Practice

In spite of the relatively secure position Oleg has established for Sibtekhnika in the local market, the directors work constantly to minimise the risk they face from arbitrary interference in order to get on with the task of selling their wares. It is not in Sibtekhnika's interest to rely on their participation in the minor coalition to guarantee a steady stream of customers, as is the way with the dominant coalition. As I have said, the minor coalition operates in the real economy, which is to say with hard budget constraints, and must meet the needs of the market in order to exist at all. In a discernible sense, therefore, Sibtekhnika's success must be viewed not as the result of privilege within a protection racket, but of years of sustained effort to comprehend and create order in ever changing and uncertain business conditions with limited (bonded) social resources and without access to state support. In Priyatnyi, new business has to be won, contracts have to be fulfilled and legal compliance is obligatory, as far as is achievable. These conditions became harder still during my fieldwork when the value of the rouble began to fall. I now examine how Oleg and his directors actually do their work with clients and suppliers, their determination to assert control over their affairs and their focus on ensuring that they are taken seriously as reliable, competent and diligent businesspeople.

Irina's resolve for control over business affairs and attention to detail is revealed in the following examples. While I was in the field, Magazinstroi was contracted by an entrepreneur from Lesnoigorodok to design and fit out his new grocery store.[3] The layout was quickly agreed upon, and the refrigeration and wall units were supplied. In addition, Irina had sub-contracted Fyodor, a carpenter, to make a set of wooden units to occupy various places on the shop floor: a wooden frame imitating a market stall to hold special offers and several tall stands for baked goods. After a couple of weeks, we visited Fyodor to check his progress, and all appeared to be on track. He called Irina a few days later to say he had finished the first bread stand, and it was ready for inspection. He brought it to the Sibtekhnika showroom. Irina was not impressed: some of the edges were finished poorly and the joints made from different woods. The shelves were also at 45-degree angles, which meant they needed rims to keep the bread from sliding off, and the current rims were insufficient. In exasperation Irina told Fyodor, 'If I was the client I would say, "*What is that*?"' By chance, the client had come in to talk about the design of the beverage section. Irina showed him the bread stand and he liked it but would have preferred the edges rounded off. Irina drew his attention closer, explaining how the quality was not right. He was an easy-going man and seemed unconcerned, leaving Irina to take care of the details. Thus, in this sense the client was happy with the product but Irina, the seller, was not and would not give it away in its current form. This is related to Irina's determination to assert control and her sense of responsibility to get it right.

A few days afterwards, Fyodor returned to go over some contractual details. He wanted Irina to pay him more for the adjustments she had demanded. He shot me a knowing glance when Irina was not looking, seeking my approval for his claim. He seemed uncommitted to the details of the contract and had underestimated Irina as a dealmaker. I had also ascertained from our previous meetings that he looked down on women. Irina, who dressed smartly and expected the same of her staff, checked her hair in her office mirror, and this seemed to fortify Fyodor's impression that she lacked seriousness. At an earlier meeting, he had taken me aside and described Irina's female office managers as 'prostitutes' when they left the room. While Fyodor pretended to study the paperwork in front of him, however, Irina in turn cast me a look indicating his uselessness. Before the meeting she had told me that she could barely understand his Caucasian dialect. Thus, both Irina and Fyodor had seen in me an opportunity to affirm their own rightness regarding the other: Fyodor sought my approval that Irina was beneath him; Irina sought it in othering Fyodor as a dim-witted oriental workman without the skills for business. I remained neutral, however, knowing Fyodor was in for a shock. He left sheepishly a few moments later after Irina repeated to him slowly, clearly, with a raised voice, what was expected of him according to their contract. A few days later, Fyodor turned up with the finished bread stands. Irina inspected them and declared, 'Look! The result of shouting!'" They certainly looked better. Fyodor was given another order for two more stands, the reward for belatedly getting it right. As he left Irina glanced at me with a 'Do you see what I have to deal with?' look of exasperation.

In this example, it is obvious that Irina feels determined to assert or display control over her business. Although there is no real need for her to show that she is right in these instances – because it was obvious that she was – she still does so. This behaviour is borne of her perception that the client should see that she is in control of his affairs and taking care of his interests in a market in which one has to be self-reliant and where people such as Fyodor will take advantage if they can. The fact that the client was relaxed is testimony to her effectiveness, while she can be sure that he believes she is reliable and trustworthy and may recommend her to his acquaintances. The assertion of control, therefore, emerges from the fact that trust has to be tangibly earned rather than believed; this is the difference between relying on informal rather than formal institutions.

Indeed, Irina often said only half-jokingly that her effectiveness as a businesswoman came down to shouting at workmen. This was borne out on visits to the construction sites (*ob"etkti*) of the kindergartens Dyetskiisad Apparat was furnishing with industrial sinks, refrigerators, washing machines, play apparatus and other miscellaneous equipment. On my first trip, I asked her en route about the purpose of our visit. 'To shout at people and everything will be OK', she replied and showed her fists. On the sites, Irina would embark on a familiar checking routine: locating the personnel responsible for the parts of the building that would receive her equipment, inspecting their work against the blueprints, identifying inevitable errors and faults and making continual demands for improvement and corrections. She invariably discovered that workmen needed to coordinate their work more carefully with her so that the equipment could be delivered and fitted and demanded their contact details so that they could be in touch. Her unlikely appearance on a construction site, clear experience in her field and quick competence comparing the architectural plans to the reality of the construction site was highly effective at ensuring she got the attention of the constructors. Often, she started directing work on the spot: on one occasion her equipment had been delivered but was not properly assembled or fitted and was in the wrong locations. She gathered the men responsible and explained that it was not her task to sort out these problems, but she needed to see that the work was done properly. One of the men said that this was his first kindergarten, as if to excuse himself from the fact that supply pipes were fitted in the wrong places. With a wry smile, Irina closed the door behind the two of them so that he could not escape as she listed what needed to be done. Then, like a traffic officer, she directed the rearrangement of the industrial fridges and basins by six men between various rooms, waving the goods to and fro and pointing out where electricity and water supplies ought to be. Her view is that only by her own personal, active, communicative intervention would things turn out right. Her assumption was to expect the worst and to be physically present to ensure people did what they had promised. In this way, Irina's biggest fear is to be associated with shoddy work because, as is now clear, Sibtekhnika's business is largely built on personal relations, so her personal integrity is constantly at stake.

Afterwards, I asked why the plans were not followed accurately. 'It's Russia', she responded bluntly. 'I wish it were better, but it is a fact'. At the time, I felt this answer was unconsidered but on reflection believe it satisfactorily explains her determination to assert her will on what she considers the predictably disappointing standards of her business partners and suppliers. Moreover, this fatalism is widely held: it is common knowledge that even the best intentions will inevitably fall short of the original tasking or finished article. Indeed, even the long-time mayor of Moscow, Yurii Luzhkov, devoted a humorous book to the subject and made particular reference to construction projects. He stated that although it is common to complete 95 per cent of a building, the last 5 per cent is almost never achieved:

> It is as though some diabolical force prevents us from doing a thing more properly and putting the finishing touches .... It may only be 5 per cent, but we'll leave something undone. But you see, as a rule, it is just this last 5 per cent that means quality!.
>
> (2005: 38)

Irina would concur with this view and responded by trying to maintain control, which required asserting her will over those responsible. On the construction site, this was not a bad-tempered process; the workers accepted the changes that needed to be made when Irina showed them. However, they could have completed the job better themselves the first time. The fact that they did not justifies and explains Irina's approach. Moreover, Irina's negative outlook was reinforced repeatedly in daily life when she encountered problems, such as a theft from her car or when the man arrived at her office demanding otkat. Such events reinforced a commitment in her not to let her guard down, which made her emphasis on control both a necessity and performance.

Oleg placed considerable emphasis on overseeing the company's business effectively. When he and I discussed his plans for the day ahead, he often replied simply with the verb 'to control' (*kontrolirovat'*). He also recruits Sibtekhnika's staff with this ability in mind too, and in this respect, Irina's determinedness to convey control over her business affairs and give the impression of competence makes sense. Before working for Sibtekhnika, Irina was a lawyer in the prosecution service, and during my observation, she frequently referred to that experience in meetings with clients or in sales pitches so that customers and suppliers knew they were dealing with a professional and serious-minded businesswoman. She also deployed her legal knowledge to placate administrators and creditors when they asked tricky questions about the business. Indeed, she gave the impression that such tasks were straightforward. When her bank manager wanted to meet to talk about why she managed three businesses instead of one, Irina became exasperated at the prospect of the meeting and claimed she would have to explain 'very slowly' how the Sibtekhnika group of companies works.

Indeed, Irina often stylised her emotions for effect. For example, when an aggressive client called about a problem with a deal she responded with aggression of her own: 'I already answered! If you want to go down that route, fine! Write a letter, bring it here!', then slammed the phone down and nonchalantly ate a piece of cake, to the appreciation and awe of her managers. Here she exhibited considerable charisma, but it was also clear that she would not tolerate aggression and returned it if negotiation was not possible. This attitude is born of a conviction that weakness has no place in business. Because formal institutions offer insufficient protection, she has to act in her own defence, which she can do with some confidence: she has both legal training and the support of the minor coalition. Here her control of the situation is both rhetorical and substantial. At the same time, she is adept at considering cost and profit on the go and decides margins quickly with a calculator on the table and the telephone against her ear. She is a master of deal-making on the telephone and baldly discusses even her suppliers' margins with them, pushing for discounts on the basis of past loyalty and potential future purchases. To her, all costs and prices are negotiable, deals are cut quickly and amiably, and she is careful not to be outdone. She conveys control with legal nous, business sense and self-confidence, which makes her an inspiring figure to her colleagues: she is able to uphold the legitimacy of the business in formal and informal terms, countering occasional doubts or threats.

Sibtekhnika is managed hierarchically, like most Russian organisations (Kets de Vries 2001: 617–18), with even basic decisions made by the directors. New employees are hired from the directors' own social networks, which ensures their reliability, trustworthiness and obedience. For example, Marina, one of Irina's managers, knows Oleg through his connections with a local university, where she had been a good student. Svetlana, another manager, is studying there part-time and was also recommended by a contact. Tanya, the third manager, is the former girlfriend of Irina's son, Misha. Misha himself is employed in the business to learn the trade before going to the local technical university to study architecture, a skill he will bring back upon graduation. Dmitrii's girlfriend, a graphic designer, works as a contractor, providing regular support to the company's retail designs and branding for clients. Indeed, Sibtekhnika's entire team had been assembled according to this method. Yet, despite this careful vetting, the directors maintain firm control, which in turn means that even capable and experienced staff defer their decisions upwards, seek their guidance on routine matters or pass them calls from clients to resolve, despite their undoubted ability to deal with such issues themselves. As a result, I often saw clients walk past the managers towards the directors' offices and wait outside until they were ready to speak to them about matters of product choice, rather than ask if the managers could help them. This, again, is the result of a system of work that privileges strict control.

In spite of this micromanagerial approach, the directors are adept at coaxing results from the staff to maintain a sufficient level of quality, although this is frequently achieved by either walking them through the job step by step or by taking over themselves, which also served to reiterate their position in control, even if it was time-consuming. For example, when Svetlana entered Irina's office with a spreadsheet she had devised for a client that even Sibtekhnika's accountant could not decipher, Irina told her to start again. 'We are trying to achieve a standard', she explained and drew columns onto some scrap paper to indicate which figures went where. She settled on a fee by calling the client to agree and told Svetlana to make the spreadsheet reach that total. Or when Anastasiya, one of Irina's senior managers, complained that she found dealing with the representative from Promstroi difficult and re-enacted a fruitless and sarcastic telephone call, Irina called them immediately to resolve the issue: such a key client must be looked after carefully. Even Anastasiya, who studied medicine, likes the atmosphere in Sibtekhnika, describing it as 'a good collective', but still deferred any significant responsibilities to Irina. Thus, the weight of responsibility for Irina's businesses falls on her personally. She makes the process of business appear controlled and simple because she is the only member of her staff that consistently makes decisions. Even as she complains about it and recruits careful, intelligent staff, this is how she likes to keep it.

In describing Oleg's entrepreneurship in practice, I have shown how old-fashioned business acumen is as necessary in Sibtekhnika as in any company. However, the ability to assert and display control in internal and external business relations to show the seriousness and credibility of the business is also critical. This serves as a signal to suppliers, clients and contractors alike and is a key factor in negotiations with business associates, such as clients or even mafiya figures, as well as within the business itself. This display is central to Oleg and Irina's strategy for maintaining the profitability and pre-eminence, reputation and autonomy of Sibtekhnika in the city's real economy. Its importance is based on their perception that the business sphere is beset with uncertainties, which I have described: Russian workers are consistently inadequate; partners will let you down if you allow them to; even with the best staff available, one has to take personal responsibility for daily tasks; and fate will strike if you let your guard down.

I argue that these actions are a response to the difficulties of business I have outlined. That is, Oleg clearly equates the assertion of his will in market relations with his longevity in business. This has meant adopting a pragmatic approach to doing business and to choosing business partners: his longstanding relationships with mafiya figures reveal his appreciation that Russian business can survive only by accepting conditions as they are encountered over time, not as he wishes them to be. Similarly, Dmitrii's description of the necessity of occasional force is a reminder that gaining a business presence in Russia has depended not only on avoiding the interference of others but also on asserting oneself. The fact that Irina uses her legal training to protect the interests of the business and promote her credibility reiterates the importance of understanding the way in which the existence of the law (if not the law itself), may be utilised in business. In this case, familiarity with the law is a fact to be vocalised as a deterrent for the purpose of conveying and asserting control. Overall, Sibtekhnika appears as an apparent exemplar of business competence in Priyatnyi. I find, particularly, that Kubik's conceptual holism, which emphasises the social construction of informants' perceptions, is particularly relevant to my interpretation of this point.

Entrepreneurship Outside the City

In this section, I describe how Oleg and Irina do business with different types of organisations engaged in the commercial scene in wider Priyatnaya oblast, with particular attention upon a business deal with state-affiliated political elites in a rural community. My purpose is to provide an empirical example of how private business functions in the 'actually existing' political economy of Siberia's interior. As I have stated, Priyatnyi is the largest settlement in Priyatnaya oblast, with a large, diversified economy compared to the region's other towns and villages, which are far smaller and isolated. Thus, in Priyatnyi small- and medium-sized enterprises (SMEs) are more common and operate under hard budget constraints, so Sibtekhnika functions as an ordinary retail business in the city, selling equipment and services to clients from the shop floor, and as a contractor, winning contracts from public and private tenders on the open market. However, Sibtekhnika also has business interests away from Priyatnyi in the rural interior where, as I show, market conditions are different. In the interior, Sibtekhnika has three types of clients. First, there are small, regional organisations and companies that buy occasional goods and services, such as kindergartens or retail stores in the provincial towns. Second, there are a few large state-affiliated resource extraction companies, such as Promstroi, headquartered in Moscow but with a huge regional infrastructure in the interior. These companies also have occasional needs for equipment that Sibtekhnika, as a regional supplier, can provide most easily. Finally, there are state-affiliated elites who have pre-eminent positions in their local communities and who, by virtue of their local power, have acquired a dominant stake in their local economies, thus requiring occasional supplies from Priyatnyi as the regional centre. As I now describe, Sibtekhnika's trade with these enterprises provides an insight into how Russian business works and the role of entrepreneurship in the wider political economy.

I begin by considering the first type of client, the small, regional enterprise. Sibtekhnika receives occasional demand for goods from these businesses but must make a decision about the profitability of supplying them, because transportation costs can be high for small orders. Obviously, there is a geographical limit beyond which costs outweigh profits. As Irina pointed out, she regularly asks herself whether particular regional sales are profitable and said that in a regional town she would normally expect a margin of 30 per cent on her sales. This, she said, is the price according to the market (*po rynku*). Some competitors, she said, might try to undercut that price by up to 20 per cent, but such businesses are one-man bands with limited logistical capabilities and no after-sales service. In contrast, Irina told me, she maintains that margin to account for the cost of future repairs in advance. For example, I once accompanied Sasha, Sibtekhnika's technician, to repair a washing machine Irina had sold to a kindergarten in the regional town of Slobodskoi. Our job was to change the machine's heating element, a task that took only a few minutes, while the return journey itself took all day. Clearly, the cost of our time and travel outweighed the price of the heating element. Even so, Oleg and Irina do their best to accommodate such clients. Irina was hard-headed about the geographical profit line, but she also had sympathy for the isolated communities that require goods from outside. In such a sparsely populated oblast, Irina also wanted to uphold Sibtekhnika's reputation, which is particularly important in the Russian market, where personal relations are critical to success.

Supplying state-affiliated companies such as Promstroi, in contrast, offers a far more lucrative opportunity. Promstroi is a notionally private corporation but is, in fact, the contemporary incarnation of two former Soviet ministries: the Ministry of Construction of Oil and Gas Industry and the Ministry of Installation and Special Construction Works (Promstroi Group 2015: 3). As a result, it is a company with continuing strategic importance. Among other projects in Priyatnaya oblast, Promstroi Group is building a gas pipeline that, according to Oleg, requires a pumping station every 70 kilometres, each of which requires a staff of seven to ten people, who in turn require a kitchen and other conveniences. During my fieldwork, Sibtekhnika was commissioned to supply equipment for the cafeteria and living quarters at one of these pumping stations. Naturally, this contract was given a high priority. As I mentioned in an earlier section, when Anastasiya had trouble communicating with one of their representatives, Irina immediately called them back and promised to visit the site and go over the paperwork later that week. Irina was keen to make a good impression, because more pumping stations could mean supplying more equipment.

The journey to the pumping station took six hours. A large digital clock on the outside of the construction office indicated that there were 114 days until the station was to be completed. While Irina entered the office for her meeting, Oleg told me to stay in the car; he did not think it would be wise for me to go with her. The site was surrounded by a distant perimeter fence to prevent terrorists, he said, and he was cautious about me taking photographs, telling me the company had its own police. Though it is hard to imagine terrorists choosing to attack a pumping station in the middle of Siberia with little but trees and swamp around for hundreds of kilometres, the protection of the site highlights its importance relative to anything else nearby. Indeed, for the nearest rural communities it could at best provide only temporary work for informal labourers, but (more likely) technical specialists would be contracted until their work was completed. To my eye, only Sibtekhnika and other distant suppliers of minor components could be the transient beneficiaries of Promstroi's construction as it moved through the territory. Thus, Promstroi is an entirely different type of commercial organisation to anything else in the oblast.

Oleg attempted to describe this difference in the car. 'Of course', he said, 'Russia cannot continue to depend on oil and gas because there are only 50 years left'. However, as I stated previously, Oleg argues that, for now, state-affiliated companies offer the most attractive form of employment, particularly for young people: 'They are attracted to the brand, steady salary and the social status given to oil and gas workers'. By chance, the following day I received a photo from a Siberian friend whom I had helped with his English language in advance of an interview for an internship with *Schlumberger*, an oil and gas services firm. In the photo, he was proudly wearing the company's uniform, having secured the position that would enable him to develop a career in Russia's most important industry. Vladimir Shlapentokh and Anna Arutunyan claim that one-third of Russian youth and 48 per cent of students wanted to become state employees in the late 2000s. They identified similar factors for this popularity as Oleg: 'social guarantees, privileges, the stability of the position, salary, and the opportunity to receive bribes and make deals', as well as 'the connections' (Shlapentokh and Arutunyan 2013: 29). In a study of the aspirations of young Siberians, Vitaly Kashpur also gathered similar responses (Kashpur 2009), and Putin himself has stated as much (see Ministry of Economic Development of the Russian Federation 2015: online).

My encounters in the field appear to show that this remains the case today. Plainly, these organisations wield incomparable political, economic and social influence in the country, yet it is characteristic of Oleg's approach to business that, while he bemoaned Promstroi's regional importance, he was happy to profit from it wherever possible.

In Chapter 1, I argued that political influence in Russia is closely associated with personal wealth. Shlapentokh and Arutunyan argue that state-affiliated companies such as Promstroi are emblematic of this relationship. According to them, access to these enterprises has, since the 1990s, become a privilege handed out to politically loyal appointees who reciprocate with lots of money (Shlapentokh and Arutunyan 2013: 23). As a result, they argue that a feudal society has emerged with liberal and authoritarian elements. The liberal element includes being able to start a business (albeit with 'impediments that are reminiscent of the Middle Ages'), accumulate money and move freely (Shlapentokh and Arutunyan 2013: 7), while authoritarianism is found in the process of privatisation that legalised 'big property' or former state assets, which allowed the former *nomenklatura* to operate those enterprises for themselves (Shlapentokh and Arutunyan 2013: 22). This argument is persuasive for my purposes because it helps to delineate between the different organisations encountered by Oleg in the course of his entrepreneurship. The transaction between Promstroi and Sibtekhnika was between two organisations working in market conditions akin, respectively, to these authoritarian and liberal feudal conditions. Still, I do not take the feudalism concept too far: Fomin has rightly cautioned that feudalism is 'not everywhere' in Russia, due to its large urban population, strategic importance in the world and scientific achievements (Fomin 2010: 140). Indeed, I propose that Promstroi is more representative of Russia's 'dominant coalition' within the country's LAO, with access to rents agreed politically among the country's elite, while Sibtekhnika, as I have already argued, participates in a 'minor coalition' whose access to resources is agreed commercially among local competitors. For all intents and purposes, the logic of both coalitions is the same: to maintain access to resources and limit competition for them. Oleg therefore replicates the coalition model to secure the place of Sibtekhnika in the market. Consequently, the transaction between the two organisations proceeds on an equal footing: Promstroi requires the goods that Sibtekhnika can supply locally. Moreover, Oleg had a strong chance of becoming Promstroi's supplier because of Sibtekhnika's dominant position over regional supplies in their market. It is undoubtedly true that Promstroi's operations provide little benefit to the rural communities of Priyatnaya oblast and far more to the members of the dominant coalition. However, the point is that Oleg managed to create the conditions that enabled him to join Promstroi's supply chain. In this respect, it is a mistake to judge Oleg's analysis of the political economy merely by his distaste for the dominance of companies such as Promstroi; in fact, it is the strength of his analysis that led him to create a minor coalition that allows him to survive and thrive in the difficult real economy under conditions of limited access. This finding, I note, could not have been identified in a study of Oleg's attitudes; an interview would only have revealed, as with most other studies of entrepreneurship, that he resented the state rather than revealing what he does about it.

I now elaborate further on the relationship between Sibtekhnika and the dominant coalition using my final example of Oleg's work in the interior of the region. One day Irina was contacted by Valentina, a businesswoman who enquired if Sibtekhnika could refurbish several grocery stores she owned with her husband, Volodya, in *Tsentralnyi*, the capital of Tsentralnyi *raion* in the centre of the oblast. Valentina had not met Oleg or Irina, but they were known to one another by reputation due to the strength of their respective positions in the region. It was agreed that we would visit Tsentralnyi and examine the stores to make more concrete plans. Tsentralnyi raion is marginally smaller than the Netherlands but has a population of only 12,000, of which the vast majority live in Tsentralnyi itself.[4] The journey from Priyatnyi by car would take at least 12 hours, mostly by dirt roads. However, to compensate for the arduous journey, Valentina incentivised our visit by promising to introduce Irina to the local officials responsible for the procurement of educational equipment and staff at the local kindergarten, which raised the prospect of further business opportunities. Moreover, she had also recently built the most comfortable hotel in the raion to cater to the regular flow of businessmen from Moscow (*Moskvichi*) visiting the regional Gazprom office and invited us to stay in it during our visit. Thus, Valentina seemed very keen that Sibtekhnika should visit, offering introductions to local officials over whom she apparently held considerable influence in addition to her own commercial requirements.

Before our arrival, Oleg and Dmitrii explained how Valentina and Volodya had acquired this influence. Oleg said that Valentina is the business partner of the wife of the leader (*Glava*) of Tsentralnyi raion, while Volodya is descended from Old Believers (*Starovery*), who wield great authority in the *taiga*. In the 19th and early 20th centuries the Old Believers were involved in the development of Russian capitalism and philanthropy,[5] and, during the Soviet period, sought positions of control within the government bodies (*gosudarstvennye organy*) that controlled taiga resources, including logging and fishing. Anyone wanting to work in the taiga today still needs their assistance and a guide (*provodnik*), he said, which endows them with continuing influence.[6] They survived in the taiga because of their toughness, he claimed, and told me to inspect Volodya's physique, which was a testament to good breeding and a cultural appetite for work. Using English, he described them as 'success-orientated', 'self-reliant' and said they have a 'protestant ethic in an orthodox society'. He also contrasted this with the majority of Russians, who 'take as they receive' and have an attitude of passivity.[7] Indeed, Dmitrii was keen to emphasise their success, describing them as among the wealthiest people in the entire oblast, with interests in forest products, milk and property. Their children live in Italy, he said, which is their first stop before London.

Oleg said that as Soviet social classes were reinvented and social positions solidified in the post-Soviet years, Russian society was divided into private interest groups. In order to overcome difficulties in business, entrepreneurs had to work between these groups. Creating bridges between them required connections or money, and Valentina and her partners were able to unite on the basis of their collective enterprise, political connections and social influence, which enabled them to reap overwhelming wealth through their dominance of the raion's economy. Characteristically, Oleg sought to relate this to academic concepts, and cited Olsen's work on group theory. According to Olsen, the formation of certain small groups allows members to provide themselves 'with collective goods without relying on coercion or any positive inducements apart from the collective good itself' (1971: 33). The entrepreneurial union of the two wives, combined with the respective political (United Russia) and social (Old Believer) influence of the husbands, presented a straightforward opportunity for all to benefit financially without significant costs or risks.

In this account, Oleg considers the good fortune of Valentina and Volodya from the same perspective that he considers his own entrepreneurial history, which is to emphasise his own agency and social capital as the cause of his success. In Valentina's and Volodya's case, however, the circumstances were entirely different, because they were the beneficiaries of political affiliation. As Shlapentokh has said, when the leaders of Russia's regions were appointed by the president in 2004–05 they were sanctioned to rule 'their regions like fiefs in the same authoritarian way as Putin ran the whole country' (2007: 130–1). Thus, while there is no doubt that Valentina's group was enterprising and well connected, it also stood to benefit enormously from this change, which sanctioned them to exercise power personally over their territory for economic gain. In other words, while I reject Shlapentokh's use of the feudal concept in preference for the concept of LAO, I accept his underlying point: Valentina and Volodya are regional members of Russia's 'dominant coalition', holding local power and wielding it for personal economic gain.

Valentina's importance in Tsentralnyi was clear upon arrival as the features of Russia's LAO became clear in miniature. Tsentralnyi is a large village mainly constructed from wood and prefabricated materials. Most residences have vegetable patches, outhouses, and a street side water supply. Valentina's hotel, overlooking the river, and the Gazprom building stood out because they were built of masonry. Valentina greeted us in a 4x4 and took us to her hotel, which seemed enormous beside the neighbouring buildings, then to her five grocery stores. She was, Oleg noted, 'very active' (*aktivnaya*), which in Russian connotes energy but also pushiness and enterprising spirit. She swept us into her stores and quickly drew our attention to dated shelving and refrigeration units that needed replacing. Her staff, the shop assistants, glanced at one another with 'here come the big shots' expressions, which cannot have escaped my companions. Still, Valentina was courteous with them, addressed them by name and asked them to describe any troubles they had with the equipment and layout of the shop floor. In other words, her command of her staff was akin to Irina's own in Priyatnyi.

As she moved between the equipment, the daily life of the store continued: a drunk man loitered at the counter before approaching a couple of men from out of town who had stopped by for provisions. The drunk had the red face, dull eyes and obliviousness of an alcoholic, but he could not buy anything to drink so began making a nuisance of himself. He asked the outsiders to buy him a drink and forcefully rubbed his forehead against the shoulder of the older man, partly to keep his balance, partly to demand his attention. Initially, the men laughed at him, but he became more vigorous and aggressive. The elder man slapped him hard on the face. Perhaps the others had not seen because they continued their inspection regardless, with Irina taking photos of the shop floor. Oleg noticed I was watching but said nothing. He was keen that I got into the social swing of things and was observing me observing, offering occasional commentary and opinion along the way. Outside, the drunk put his foot on the bumper of the men's car but was threatened with the elder's fist, and they drove off. He staggered over the road to another wretched bystander holding a bottle of vodka and related his story. Thus, although we were among the poor and drunken Russian peasantry of the Siberian interior, we were also disconnected from any meaningful interaction with them. Indeed, as the wealthier men drove away, they left the sad poverty of the village, not with pity but relief. In this way, the disconnection between Valentina's membership in the dominant coalition – concerned with the modernisation of her shop floor – and the misery of many locals was revealed. I followed Irina and Oleg as they trailed Valentina out of the store, continuing the discussion, and we drove to the next. Although I felt ill at ease with my temporary position among the privileged, I was also relieved to be in the car away from the swarms of mosquitoes, four-winged dragonflies and three-inch hornets with luminous green eyes that thickened the air and made street life immensely uncomfortable. These experiences caused me to consider what it takes to be enterprising in the taiga, and I pondered Volodya's Old Believer resolve and toughness with new admiration: it is not only good fortune that allowed them to join the dominant coalition but hard work and an eye for pouncing on the chances that came their way.

After looking at the stores, Valentina turned her attention to showing us a good time with an evening of corporate entertainment. Volodya took us on his speedboat upstream to where he had constructed a short boardwalk between the rivers and a tributary, and several log cabins with hot baths, where we were treated to a large meal and vodka. Volodya had built the site to offer entertainment and relaxation for Russian tourists and Moskvichi. Indeed, this wealthy demographic emerged as prominent in Valentina's strategy for the development of her business. It emerged that she deplored the incapacity of the locals to contribute much to the development of the local economy, saying that there is no hope for young people who 'do not work and do not want to! They are happy to receive 50,000 roubles per month and that's it!' On this basis, I reflect, she knew that the redevelopment of her stores would not increase her profits substantially because the market in Tsentralnyi was not growing, nor was the purchasing power of its residents.

Consequently, her focus for business growth was her new hotel and riverside cabins, based on the spending power of wealthy outsiders. As such, the renovation of her shops may be seen more as a gesture to the locals, giving the impression of modernisation, rather than because it was essential or promised further development. This reflects the government's own rhetorical commitment to improving business conditions without much tangible change.

Reflecting on our time with Valentina and Volodya a few days later, Oleg said that although they do not have a monopoly on local trade, they do monopolise power. 'In Russia there are two social worlds', he explained, 'a poor majority and a very rich minority, which never meet one another'. He called this the 'Haitian model' ('*Gaityanskii model*') in which power is hoarded both regionally and centrally. His analogy is useful to the extent that it acknowledges the marginalisation of the Tsentralnyi population from political and economic influence, but the 'Haitian' aspect is only figurative, likening Russia to a developing country, prone to dependence on resource exports, political elitism, violence and the marginalisation of the people. As I have indicated above, however, I find a more accurate description for them as regional members of the country's 'dominant coalition' in Russia's LAO. This is a concept to which I will specifically return in Chapter 6. Nevertheless, Oleg is right in the sense that Russia's social and economic inequality is integral to the country's institutional structure and that this is politically legitimate. As I now describe, Valentina does not hide her political influence or connections.

Following our inspection of her stores, Valentina introduced us to her political contacts at the House of Soviets (*Dom Sovietov*), where the local parliament (*rayonnaya Duma*) and local administration are located. She walked through the building as if it was her own, knocking on doors and entering offices, compelling officials to meet us. We were introduced to a young bureaucrat coordinating raion kindergarten provisions, who listened as Irina gave a polite and polished sales pitch, supported by brochures, highlighting her legal training and 13 years with Sibtekhnika. She described her team, their expertise and the services they could offer. The bureaucrat hardly said a word, but accepted Irina's card and said she would be in touch if needed. She did not demand an introduction from me because I was welcome simply by association with Valentina. She only raised an eyebrow when Irina introduced me as a student and former lobbyist. Everyone politely agreed that lobbying was a fine idea but were sure such an industry could not exist in Russia. Although we did not talk about politics, it is ironic that using her political clout to lobby decision makers was exactly what Valentina was doing for Sibtekhnika at that moment.

As word of our presence in the Duma spread, we were joined by a woman responsible for the development of business in the raion. Irina said that she chairs an interest group of businesses working with the Priyatnyi city government and invited her to speak at a future meeting. The woman replied that, on the contrary, Irina should bring her colleagues to Tsentralnyi for the meeting, which attracted ironic smiles all round; bringing these businesses here would be impossible and futile. All the same, this conversation underlined that some bureaucrats *do* try to promote business development in Russia in spite of the difficulties. However, just as I indicated in Chapter 1, this policy does not really work in practice. In Tsentralnyi, it is Valentina's entrepreneurship that is pre-eminent; the only reason Sibtekhnika was present here was because Valentina temporarily required it. Indeed, the difference between those inside and outside the 'dominant coalition' was exposed in our next meeting with the manager of a local kindergarten, to whom Irina handed brochures and spoke about Sibtekhnika's product range. The director flicked admiringly through the materials, but said her budget of 7 million roubles (approximately 140,000 pounds in summer 2014) was all she had to pay wages, maintain the site and buy equipment, so she could not afford anything more at present. It was clear to me that the main investment in the village would be Valentina's new shop floors.

Despite the disparity between the resources available to the kindergarten and those available to Valentina, the kindergarten director deplored the Tsentralnyi parents as much as Valentina had bemoaned the local workforce. 'Some fathers', she said, are 'cunning, and never around, and many mothers are alcoholics'. She introduced us to two toddlers who live in the kindergarten because their parents cannot be relied on. Valentina nodded and shrugged with a resigned expression, showing she hears such stories all the time. In this way, it was clear that Tsentralnyi's citizens have little hope for its further development within the wider economy, and only Valentina and Volodya had reason to expect better prospects. This realism reflected Oleg's acknowledgement that he must deal with his own affairs rather than expect the government to bring about changes.

The influence of Valentina and Volodya in Tsentralnyi reveals the role of Russia's 'dominant coalition' in the political economy as it actually exists in the regions. Their status derives from the convergence of the power of the state (*vlast'*), which in Russian connotes the right and capacity to rule, embodied by their partner the mayor, the local personal or de facto power (*avtoritet*) of Volodya (the descendent of Old Believers) and the business acumen of their wives. Moreover, their economic success is *not* derived from the small stores we visited in Tsentralnyi, even though they face slim competition in the groceries market. Rather, the vast majority is derived from their ability to exercise authority over the natural resources of a large territory, just as Promstroi controls the transportation of oil and gas across the oblast. Therefore, as with Russia's strategic industries, their membership of the dominant coalition is, de facto, a political right to derive financial benefit from the territory under their control. This is the way power and wealth are distributed between ministries, strategic industries and regional territories across the country from the president down.

Sibtekhnika, however, also provided Valentina and Volodya with services they could not obtain locally. These goods, I argue, are essential because Valentina and Volodya are morally obliged to maintain a degree of local service provision for the community and, over time, some sense of development or modernisation. Another plausible explanation for the grocery store expenditure is that it would enable them to show less profit within their wider business, leaving them liable for less tax, although we did not discuss this matter specifically. As Inozemtsev has argued, in contemporary Russia, 'politics is just another kind of business. Political problems are solved as if they are commercial ones, and commercial ones as if they are political' (2011: online). Thus, despite their regional dominance, Valentina and Volodya were, in a sense, dependent upon access to the open market, which is to say they depend on occasional trade with companies like Sibtekhnika. Sibtekhnika also welcomed the business: Oleg and Irina gained a substantial and competition-free sale, corporate entertainment, luxurious accommodation and new political contacts from the invitation. To this extent, there was mutual benefit in the deal; however, Sibtekhnika did not depend on it. The dependence, in fact, was all on the side of Valentina and Volodya. Therefore, even though Valentina was politically stronger as a member of the country's 'dominant coalition', in fact she was in a relatively weak position in this transaction.

In this section, I situated Oleg's entrepreneurship in the context of the regional political economy by examining his interactions with other types of commercial organisation, which showed how business conditions in the interior differ from those in Priyatnyi. Because Oleg is able to survive and profit in the city (described earlier in this chapter), he has little need to extend his business into the interior; however, two motivations push him to do so. First, small regional enterprises require goods and services, and Oleg and Irina do what they can to supply them, even if the profit is not always high. This type of trade provides a regular stream of business, a reputation for reliability and customer service and serves a community need. Second, and in contrast, business with state-affiliated enterprises in the interior or with regional elites can be very profitable. Most significantly, I showed that the terms of trade between Oleg and these elites can be in his favour and not theirs, which is an unexpected but significant finding given what is known about the difficulties facing entrepreneurs. Despite their political power, these elites require occasional goods and services from the private sector, a need that benefits Sibtekhnika because of the dominant stake Oleg has established as a regional supplier. Sibtekhnika was invited to help Valentina and Volodya and won a significant contract without competition, profiting handsomely, increasing its social capital and adding to its share of the regional market without any significant effort. I therefore find Oleg a highly effective entrepreneur in spite of the impediments he faces. He does not depend on trade in the interior but knows it is profitable if he can get it, and he is in the rare position of knowing that elites there may require entrepreneurs more than vice versa. Thus, Oleg operates more from a position of strength in his regional market than weakness. To achieve this position, I argue that he has worked according to the same logic of the dominant coalition, which ensures continued access to economic resources and limits outsiders' access to supply in his market. This gives him improved terms of trade vis-à-vis the ostensibly more powerful state-affiliated elites of the interior.

Social Entrepreneurship

In the first sections of this case study, I emphasised a dichotomy between Oleg's disdain for political economic conditions on the one hand and his pragmatic approach to working within them on the other. However, Oleg's pragmatism does not mean that he accepts the political economic status quo (that he describes as 'imperialism') in which private business is vulnerable. On the contrary, in this section I describe his quiet efforts to challenge it through a philanthropic initiative he has established called the Cooperative. The Cooperative is a community centre ostensibly devoted to providing low-cost social educational activities, but Oleg also intends for it to enable individuals to think and learn independently, as a way to counter the narrative of the state. I begin by discussing what the Cooperative is and the factors in its development, which I observed during my fieldwork, before considering its implications for interpreting Oleg's entrepreneurship as a whole.

The Cooperative is a community centre funded by Oleg in a refurbished building adjacent to the Sibtekhnika showroom. It resembles a village hall with two large rooms, a kitchen and an office, and was officially established to provide a co-working area for young entrepreneurs, a community space for events, a series of educational and lifestyle courses and a sports court for ball games. However, as I now describe, the Cooperative is actually a determined response by Oleg to his disdain for the political economic status quo. Specifically, Oleg explained that his ambition for the Cooperative is that it instigates the development of local civil society, by nurturing independent thought and learning, which he believes is absent in Russia. Indeed, this assertion is not without foundation; Schrader has argued that civil society is missing in Russia because it requires solidarity between people who do not personally know one another and a 'personal commitment across network boundaries', which are absent. (This fits with Oleg's assertion that bonded social capital defines the way Russians cooperate with one another.) Bringing this about, Schrader argues, requires not the implementation of market institutions but 'longer socialisation' (2004: 407). Thus, Oleg wants to instigate a sense of solidarity and development in the community. This finding offers another reminder that ethnography with contextual holism can draw specific attention to the difference between attitudes and behaviours of individuals in a situation of formal and informal hybridity (institutional asymmetry). In this case, the Cooperative is Oleg's attempt to bridge that asymmetry with his own resources.

Oleg does not, of course, market the Cooperative on the basis of developing civil society. Rather, he has both public and private narratives for it. The public purpose is to provide educational and personal development opportunities to youngsters, which are otherwise unavailable or out of reach, in order to broaden their horizons. The private purpose for providing these services is to set up a small bulwark against what he perceives to be the uninspiring and politicised education provided by the state and creeping political lethargy among the young. Moreover, Oleg sees the Cooperative as a potential site for the identification and development of talent for business, particularly Sibtekhnika. He therefore established the Cooperative to be both a genuinely useful and politically acceptable community centre, but at the same time provide an alternative to Russian political narratives, establish some roots for civil society and advance his own interests.

While the Cooperative was under development, I observed as Oleg and the Sibtekhnika team drew on their contacts to establish a cadre of teachers who would offer lessons and activities, and as they engaged with local officials to secure their endorsement. In the course of this process, Oleg revealed his specific ambitions for the centre. His plan was not merely to provide extra-curricular activities but to enable locals, and youngsters particularly, to think creatively and for themselves by giving them access to innovative people and teachers in the city from a variety of fields. In his view this was important not for its own sake but because of his dissatisfaction with the Russian system of education, and particularly its inadequacy for providing the right type of skills and motivations for business. 'Schools and universities', he said, 'just provide badges. Diplomas are meaningless. It is impossible to differentiate between candidates from a business perspective'. In this sense, the Cooperative was more than a philanthropic gift to the community; it was an attempt to compensate for and subvert a state system he considered inadequate and unfair and was a means to identify and nurture those with the potential to become freethinking entrepreneurs. 'The Russian market', he said, 'cannot reliably supply the people my business requires. Russians have to make their own communities. I am forced to make my own way'. In this statement, Oleg resolves to create the means for his own survival and development in business due to the inadequacy of the state. At the same time, the Cooperative may be viewed as Oleg's response to his perception that the youth are turning towards the state and away from other possibilities, particularly personal responsibility for their own destinies and private enterprise. Therefore, the purpose of the Cooperative is to provide an alternative in a country where these are few. Needless to say, Oleg kept these objectives 'private' in order to keep them from local bureaucrats who might consider the Cooperative a provocation or even confrontational.

On the other hand, drawing on the public objectives, Oleg did seek to win local government approval for the Cooperative because he wanted them to support his initiative. In his meetings with local officials he drew, characteristically, on a sociological concept to impress them: gentrification. 'The word sounds good', he said. 'It is new to Russia and will be attractive to local officials'. Using this concept, he sold the benefits of the Cooperative in terms of local development. He argued that improving the prospects of the young could spur other advances, such as attracting property developers, new inhabitants and businesses. Gentrification, he explained, is based on education and, according to him, 'Education is the same thing as entrepreneurship in post-industrial society because entrepreneurs must exploit knowledge'. Therefore, he concluded, 'Gentrification is a commercial technology' that can bring about economic development once it is initiated. In this way, Oleg's public justification for the Cooperative was that it serves to gentrify the area.

I do not overplay the distinction between Oleg's public and private justifications for the Cooperative. He genuinely believed in the importance of gentrification and felt the Cooperative could assist with it, just as improving the educational opportunities for youngsters was unlikely to be very controversial, even to state officials. However, the dichotomy is important because it underlines the relevance of political correctness in the development of private enterprise and education in modern Russia. Oleg was angered by what he believes is the deliberate politicisation of education by the state. In his view, Russian education falls not only technically short but is also propagandistic. For example, he frequently discussed the Cooperative in contradistinction to a regional state-run summer camp, the Integrator, run by the local Department for Youth Policy, Physical Culture and Sport, as part of its 'Integration' programme for young people in the region. Integrator is held over two weeks for specially selected young people aged between 14 and 30 and offers lectures from popular figures, some flown in from Moscow, and numerous development activities. Monika, who assisted Oleg with the development of the Cooperative, also attended the Integrator and enjoyed it tremendously: 'It gives young people opportunities to reconsider and think critically about their futures', she said, 'and involves experts from different spheres'. She introduced me to two friends, who also attended and had since been 'reconsidering their own futures', though they had not decided on anything specific. Schwenk has noted these factors in her research into state-run summer camps in Omsk oblast (also in Western Siberia), where young people are attracted by inspirational figures and attendance is considered a 'life opportunity' for a lucky few. According to her, attendees do not perceive the camps as political events; however, lectures and events emphasise economic patriotism, in which work should be done above all for Russia, and one should not leave the country permanently but return to build their own success at home (Schwenk 2015). Oleg was damning, describing the Integrator as 'the new *komsomol*', with the purpose of 'creating new cadres, recruits to the state', and confided that he was not sure what to do about Monika, who had been corrupted. Attendees are 'attracted by power', he complained. 'The big opposition figures in Moscow, Kasparov and so on, don't have any support. Young people don't see anything wrong in Russia'.

In practice, Oleg concealed his subversive intentions from bureaucrats by simply not mentioning them. Moreover, winning the support of officialdom was not difficult. He made contact with the Department for Social Initiatives (DSI)[8] within the Priyatnyi administration and sought its endorsement. Their representative, Yulia, responded positively, because privately funded social initiatives are uncommon, and said that the DSI even had resources it could offer the centre, such as 6,000 roubles a month to pay a local coach to help organise sports events and training. Such support came at a cost, however. As Oleg put it, the administration does not normally give money away unless it is to somebody they know. Therefore, his cultivation of Yulia was essential, and she visited the Cooperative several times for tea and biscuits. In time, Oleg reported that he had paid Yulia to facilitate DSI's support. Thus, formal support for the Cooperative was gained through otkat, revealing again the personalisation of the state.

Oleg sought direct political approval too because with this, he could claim real legitimacy for the centre even as he sought to undermine the political system. He approached three local representatives from the Priyatnaya oblast Duma (all United Russia) and invited them to attend the Cooperative's inaugural party. To his dismay, none of them did. One made the unexpected excuse that he had cut his finger off in a DIY accident, but the others simply did not show up. Here, the political significance of the Cooperative is revealed to be small. Although it represents a generous, innovative and unusual investment in the community, public recognition was granted by bureaucrats, not politicians, with bureaucratic support granted for a fee. This might not seem a bad thing given Oleg's aims, but the absence of political interest in the initiative is also indicative of the contempt Oleg sees in the attitude of the country's rulers towards private initiatives and civil society.

Oleg's frustration with the lack of political interest is also related to the fact that working in partnership with the bureaucratic organs is arduous and offers little benefit. The problem, as he sees it, is that bureaucracy oversees public events and festivals. 'The government has a monopoly over legitimate public actions', he complained. 'It would be unthinkable', he said, 'to hold the inaugural party without them'. Moreover, in Oleg's mind, the representatives of these organs are 'simple people', pencil pushers who 'run the state'. To illustrate his point, Oleg recalled a recent volleyball tournament he had organised to encourage locals to start using the Cooperative court. Disappointingly, only three teams came: a group of seasonal workers from Tajikistan, the second from Sibtekhnika and the other a team of retired colleagues from the city administration. The retirees immediately assumed control, Oleg says. They made all the players write their names and dates of birth on a clipboard they had brought along, for reasons unknown, and dismissed latecomers. They also officiated the games pedantically, and everybody had to stand around afterwards while they handed out pathetic plastic medals and commented on individual performances. Even though the court is Oleg's property and he had initiated the event, 'It is in their nature to control', he said. 'Putin gives these people the laws they want. They are the implementers. They are simple people, but you cannot act in public without their approval'. In this sense, Oleg's hope for brief public recognition by local politicians is more obvious. With the involvement of only bureaucrats, the Cooperative is, in his view, more prone to unnecessary interference.

While Oleg's wish for political recognition was frustrated, readying the Cooperative to begin its work was a greater priority. Oleg sought the support of acquaintances he believed could offer the right sort of teaching, offering them cognac, tea and chocolate in order to entice them to his cause. He outlined his vision that students would receive one-to-one tuition in the Oxbridge style. Over time, he secured the services of several tutors, including an artist, a photographer, an actor, a professor of psychology, an art therapist, an English teacher, an expert in speaking and writing clearly, a yoga instructor, an expert on women's health and the municipal sports coach promised by the DSI. An inaugural party was held offering them the chance to showcase their wares, and leaflets were posted locally to attract potential clients. The event attracted a large crowd. Local interest in the Cooperative was growing as I left the field.

How should the Cooperative be interpreted in the context of Oleg's entrepreneurship? In one respect, the Cooperative is a business project for finding the right type of staff: given Oleg's disdain for state education, it provides a mechanism for attracting and vetting potential employees. This makes sense in light of what I have written about Oleg's approach to business, which is to create the conditions for success himself rather than getting by with the minimal support available. In another respect, the Cooperative is a philanthropic initiative, born out of Oleg's wish to improve local social conditions with his own resources. In a final respect one might consider Oleg as a 'social entrepreneur', which is someone who, to paraphrase Martin and Osberg, targets an 'unfortunate but stable equilibrium that causes the neglect, marginalization, or suffering of a segment of humanity' and brings their resources to bear in order to bring about 'permanent benefit' for that group or society as a whole (2007: 39). However, I do not find this fully persuasive because Oleg does not believe he will bring about such a change, even if the majority of society is marginalised from the entitlements granted to the Russian elite. Rather, I prefer to consider the Cooperative as a way for Oleg to challenge and resist the political economic status quo that has made entrepreneurship a marginal and dangerous occupation and which has a determinant effect on his everyday behaviour (in spite of his relative success). In other words, the Cooperative offers him cover for undermining the authority of the state in a normative way. Overall, the Cooperative is a project of choice funded using Oleg's own resources. He did not have to go to the trouble of furnishing a new building, seeking new staff, negotiating, bribing and ingratiating himself with state representatives but did so, not for business reasons, but to raise a challenge and offer something different in the community. The Cooperative was a mechanism for channelling his rejection of the status quo, and stood in stark contrast to his business, which operated, to the contrary, according to the logic of Russia's limited access order.

Summary

In this chapter, I set out the factors that have enabled Oleg to become a successful businessman in spite of the difficulties facing entrepreneurs. He is antagonistic towards the political economic status quo, but he developed a pragmatic approach to his entrepreneurship. In his assessment, social capital and self-reliance are essential factors to his survival and success. However, Oleg's longevity in business and strong market position are also due to his recognition that a degree of control over one's competition is critical to survival in the contemporary political economy. To this end, Oleg participates in what I described, drawing on LAO theory, as a minor coalition, in which he shares domination of supply of goods (office, retail and commercial equipment) in his local market: he does not seek to outdo his local competitors per se, but to collaborate with them to uphold their mutual security and deter outsiders. To be clear, the minor coalition works in direct contrast to the open economy he himself privately advocates: this protection racket (for it is such) does not bring about the development of competition he wants (and the government claims to want too) but is a direct reflection of the dominant coalition of the country's elite, which is cooperating to limit access to profitable resources. In other words, both the government and Oleg publicly seek a 'modernised' business sector and privately act differently to maximise personal gains. Therefore, the basis of Oleg's entrepreneurial success is replicating the political economic system to which he is politically and morally opposed and which makes entrepreneurship challenging.

Oleg also has a pragmatic approach to business relations. He is prepared to pay backhanders to state representatives for them to do their own job, negotiate with indebted mafiya bosses, pay off aggressors who threaten his staff and build relationships with state-affiliated elites. These activities appear to be the necessary, common-sense actions for a businessman who wants to protect his interests and quietly proceed in the real economy of contemporary Russia. Upholding this pragmatism, Oleg and his directors maintain a focus on organisational order and customer service that is itself a reaction to the perception that things tend to go wrong and fate can strike the careless. They work to reduce the potential for problems to arise by emphasising competence and control within Sibtekhnika and in their public persona. This competence is a result of their long experience, pragmatism in deal making, self-assertion and confidence, in employing and drawing on allies, in legal understanding (or understanding what can and cannot be done in practice) and in focusing on detail. These factors do not mean that Sibtekhnika is not prone to interference, but that minimising of the possibility of interference underpins their everyday entrepreneurship.

In considering Sibtekhnika's business outside Priyatnyi, I showed that the profitable market has geographical limits, but opportunities can also occasionally arise to supply the region's dominant elites very profitably without competition. These opportunities do not arise by chance but as a consequence of the scale and reputation of Sibtekhnika established in the city. The most interesting feature of these transactions, nonetheless, is they reveal that Sibtekhnika is able to act independently and without necessity or coercion with notionally more powerful elites, whereas, perhaps counter-intuitively, it was the elites who required the supplies that are only available on the open market from a few suppliers such as Sibtekhnika. Thus, Valentina and Volodya went to considerable lengths to attract Oleg and Irina to Tsentralnyi.

In the final section, I showed that although Oleg's business activities do not reveal his distaste for and will to resist the status quo, his efforts developing the Cooperative show that this is in reality one of his personal priorities.

Oleg's public hopes for the Cooperative are philanthropic: he wants to improve the educational opportunities available to local youngsters, and with this objective, he has won the support of the local authorities. Privately, however, he also wants to create a community of free thinkers with independence from the state and personal ambition, responsibility and suitability for work in private enterprise, potentially within Sibtekhnika. Oleg does not seek substantial change, of course: he knows it is not within his gift. Yet, with the Cooperative, he can set his own agenda and quietly promote his own worldview.

What, then, is the answer to the question I posed at the outset of this chapter – how has Oleg been so successful? His objective, which he has instilled in Irina and Dmitrii, is to realise that success as an entrepreneur means to function with autonomy from the state, which requires hard work and vigilance. Through constant effort he has maximised his chances of survival by developing the capacity to work and profit without interference and live with a high degree of autonomy. This clearly reveals the continuing relevance of Yurchak's concept of 'entrepreneurial governmentality' (as described in Chapter 2) 15 years after he conceived it. However, Oleg has not succumbed to accepting the inevitability of the status quo even if he is too weak to change it. Rather, he advances his own vision by investing in the Cooperative, which offers alternative sources of information and inspiration (of his choice) in the community. With this, he resists the state in a way that is not possible in business. Oleg's entrepreneurial work for autonomy and resistance are themes I return to in Chapter 6 when I draw the case studies together.

Notes

1 Oleg used the term 'mafiya' to refer to men working notionally in business but who in fact have criminal intent and methods. Therefore, extortion, violence, protection rackets and criminal codes of behaviour are taken here as read.

2 Varese first noted that Russian firms made up for the absence of secure property rights by 'internalising' or buying protection from an outsider (1994: 251).

3 Because all deliveries and visitors are subjected to checks before entering Lesnoigorodok, and all residents have specific permission to live there, my entry was out of the question. However, Irina had acquired a pass based on old relationships in the city, which meant she could consult with clients there rather than rely on their approaches, therefore providing greater access not only to a larger regional market, but one in which competition is severely limited.

4 In reality, Oleg joked, it is ten times larger than the Netherlands, because it is impenetrable except by dirt road or by riverboat.

5 The renowned hardiness of the Old Believers is often described through the story of the Lykov family. See, for example, Dash 2013: online; *Vice* 2013: online. See also Roschin on the role of the Old Believers in 'opening-up Siberia' (1995).

6 There is little evidence behind Oleg's claim that the Old Believers accessed positions of power in the Soviet bureaucracy because, as Humphrey argues, the majority were hostile to the Soviet government (2014: S218) and industrialisation

(Dunn and Dunn 1964: 478), although they were praised as sober workers and did develop personal strategies for interacting with officialdom (see Paert 2004: 202–5). In any case, the extent to which Volodya could be considered a practicing Old Believer is negligible today. At best, he has assumed the cultural traits without the religion. Although he was certainly a hard worker in my observations, he was not obviously pious and was a committed Putin supporter and vodka drinker. Oleg said he would quickly sober up in the presence of elders, though I did not have the chance to find out.

7 Oleg's opinion on Russian passivity is not unique. The supposed inertia and apathy in the Russian character is sometimes referred to as Oblomovism, after the character in Goncharov's novel (Goncharov 1915; Kets de Vries 2001: 609).

8 This department is responsible for organising the infrastructure for 'physical culture' in residential areas, the municipal sports fields and sports instruction in the community, for working with disabled people, for 'healthy groups' for the elderly and the development of urban and regional sports events.

4 Case Study
Anna

This second case study draws on observation within the Centre for Small Business Growth (CSBG), a business established by Anna in 2001 in the city I call Oblomov. Anna established CSBG to assist small businesses with their development, and for several years she employed two members of staff and achieved some commercial success. However, over the past four years, Anna has endured a significant business crisis partly of her own making and partly a consequence of the malicious actions of former clients and local prosecution service officials. As a result, she now runs CSBG on her own, moving between the formal and shadow economies.[1] I argue that Anna's crisis experience provides an example par excellence of the difficulties facing entrepreneurs that I outlined in Chapter 1. I, therefore, set out the events that led to the crisis and the factors that enable her to survive as an entrepreneur today.

I begin the case study by outlining Anna's attitude towards business and the history of her company. She started CSBG with the goal of assisting the development of business in the Western image, an objective she then believed was mirrored by Russian government policy. I describe how she came to form this view and its implications for her entrepreneurship. During her first year in business, she secured the support of a Western sponsor, which ensured that CSBG grew in the early 2000s as the Russian economy recovered. However, when this support was withdrawn, she was left with insufficient funds to continue with her core business services. This led her into a poorly judged business deal she could not honour that made her indebted to former clients, sparking a crisis she could not control and leaving a business with little prospect of recovery or future development. In spite of this, Anna has remained committed to the Western vision of entrepreneurship and maintains a façade that her business is representative of it.

In the following section, I describe Anna's current situation as an entrepreneur enduring a significant crisis. The crisis presents her with two particular challenges. First, she faces persecution from a group of her former clients who seek to intimidate and harass her until she repays her debt, which she is unable to do. Second, these clients have also secured the support of prosecution service officials who have launched a legal case against her that, they say, will end with her inevitable imprisonment, but about which she has very little

DOI: 10.4324/9780429469176-4

information. I outline the characteristics of this persecution and prosecution, consider how it has affected her entrepreneurship and assess the personal and financial toll they have taken.

In the remaining sections, I describe how Anna has responded to the crisis by examining her entrepreneurship in practice. I explain how she 'gets by' in these conditions and what this reveals about the 'actually existing' conditions of entrepreneurship in Russia. I begin by showing how she dedicates significant time to dealing with and responding to her persecutors and prosecutors and how this requires a high degree of entrepreneurialism in itself. I find that Anna's appeal, in which she declares her innocence, is based on invoking the arguments for which she established CSBG in the first place, namely that the government needs to continue to support the development of business and protect entrepreneurs. In other words, she invokes her longstanding support for the improvement of business conditions as the basis of her claim that she has not done anything wrong. Indeed, even though her crisis reveals the fallacy of the government's rhetorical support for business, her self-defence effectively invokes the government's own formal policy in a way that has tangibly stabilised her situation. In sum, I show that her accusers have built a case against her by simulating the legality of their case, and she has defended herself by simulating her own compliance with the government. I therefore find that her entrepreneurship is defined in part by an ongoing argument about the degree to which her activities are legitimate.

Next, I focus on Anna's specific commercial activities. These have changed significantly since the crisis began. Her objective is now to generate enough money to 'get by', support her teenage daughter, and pay off her debts. In order to achieve this, she has retained CSBG as a formal business shell but in practice works mainly in the shadow economy – partly because her reputation is decimated, so business is weak, but also to keep cash flow off the books. To this end, she has registered two further companies through which she can divert resources, if needed. To generate money, she holds periodical executive training seminars, which allows her to keep up appearances, but her main business is now informal and includes translation services for cash, assistance with visa applications to Western countries, as well as participation in two multilevel marketing (MLM) companies and other opportunistic activities. I show that, through these activities, Anna is able to scrape by and must therefore be considered a successful entrepreneur in the context of her situation.

Finally, I account for the difference between Anna's attitude towards business, based on support for Western business norms, with her entrepreneurial behaviour, which is determined by her crisis and a consequence of Russia's institutional asymmetry. CSBG failed as a legitimate business of a Western type, meaning that Anna has not lived up to her ambition to assist in the transformation of business conditions, or even become a competent 'Western' businesswoman herself. However, in the context of crisis, she became a far more effective entrepreneur by being forced to deal with the political economic circumstances as she finds them, rather than as she would like them to be. I draw on the concept of 'entrepreneurial governmentality', to show how Anna's entrepreneurship improved during the crisis as she recognised how to do business in ways that allowed her to survive and remain independent. Moreover, the crisis has provided her with a new opportunity to show that business conditions can and should improve for entrepreneurs, which was her original purpose for becoming an entrepreneur. In this way, I argue that Anna's entrepreneurship retains its original purpose in spite of her changing circumstances. Consequently, her entrepreneurship remains a vehicle not primarily for commerce but for upholding her independence and resisting the status quo.

Anna's Attitude Towards Business

Following the completion of a doctorate in Europe, which focused on the problems facing businesses in Russia, Anna worked as a research fellow for a Western non-governmental organisation (NGO) promoting democratic and economic transition in the former Soviet Union (FSU). There, she wrote a report detailing how business could be supported in Russia. As her contract ended, she drew on her recommendations to ask for support from her employer to start a company supporting businesses in Oblomov, her hometown, and was granted sponsorship for a year to establish CSBG. During that year, she looked for ways to make the business sustainable and won further assistance from the US State Department to establish a programme enabling Russian entrepreneurs to participate in internships with companies in Europe and America where they would learn to improve their business skills. Thanks to that assistance, these internships were offered for a fraction of their real cost and became very popular. Anna's clients spent three weeks with businesses operating in their sector in America or Europe, then brought Western business acumen home, enabling them to develop their own companies, which over time would become models of free market capitalism.

Anna is a true believer in the need for Russia to become a free market economy in the Western model. As she argued,

> It is often said that business is for the Americans or English and not in our mentality. Sometimes people love to justify their lack of success on the basis of a lack of business mentality. For me, sending clients abroad is the best example. Or, Western companies come here, employ our people and quickly set high standards. Therefore, it is a question of management. In America people have come from every country, and they succeed. They are integrated, work at it and believe in business. This will be achieved here when the management standards we need are adopted to get people working.

Thus, Anna's commitment to importing Western business practices is unambiguous, determined not only by the values of her sponsor and patron but also her experience studying Russian business in Europe. She looked upon Russian businesses as inherently poor in comparison. When an American opened a coffee shop in the city, for example, she described a 'spirit of celebration' and the 'good attitude' there, compared to the dismal 'Russian mentality' she encountered in *DomKoffi*, a café opened by a Russian nearby. Her self- appointed role was 'to break the Russian stereotype' that there can only be businesses of a Russian, American or British type, but that Russian entrepreneurs can and should be like those in the West. She claimed that her work was at the forefront of bringing this change about in Oblomov because, when clients joined her programmes, they immediately saw the benefits of a Western approach. 'For them it was such a surprise, a new ideology. Earlier there had been a boss in control but now the leader had to work in a cooperative spirit'. One client, so inspired, decided to introduce ATMs to Oblomov. At first he thought it would be impossible in Russia because people would steal them, or they would be destroyed, she said, but she persuaded him to try. As a result, she claimed, 'We did not even have cheque books, because we went straight to Visa cards'.

In Anna's view, her programmes also gave clients the chance to see how Western society works too by staying with a Western family. To her mind, Western families relate to one another more effectively and value one another more than Russian families. The Western family model, she believes, has provided the basis for many successful businesses and a thriving economy. As she put it, 'It is one thing to arrive and have a look but another to speak with people, with leaders, see how differently they operate in the company, how they talk to people, how their system values business'. Clearly Anna's enthusiasm for the West contrasts with her rather pessimistic view of Russia. To her, the more her clients learnt from Westerners, the better for themselves, their families, the economy and the country as a whole.

During the early years, Anna also established a seminar, workshop and roundtable event programme in the city in which consultants, business trainers and, as she put it, 'those who had already achieved something' in different fields of business gave talks to her clients. According to Anna, these speakers passed on 'an ideology, the high standards and phrases that you have to introduce directly to salesmen'. In this way, Anna meant the training to be transformative, not only of business practice but of the attitudes local entrepreneurs had towards their work. However, for her, the most important aspect of her training was to offer advice on how her clients should improve their relations with the local authorities. To achieve this, she invited members of the local government to attend. 'Everything is connected with corruption', she said. Because the authorities did not know how the relationship should work, she said, businesses must tell them. 'If businesses do not demand and encourage better relations with the authorities, nothing will change because they will continue to act as before'. The responsibility was on businesses to define a new working relationship with officialdom, she argued.

> We had many roundtables, she said, where people spoke about how it works in America, for example, how their Chambers of Commerce work to help businesses as much as possible, and when people realised that this is the best way, it became simpler to achieve it here.

Anna, therefore, conceived of her roundtables as forging contact between entrepreneurs and bureaucrats and portrayed the Western model as an ideal, achievable example for Russia.

The final aspect of CSBG's early work began when Anna found out that the local administration had established initiatives to tackle corruption, which enhanced her conviction that political-economic change was underway. She gathered information about these initiatives under the banner of an 'anti-corruption programme' and offered it to her clients for a small fee to cover her administrative costs. Considering the early work of CSBG together, the influence of the idea of 'transition' (see Chapter 2), in which Russia moves inexorably from a planned economy to a Western-type free market, is unmistakable. Anna established CSBG as an exemplar of transition thinking in her city; she literally *sold* the transition. In this respect, her business has a clear ideological underpinning, one that rejected the status quo in Russia and aspired to Western norms. Her feeling was that Russian political economic conditions and social attitudes would have to change, and as her anti-corruption programme appeared to show, the state was already orientating itself to this end. Anna therefore positioned herself as an advocate of this change, based on her expertise (having interviewed many of the first generation of businesspeople in Oblomov) and experience (having worked for an NGO in the vanguard of transition advocacy).

During the course of Putin's first presidency, CSBG achieved some commercial success. Anna acquired a modern apartment in the centre of the city and a foreign car. She took on two employees and acquired an office with an adjacent conference room for her seminars. Moreover, her professional network also grew extensively as several of her internship alumni built successful businesses. She was also well known among local officials as an entrepreneur working hard for the city. Today, her office displays the values for which she toiled: posters of both the Russian and American presidents, flags, photos from clients and associates, and letters of gratitude, including one from a former US ambassador, adorn the wall. However, after this initial success, CSBG was threatened by a variety of factors. The sponsorship that was the basis of her commercial success could not last indefinitely, and business became far more challenging when it was withdrawn. As Anna put it, 'we had partners in the West, we worked together, but the programme became more expensive and the number of clients fell immediately'. Although Anna did not say so, the withdrawal of assistance was undoubtedly related to the dawning realisation among Western donors that Russian transition was not happening as expected. In truth, transition had not been happening for several years: CSBG was established four years after Yeltsin effectively formalised a new kleptocracy in the loans for shares deal (Barnes 2006: 104; Green 2009: 202–4; Lovell 2006: 96–99; Nellis 2002: 48), and serious doubts had already been raised about the relevance of the concept of 'transition' (Pine and Bridger 1998: 2–7). By 2003, there was little doubt at all that transition was conspicuously absent (Carothers 2002: 13).

It is reasonable to ask why Anna, a student of Russian business, did not see this coming. However, within Oblomov's business scene, the continuing difficulties facing entrepreneurs made her more convinced of the need for change, rather than less convinced that change was happening. While academics may have started to find the concept irrelevant, she viewed it as incomplete. This is why I describe her as a transition believer. For her, transition was an ambition and her main business chance, even if, in reality, it was a receding prospect she did not comprehend or refused to acknowledge. I argue that Anna's experience underlines what Charlie Walker has described as the 'transition to nowhere'. In his study of working-class Russian youth, traditional routes to work are available yet unviable as a result of the collapse of the state-led economic system (2009: 531–2). Building on this, I contend that the aspirations of Russia's emergent middle class appear to be equally limited, if not by economic collapse, then by the failure of the state to enable the emergence of the market economy it promised. Thus, Walker's conclusion that 'institutional inertia and economic decline have rendered "old" transitions simultaneously available and yet unviable' (Walker 2009: 544) is equally valid in Anna's case: her identity has been 'disembedded' by the fact that she must function between 'old and new modernities' (Walker 2009: 544).

For Anna, the state's advancement of entrepreneurship in its rhetoric about economic development and 'modernisation' (*The Economist* 2009: online; Hill 2010: online; Medvedev 2009: online; Merry 2011: online; Ruptly TV 2015: online), offered her hope and served to legitimate her convictions about the need for transition. The fact of the matter was, however, that the number of Anna's clients fell as their interest in Western perspectives declined. Businessmen found that the situation they encountered in the Russian market bore little resemblance to the Western experiences Anna shared in her seminars. The increasingly widespread accessibility of the internet also meant that the materials Anna marketed could also often be found online. In one seminar I attended, participants laughed as one circulated his smartphone revealing that the lessons Anna was translating from a DVD were available free in Russian on the Internet. At the same time, securing a visa to the West remained a difficult and unpredictable process, while the cost of foreign travel in the West stayed high for ordinary businesspeople. These problems presented a significant challenge for Anna to continue to meet the goals for which she had established CSBG.

Despite these challenges, Anna decided to persevere with the internship programme, so she looked for ways to reduce the cost in order to attract new clients and enter what she described as 'the mass market'. She judged that this was possible if she used travel websites to find cheap flights and accommodation. These costs had not been a priority when she had financial support, so her idea was to try to reduce them in order to make the programmes accessible to a wider client base. However, this turned out to be risky. Anna had to spend much time identifying savings online, which proved exhausting. Moreover, by reducing her costs, she also reduced her margins, so her profits were smaller and unpredictable. It soon became clear that the programmes were unprofitable compared to the effort expended making them affordable for her clients. Furthermore, Anna continued to market the packages as a premium product, which, to her dismay, meant that clients valued their travel experience at least as much as the training and contacted her at all hours with various demands, even when they were in the hands of Western hosts or establishments. This model was unsustainable: CSBG could not deliver, administer or profit from the high-quality travel packages it was selling, and the business was becoming heavily indebted with the runaway costs. Anna found herself spending new clients' money to pay for services for existing clients. Desperate, she finally called a halt to the provision of travel services in order to concentrate on running the training aspects of the programme. However, this decision meant she owed several hundred thousand roubles to clients who had bought packages only for them to be unfulfilled, and she was unable to compensate them. Anna admitted that she had made a mistake, but instead of filing for bankruptcy, she declared herself innocent of wrongdoing based on a conviction that she had the right to repay the debt on her own terms. This, she claimed, is how business should work, even though, as I show below, the law is prone to interpretation. Thereafter, she informed her clients that she could not repay them in the hope and with the assumption that she could make personal repayment arrangements with them. Instead, they took matters into their own hands and instigated the crisis that continues to engulf her over three years later, and which I outline in the next section.

In this section, I have described Anna's attitude to entrepreneurship as bound to the idea of transition that was influential in academic and policy circles during the Yeltsin period, when she studied in Europe. This view was reinforced when she then continued her research within a prominent NGO. In hindsight, it seems inevitable that her own transition into Russian business would draw on that ideological framework, and her success at securing funding to develop CSBG from significant foreign sources is indicative of the importance and relevance of those ideas at the time. Despite the fact that the 'Westernisation' of Russian business seems flawed today, it continues to carry influence. As Oleg's case study also revealed, the improvement of business conditions is a rational aspiration for Russian entrepreneurs. Because business conditions in Russia did not improve substantially through the first Putin decade (see Chapter 1), it seemed appropriate to Anna that she could continue offering these services even after her sponsor withdrew its support and her market diminished. Nevertheless, it is also clear that Anna did not develop the business qualities she advocated and was unable to maintain a profitable business. Her argument that she did not defraud her clients illegally is a spurious one, but as I show in the following sections, the argument could not be effectively countered, which indicates that her intuition and understanding of how business can survive under such conditions (as a consequence of institutional asymmetry) is not quite as bad as it seems.

Entrepreneurship Through a Crisis

When Anna informed her clients that she could not repay them immediately, several of them formed an ad hoc group and signed a document in which they accused her of stealing their money. Then, using personal connections to gain the support of influential police staff, an investigation was launched against her that is now with city prosecutors. Although Anna secured an agreement with some clients through the court to repay their debts according to a repayment schedule, this was insufficient for others who, working together or alone, preferred to pressure her personally in pursuit of their money. As a result, Anna now faces a crisis with legal and informal dimensions: she endures threats and intimidation to herself, her family, her property and her business and remains under prolonged investigation without much knowledge of the actual case against her or its likely outcome. Both have taken a significant personal and financial toll, but the most intolerable aspect of the crisis is the ongoing uncertainty it has created. According to her, some prosecutors connected with her accusers assume she is guilty, while others take it that she is innocent until proven guilty. This is a fair assessment, regardless of whether she is guilty or not. She has been threatened with inevitable jail by some, while others have assured her that the case would be resolved in a matter of days, only for it to roll on, now into its fourth year. Indeed, despite what ostensibly appears to be a simple case of business debt, the specific charges against Anna still remain unknown. Given that she has already admitted her debts and secured a court-approved agreement for gradual repayment with some clients, the prolonged nature of the case likely stems from the connections between Anna's accusers and prosecution staff. Anna is now confronted with the fact that the transition she sought did not happen, and as will now become clear, her advocacy of Western ideas may have even aggravated those now plotting against her. During my months with her, Anna spent a great deal of time speculating about who is against her, who is for her, and how to persuade the most sympathetic people of her innocence. In this section, I begin with a description of the persecution Anna faces before turning to the prosecution.

Anna has faced several forms of persecution since her accusers began their campaign against her. Their main tactic is to intimidate her, which began as soon as she informed them that she could not repay them. Within a few days, two armed men entered her office and said she needed to pay, or her family would be hurt, which indicates that they had followed her to identify that she had a father and daughter at home. She pleaded that she could not pay immediately. Later, a man entered the office and demanded Anna gave him her internal and international passports, which would prevent her from fleeing. Her clients apparently believed that her connections in America and Europe or the fact that she is Jewish and could leave for Israel meant she could take flight, even though she had admitted her debt and was willing to strike a deal to repay it over time. Anna told me that her external passport had expired, but she chose to give it up anyway to avoid violence: she quickly decided that she would not be able to prevent these people from acting as they wished, so she would have to conform to their demands wherever possible without actually being able to give them the money.

Sometimes intimidation failed. One evening, a man arrived at her office drunk and claimed to be a sniper. He said he was flying to the Netherlands the following day on business, implying that he was on some kind of secret mission. Knowing he was trying to intimidate her, Anna bravely replied, 'Yes, you look like James Bond'. The man changed tack and claimed he was representing one of Anna's clients. Anna said she would call her and arrange gradual repayments, to which he said, 'No, that's too easy. Why don't we talk? I can help you'. Having failed to intimidate her, he attempted to appeal to what he apparently believed were her intellectual pretensions. He said that he was sleeping with the client and knew that she was 'simple and working class'. He told Anna that she should hand him the money so that he could pass it on to her, and if she did, he would let her keep some for herself. Anna replied that she could resolve the dispute herself, and when the man had reluctantly left, called the client directly to offer gradual repayment. The client said that she was waiting for the money to be returned all at once and would not accept Anna's offer. Several days later, the 'sniper' returned and said, 'You did not accept my suggestion so what can I have from this office?' He pointed to a plant in the corner, 'Maybe this tree?' Anna responded, 'The other day you were trying to offer me money and now you want my tree?' He left again empty-handed. In these tragicomic episodes, it is again clear that, contrary to Anna's hopes, the formalisation of the business sphere has not taken place; several of her former clients are resorting to individual tactics based on brute force rather than negotiation or recourse to the law.

Another mode of intimidation used by Anna's accusers is anonymous phone calls. On one occasion she received a call from a man who claimed he was from a neighbouring oblast. He said that he wanted to go to New York for business training and asked her where he should send the fee. Anna responded by asking if he wanted to know more about the training packages, to which he replied, 'Just tell me where I can send the money'. Anna wondered why he would not want to know more about what he was buying, so asked him again, and got the same response. After a time, she put the telephone down. In relating this episode to me, Anna said the caller was trying to entrap her. This type of intimidation did not stop at the office, however. One evening, Anna left her flat without warning, leaving me with her father, Boris. A few minutes later, Boris answered the door and admitted a huge, strong-looking man with a woman and children. He proceeded to show them eagerly around the flat as if it were for sale. The man scowled as he moved between rooms. After they had left, Anna returned and, in some distress, called a friend, while Boris busied himself in the kitchen. Anna had not told me about the visit, so I assumed that she had decided to sell the apartment in order to repay her debt. However, when Anna recovered, she told me it was not her choice but forced upon her by an accuser, who threatened that he was going to take her flat away; she had been intimidated into the viewing even though she did not intend to sell it.

These intimidation tactics are also accompanied by attempts to humiliate Anna publicly and cast aspersions on her character. On local TV news and on internet forums, her accusers cast doubt on her credibility as an entrepreneur and business history and portrayed themselves as her victims. They claim that she is manipulative and calculating with dubious international connections and that she lied to her clients about 'partnerships' she had never had with reputable airlines in order to force them into deals she could not honour. Remarkably, the group also sought to turn her reputation for supporting business against her by claiming that her numerous initiatives over the years showed that she tried to develop a large pyramid scheme to defraud ordinary people and that her seminars introduced Scientology influences into the city.[2] Considered together, Anna faces persecution ranging from physical intimidation to slurs on her reputation, with a significant impact on her well-being and business. These attacks have been calculated, constant and unpredictable. The accusations against her have also been invented, vindictive, defamatory and, though it is difficult to comment on every incident, probably illegal.

Anna is vulnerable in a way that Oleg is not, due to his emphasis on self-protection. Yet, two factors undoubtedly make her predicament worse still: she is a woman and a Jew. Female entrepreneurs are not unusual of course; many women are engaged in small- and medium-sized enterprises (SMEs) as opposed to larger companies, and the majority work in the service sector like Anna (Salmenniemi, Karhunen and Kosonen 2011: 83). However, her ideological drive to be an entrepreneur appears quite unusual: in a study of 27 female Russian entrepreneurs, Salmenniemi, Karhunen and Kosonen found that only two of their sample aspired to entrepreneurship, and the remainder were driven to it out of necessity. On the other hand, a majority encountered gender-based discrimination, ranging from the common sentiment that women belong at home (where Anna had to be anyway as a single mother) to sceptical attitudes towards female entrepreneurs (Salmenniemi, Karhunen and Kosonen 2011: 87). However, Anna is not only a failing female entrepreneur with a family to support, which leave her vulnerable enough to intimidation and bullying. As becomes clear throughout this chapter, Anna's particular attitude towards business – her invocation of the Western model, her rejection of Russianness in business, her determination to show Russians how to be entrepreneurial (even when she fails) – is deployed by her accusers against her. In her attempt to be a progressive path breaker, she has isolated herself further from her contemporaries. Her case does nothing to improve the view that Russian women have had a particularly hard time in business, notwithstanding her commercial errors.

To Anna's isolation must also be added the fact that she is almost certainly the victim of thinly veiled anti-Semitism. Like most of Siberia's Jews, her family is non-practicing and assimilated, but their religious-ethnic identity is not unknown. She also has a daughter and a mother in Israel, and this is likely to be the reason that her passport was requested. When I specifically asked her if anti-Semitism was behind the attacks against her, she denied it and pointed out that there are many successful Russian Jews, including the former regional governor. Nevertheless, a number of 'successes' does not discount the existence of anti-Semitism in wider society. Indeed, numerous Russian oligarchs of Anna's generation have Jewish parentage (for example Harding 2007: online; Hoffman 2002: 359; Weaver 2012: online), a fact that has not resulted in overt public resentment against Jews (Rutland 2005: online). Yet, Anna's denial prompts me to justify my argument. Anti-Semitism is alive and well in contemporary Russia, because Jews are still widely considered to be outsiders working against the interests of the country and its people, which Howard and Gibson describe as a result of dogmatism and xenophobia (2007: 195).[3] During the early 2000s, anti-Semitic feelings were 'running high', but Putin expressed considerable and unprecedented support for Jews (Shlapentokh and Arutunyan 2013: 57), while retaining a 'niche for anti-Semitism' in Kremlin propaganda so that 'the Jewish card could be played if the danger to Putin's elites from Russian nationalists increased', in order to deprive them of the ability to use anti-Semitism (Shlapentokh and Arutunyan 2013: 57–59). Meanwhile, in Russian society, anti-Semitism remains ingrained. Increasing state control of the media has not prevented the publication of slurs associating Jews with opposition to the state (Cantorovitch 2014: 17), while the resurgent Orthodox church seeks to 'other' Jews. The church refers to Jews like the Russians – a people as well as a religious group – which makes them 'a rival chosen people' (Kornblatt 1999: 416). Accordingly, while Russia formally accepts and supports Jews, open anti-Semitism exists in various public institutions. This reflects the situation for entrepreneurs, who are formally supported yet in reality frequently exploited. I therefore argue that, as a Jew and an entrepreneur, the persecution Anna endures has undeniably racist undertones. In the face of all this, there have been no legal implications or repercussions for her persecutors or any protections given to Anna. She faces their aggression alone. As she put it, 'Well, my situation simply shows that in our country the presumption of the guilt of business is dominant'.

What ultimately lies behind the attacks on Anna if it is obvious that she cannot repay her accusers? In a tangible sense, Anna promised her clients an opportunity to improve themselves – to make themselves more successful in the post-Soviet market. As such, when her business collapsed, she not only failed to achieve her own aspirations but also let her clients down too. Thus, in selling the transition but not delivering it, Anna demonstrated to her clients that the promise of the market was too good to be true. Like her, they had wanted to believe they could change their lives with business training in the West, but it proved impossible, and they lost their money in the process. This gave them the opportunity to revert to old 'truths' about rampant Western capitalism, Jews and entrepreneurship. Thus, the market emerges as less than hegemonic in the way that the planned economy was but, rather, as something that might have been but is no longer possible (or possible for everyone) under current LAO conditions. This is the case even when individuals such as Anna, or her clients, have done all the right preparation with training or study. Thus, Anna and her clients are unable to attain the market they have been promised. This is the 'transition to nowhere' described by Walker (see above) and is visible in the contemporary aspirant middle class: the promise of progress is restricted for entrepreneurs too.

I now turn to Anna's prosecution, which has been created by a plot between her accusers and their allies within the state prosecution service. I will not provide an appraisal of the specific legality of Anna's position because 'legality' is relative under conditions of institutional asymmetry: the fact is that, although Anna has been the subject of a legal investigation since her former clients accused her of taking their money, the specific grounds for the investigation have remained unclear. Instead, I describe her situation as I observed it as regards the investigation. Anna told me that when the police first responded to the allegations of her accusers and seized the computers from her office, they did so in order to search for evidence of fraud. Investigators also accessed CSBG's bank account to determine from and to whom money had travelled. In my assessment, these actions appear to be a legitimate course of action for investigators under the circumstances and proportionate to the alleged crime. However, when I left the field, officials had yet to return Anna's computers, and it is not altogether clear what data was recovered through these actions or what they have been doing on the investigation since, with the exception of periodical and unpredictable demands for further paperwork. In other words, Anna appears to remain under investigation without knowing its legal basis and, therefore, has no idea of her prospects. In this respect, she endures the crisis as much a victim of the law as a subject to it, and, indeed, this applies whether she has broken the law or not. The prosecutors are unable or unwilling to present clearly the legal case against her.

Moreover, some prosecution officials have engaged in intimidation tactics resembling those used by her accusers, which indicates that they have little intention of building a robust legal case against her anyway. For example, Anna has been called to the prosecution service offices to be told that Russia's prisons are empty and need filling, and that the only way to reduce her sentence was to immediately admit her guilt. In other words, Anna was asked to plead guilty to a crime for which she had not been charged. If she refused, the official warned her, the process of building a case against her would take longer, but her imprisonment was certain. Remarkably, Anna did not blame the state for this situation, but said it only proved her belief that influential individuals within the prosecution service were in cahoots with her accusers and out to ruin her.

The compelling case that the investigation was being manipulated to implicate her did not make Anna's defence any simpler. Rather, building a case for her defence proved to be extremely difficult. By the time I left the field, she had employed (and dismissed) four separate lawyers to help her understand her legal situation, but each had offered conflicting advice, and the investigation was no further towards a resolution. The first recommended that Anna develop a specific 'strategy' and 'play a game of chess' with prosecutors in order to proceed carefully through the crisis. Anna quickly rejected this. 'I did not want my life to be a strategy', she said, 'but only wanted to tell the truth'. The second lawyer proved to be ineffective too. When we met her, for example, Anna asked her to visit the prosecutor's office to draw their attention to a recent presidential declaration stating that if a business debt is being repaid, the process of repayment should not be interfered with. However, the lawyer was inexplicably hesitant and said she was about to travel to Moscow for a month so refused to help. Instead, she recommended another lawyer whose daughter worked in the prosecutor's office, which might provide a better way of influencing the process. It did not, and two further lawyers have not advanced the case any further. Overall, their contribution has been educated guesswork at best rather than effective legal assistance.

Thus, Anna has encountered the legal process as ineffectual from the perspective of both prosecution and defence. Just as the prosecution service cannot build or has avoided building a decisive case against Anna, so have her lawyers proven more concerned with strategising and offering connections rather than developing a proper defence case or counselling. Within this perplexing and apparently interminable legal process, Anna's uncertain prosecution continues. This is clear empirical evidence, if it were needed, of the institutional asymmetry in Russian society. In this situation, individuals simulate formal processes for personal rather than legal gains. That is, prosecution officials appear to be simulating a prosecution for their acquaintances and, presumably, some eventual material reward. This is a point I return to below. As it happens, the major consequence for Anna is that she remains isolated from support or advice, alone to respond to the persecution and prosecution. Outlining the ways in which she does so is the purpose of the next sections.

Before continuing, I wish to consider what it means to say that Anna is in a 'crisis', even if it appears self-explanatory. I use this term because it has come to define the essential characteristics of her everyday life and the situation that determines her everyday activities. At the time of writing, she has experienced the persecution and prosecution I have described for over four years, so her nerves are frayed, and she is often exhausted. Her mood fluctuates between elation, when she manages to resist pressure or receives some encouraging news, and depression, when she is threatened or has to respond quickly to placate a former client. She is at the mercy of her doubts because she does not have a real sense of whether she is making progress. Her days cannot be planned because she is constantly responding to various demands. Her family life is strained, with Boris, her septuagenarian father, her only practical help. Her remaining employee has resigned because she was scared and gave up hope. Her home is under threat because her income is not sufficient to pay her bills. Walker has argued that the Russian working class has disproportionately borne the brunt of Russia's economic adjustment on their bodies and minds and 'are forced back to the same strategies of the early post-Soviet period' (2015: 34). I suggest that Anna's experience shows the entrepreneurial class to be similarly vulnerable, particularly women, as I argue further below. While there is no denying that she made a mistake and lost the money of numerous clients, her situation now can be fairly likened to that of Joseph K, the respectable banker accused of an unknown crime in Kafka's fictional *The Trial* (reprinted 1998). I draw on Shevchenko's definition of a crisis, drawing on her ethnography of post-socialist Moscow in the late 1990s:

> A crisis may be perceived as a routine and unchanging condition. In such circumstances, the crisis evolves from a singular and alien happening into the very stuff of everyday life, the immediate context of decisions and actions, and, at a certain point, the only reality with which individuals have the social and cultural tools to deal. Crisis may become the default expectation that organises people's priorities and desires, as well as the benchmark against which they measure their successes or failures.
>
> (Shevchenko 2009: 2)

Over two decades after Shevchenko's fieldwork, this definition of crisis appears to sum up Anna's everyday experience very well. Anna has come to consider, for example, that the conditions of her crisis are at their worst during the full moon, when, she says, 'the wolves howl and emotions dominate'. In this way, the crisis has become the defining feature of her life and, as I show in the next section, the key determinant of her everyday activities.

In this section, I have described the specific conditions of Anna's crisis. There is no doubt that she is responsible for her debts; nevertheless, the reaction by her clients and their allies in the prosecution service could not have been predicted. Anna admitted that she had made a mistake but, believing she had a legitimate claim to repay the debt on her own terms, prompted an aggressive reaction from her clients, who took the case into their own hands. At the same time, the legal process, such as it is, has been manipulated by officials themselves. Anna, it seems, is not even guilty until proven innocent because the prosecution service is not interested in whether she is innocent. Overall, the circumstances of Anna's crisis exemplify the conditions of institutional asymmetry that I described in Chapter 1. Specifically, in an environment in which formal rules are uncertain or prone to manipulation, those in charge of their enforcement manipulate them to their own advantage. This was the case when Anna refused to proceed down a repayment path that suited her former clients, and it was again the case in the way they responded according to informal rules. At the time of writing, both sides continue to try to overcome the other between the formal and informal spheres. Meanwhile, Anna has managed to strike informal deals for periodical repayment with several former clients, paid for by her new business ventures, which shows that others are prepared to work with rather than against her to reduce the debt. As I now explain, by working between the formal and shadow economies, she has managed to restart her entrepreneurial career, even as she deals with the ongoing travails of the crisis.

Responding to Crisis

In this section, I outline how Anna has responded to the crisis I have described. I specifically focus on the activities she undertakes to counter the case against her, as opposed to the activities she undertakes to make a living, which follow in the next section. I first discuss the time and effort she devotes to interpreting and making sense of her situation by seeking advice and counsel from various sources, and then discuss how she seeks to improve it. With her persecutors, Anna's activity is mainly reactive because she does not want to aggravate them. With her prosecutors, in contrast, she is far more proactive and devotes great effort to trying to persuade them of her innocence. Only by achieving this does she hope to resolve the crisis. In addition, Anna has also decided that she should seek to win the support of the presidential administration itself, which she believes will be able to examine her case objectively, see that she is right and intervene to stop those against her. In this section, I examine these efforts in turn.

Given the uncertainties of her situation and progress, Anna devotes much time to seeking advice in order to cope. She often attempts to draw on advice from old contacts, but the damage to her reputation caused by her debt and the negative publicity advanced by her persecutors has limited her social capital. However, some contacts have remained notionally loyal. For example, she places great stock on the information she receives from a friend, a retired policeman. His advice does not come free, however, and in return, she gives him English lessons. One piece of information he offered was that one of Anna's prosecutors, a woman, is 'essentially a good person', so she must be under pressure to advance the case from her superiors. Although this hearsay is vague and possibly false, Anna valued it because it gave her confidence and specific direction for her appeals, which I discuss later. However, more often, her contacts let her down. When, for example, she asked the retired policeman if he would go to the prosecutor's office and vouch for her character, he became unavailable. Indeed, few of Anna's advisors have been prepared to support her in person, apparently because they fear association with a potentially guilty businesswoman. When, for example, she asked some loyal clients to go to the prosecutor's office as a group, some made excuses, some went quiet for days and others agreed but then backtracked. Anna believes that men are particularly weak in this regard. In contrast, she told me, one loyal female friend went alone and voluntarily to the prosecutor's office as a character witness. She told them they were wasting their time, that Anna was not a criminal and that she felt sorry for them chasing her because it was all so insignificant. Anna also seeks advice from fellow entrepreneurs who have endured similar crises, on the basis that their insights might offer the best course of action. However, because each case ends differently, it is difficult to know which to emulate: some went to prison, others gave up their assets in order to avoid violence and still others did not give up but worked relentlessly until they were somehow vindicated.

To make up for the lack of quality information from her personal acquaintances, Anna tries to gather as much as possible from different sources and draws particular motivation and guidance from the American life coaching audio courses she uses in her seminars. These courses emphasise personal and psychological transformation in a step-by-step process that encourages listeners to take control of their destiny and become mentally and financially successful. Anna plays these late at night and first thing in the morning. Unsurprisingly, when her daily circumstances appear to match the messages in her courses, this reinforces her chosen course of action. Salmenniemi and Vorona have described this in readers of Russian self-help literature as 'a pick and mix method', where certain points are selected when they are experienced as useful (2014: 51). According to their research, some Russian women have embraced positive thinking on the basis that if they change themselves, the world around them will change too: 'such an individual-centred conception of social change has a certain appeal since it resonates with the widespread sense of powerlessness and inability to influence the structural conditions of everyday existence in Russian society' (Salmenniemi and Vorona 2014: 54–55). Salmenniemi has also found that popular Russian self-help literature has done 'important ideological work by making sense of and legitimising social inequalities with a psychological repertoire. With its emphasis on self-reliance and autonomy, this repertoire resonates with the acute sense of political disenfranchisement that exists amongst the Russian population today' (2013: 23). Salmenniemi argues that 'this psychologisation of social inequalities is not particularly Russian, but can be seen as part of neoliberal rationality' (2013: 12). In this vein, Anna's image of society as one in which inequality exists but in which anyone can achieve the American Dream if they take the right steps is reified by her American courses. The cyclical power of these courses lies in the fact that if one does not achieve their results, it is still in their power to gain control over their situations.

Although American life coaches offer a rational path to success, Anna also seeks emotional and psychological support and reassurance, so she periodically turns to a palm reader (*ekstrasens*). Unlike the coaching tapes, Anna can ask questions of her ekstrasens and seek some guidance. As I have shown, there are very few other people listening to her elsewhere. The ekstrasens, a former waitress, predicts Anna's future using tarot cards for 1000 roubles a session. She told me that she had enough demand to start a business seeing clients daily every half an hour between four and seven o'clock, which suggests that Anna is far from alone in wondering about her security and prospects. Before the palm reading began, the ekstrasens comforted Anna by saying that she had once had cancer but had survived because she had to look after her daughter, a story that Anna, whose daughter was the same age, found inspiring. Indeed, Anna took the insights she received from her as seriously as those from other sources. Galina Lindquist has also noted the importance of magic in her anthropology of post-socialist Russia:

> Magic has an obvious connection with the structures of power. Magic practices thrive where power is brutal and overwhelming, where the rational channels of agency are insufficient or of limited value, and where the uncertainty of life calls for methods of existential reassurance and control that rational and technical means cannot offer.
>
> (Lindquist 2006: 2)

Moreover, as Borenstein noted, it is 'not at all uncommon' in post-Soviet Russia for an intellectual woman to give credence to the powers of her ekstrasensory consultant (Borenstein 1999b: 439–40). Anna's visit certainly had a cathartic effect: when the ekstrasens asked how she was, Anna began to cry. She took Anna's hands, shuffled her cards clumsily and allowed Anna to collect herself. She laid out the cards and turned several over consecutively before telling Anna that, although things were difficult, she would get through it. She said that Anna was currently working with a man and a woman and should continue to do so. Afterwards Anna identified these people as two contacts who had been involved in a recent seminar and with whom she hoped to start working. Later, it turned out that they were in fact rivals plotting to take Anna's remaining clients for their own seminar programme. Even though the ekstrasens had appeared to be wrong in that prediction, however, Anna blamed herself and speculated that she had identified the wrong contacts. Indeed, in a later session the ekstrasens told her that a previously supportive man would turn against her. In any case, Anna always emerged from these sessions with a feeling of relief: the advice was delivered in a way that acknowledged Anna's problems and told her that, after a few twists and turns, things would turn out all right.

Anna's lone vulnerability led her to put great emphasis on all the advice she received. The relief she experienced during the moments when others considered her problems was palpable, and for a short time afterwards, her mood vastly improved. Moreover, even if the information she received was not useful, it did have personal value to her: her retired police contact had knowledge of the prosecution system that she did not; those who had endured crises showed her it could be done; the life coaches made it seem as though she had power over her destiny and the ekstrasens gave her perspective about the journey. Magic in Russia, Lindquist argues, is one of the

> Cultural tools to change people's subjectivity in ways that make their lives livable. It is about hope, the existential and affective counterpart of agency that replaces it where channels for agency are blocked, and presence in the world becomes precarious.
>
> (2006: 4)

In Anna's case, each of her sources serves a similar function.

Anna's response to her persecutors is mainly appeasing, meaning that she attempts to placate them when they try to intimidate her. Her overriding objective is not to buckle under pressure. It is vital to her that she does not yield, she said, because this would be interpreted as an admission of guilt and strengthen their will. However, because she cannot repay her debt, she must hope that they do not take rash measures or resort to violence. To do this, she tends to submit to their demands, no matter how uncomfortable or problematic, or attempts to negotiate a slower repayment plan. As I will describe in the next section, several accusers have already agreed to such plans with her, and relations between them and Anna are no longer antagonistic. However, others still aim to intimidate her at random as part of their campaigns against her.

Anna's determination to respond to the whims of her persecutors is extremely time consuming and often prevents her from getting on with more productive tasks. Nevertheless, she has little choice if she is not to anger them further. Her decision to let one of her accusers look around her house as if it were for sale is a case in point. She did not resist this in the hope that it would prevent a more aggressive episode. There are plenty of other examples. For example, late one night, Anna received a call then suddenly asked me to accompany her to a chemist to buy some medicine. En route, she added that a member of the group of accusers had called to demand 500 roubles immediately (approximately £10 in early 2014) and that we were going to give it to him near the chemist. Anna was extremely nervous as we waited on the freezing street for a few minutes before a young woman turned up with a tough looking man. He was not expecting me to be there, so shook my hand far longer and more firmly than necessary, while smiling menacingly and asking about my business in Russia. However, my foreignness seemed to stifle him, and because he was not really looking for conversation, we instead stood beside the women awkwardly, he with an aggressive stance, me with a frown. Meanwhile, Anna gave the woman the cash then wrote out a receipt, which they both signed. Anna, with her debt marginally reduced, thanked me for my help as we walked home. She had to run numerous such errands at short notice for little gain all the time.

A few days later, Anna was called to meet another member of the group, a successful investment banker, in his office at one of the country's largest banks. When we arrived, he asked about her progress repaying the debt. She said that she was working on it and described the informal repayments she had agreed to with some clients. She also mentioned that some clients were accepting cosmetics or discounted participation in her business training seminars in lieu of cash (described in the next section). The banker replied that cosmetics could not help him, and it went without saying that he did not need her seminars. Instead, he took a notepad and started to write a list of administrative tasks she would do for him, then requested the translation from English of two articles on banking and gave her until the next day to send them over. At over 20 pages each, this was a tall order. Finally, he then told her be ready in case he thought of anything else. It was not clear whether this work counted as repayment or a punishment while he waited for his cash, and Anna did not seek clarification. She was obviously fearful. Afterwards, she said Boris would complete the translations using Google Translate, and, in any case, he liked doing it. She would remain available in case he wanted anything else. By responding to her persecutors in this way, Anna hopes to placate them while she gets on with her defence.

Anna is far more proactive in her response to her prosecution. She makes regular visits to the prosecutors' office to make representations and petitions on the grounds that she is innocent of wrongdoing and has the government's own support for business on her side. By drawing on the government's rhetorical support for the improvement of business conditions and highlighting her own victimisation as an entrepreneur, she aims to show that her way of doing business is aligned with the state's policy and that the persecution and prosecution she faces is unfounded, typifying the need for reform. Moreover, by making this argument regularly, she aims to demonstrate that she will not give up. This approach has proven reasonably successful to the extent that Anna has maintained an ongoing argument with the prosecution service, rather than admitting defeat. This has been a tangible factor in her survival and continuing freedom and, I argue, may be understood as 'entrepreneurial governmentality', aimed more at independence than commercial objectives.

Despite Anna's ability to maintain occasional communications with the prosecution service, her everyday experience has not improved as a result: she must consistently argue her case until the investigation against her is dropped. As a result, she is often unsure how to proceed. During my observations, an idea would often cross her mind, making her suddenly concerned that it offered a new or better way to promote her innocence or that the prosecutors might have overlooked some important aspect of her case. She also frequently sought to inform them of a recent presidential declaration about the development of business or a new law that they might not be aware of. On these occasions, her angst would increase, and she became fixated on the possibility that this new information might bring her troubles to a close, coupled with the great nervousness that accompanied confronting officials. Anna usually asked me to accompany her on these visits for moral support, and, though I decided not to refuse, they did cause some anxiety. I was wary of highlighting my connection with her affairs and raising suspicion against her, especially given the 'foreign agents' law, which was passed just prior to my fieldwork and which, as I highlighted in Chapter 2, effectively legalised hostility to foreigners' interest, real or perceived, in Russian politics (see Machalek no date: online).

Besides, the specific utility of Anna's representations was also unclear. They served to underline her awareness of the law and determination to fight, but it is also likely that they aggravated the prosecutors already set against her. Nevertheless, it is certain that they did have some effect. On one occasion, we visited when Anna was more confident. A member of the accusing group had withdrawn their support and Anna had also identified mistakes in the group's statement against her. She turned up unannounced to speak to an official she believed was torn between his conscience and the demands of his corrupted superiors. She told him about the mistakes and revealed the name of the woman no longer against her. The official was visibly ill at ease and said that he had also been trying to get hold of some of Anna's accusers to verify their statements but had not succeeded. On the way back to the office, Anna was ecstatic, sure that she was on the right track. Later she decided to visit him again to give him documentation that she believed would advance her case. She cornered him in his office and explained about her ongoing effort to repay the money through legal and personal arrangements, which demonstrated her innocence and good intentions. The official could not disagree. Afterwards, Anna was again delighted at his agreement, which she saw as a positive sign of the way the case was moving. She was sure that, by convincing this particular official, he would fight for her cause. Whether this was the case or not, Anna's brave personal campaign also reveals her isolation and its impact on her well-being. Without legal guidance or reliable legal processes, her own interpretation of her case forms the basis of her approach, which makes it highly fraught and uncertain.

Anna's campaigning was not only focused on proving her innocence, but speculative attempts at winning her prosecutors over. For example, when she heard that the government planned to offer an amnesty to coincide with the 20th anniversary of the Russian Constitution (Prezident Rossii 2013: online), she visited the prosecutors again to make her case. She became sure that this offered her a chance to secure her freedom, even though she did not wish to imply that she required an amnesty. Of course, as before, this amnesty did not bring about any material change in her situation. Rather, it shows how Anna's campaign of defence attempts to balance the idea that she is innocent with any opportunity to extricate herself from the crisis. However, this lobbying did have some effect, if only by causing consternation among her prosecutors. As Peter Pomerantsev has written about the unfounded prosecution of the entrepreneur Yana Yakovleva, her eventual release would not have been possible without her 'dissident impulse' or will 'to fight back in the first place … To make something happen in Russia, you have to be both valiant protester and Machiavellian, playing one clan off against the other' (Pomerantsev 2015: 117).

The final dimension of Anna's response to her prosecutors is her attempt to secure the support of senior political elites for her cause. Although this effort may seem absurdly optimistic, she gives this campaign a great deal of time and attention. She is convinced of the essential virtue of these elites and believes that, if they hear about her case, they will be clear about her innocence. Her work in this regard is both speculative and coordinated. The speculative aspect involves taking any opportunity, however remote, to secure the support of powerful leaders. For example, when she heard that the former deputy prime minister and current head of *Rosnanotech*, Anatoly Chubais, was visiting the city, she called an influential local businessman to ask if he would make representations to him on her behalf. She told me that because Chubais had led Russia's privatisation drive (Freeland 2000: 48–68; Hoffman 2002: 99), he would understand her situation best of all. While I was astonished that she thought her acquaintance would do anything of the sort, Anna became visibly enthused by the prospect. When he told her to fight her own corner, she promptly slumped again.

Anna's most coordinated appeal is to President Putin himself. She told me that she once met him through her work and was convinced that he is coordinating a strong anti-corruption drive.[4] She therefore places great faith in him as a fair arbiter and fellow transition believer. Her appeals to him are also made on the basis that she is being unfairly persecuted and that an intervention from Moscow could resolve the crisis. In order to reach him, she spent several days preparing a letter in which she drew attention to her problems, asked for his help to resolve them, and offered her services with his anti-corruption activities in the region. She even mentioned that she had been approached by both the Russian and American security services in the course of her travels to acquire information about the other but had turned them down. Anna told me this information would demonstrate her honesty and good intentions for business and Russia. Anna's lawyer took the letter to Moscow when she visited and made an appointment at the Kremlin. Anna also sent a copy to the president's regional office. The very act of sending the letter lifted her spirits, and she received a reply after a few weeks asking for more information. This put Anna in a fine mood for days: she could wield the letter in front of the local prosecutors to show them that she was in contact with representatives of the president himself. In order to be sure that the additional documents reached Moscow she dispatched Boris himself to deliver them. He called on his arrival to say he had taken a ticket in the administrative offices and was waiting his turn to make their case.

Appeals to Moscow have a long historical lineage in Russia, but the Putin administration has worked to formalise the petitioning process itself. According to Arutunyan, the government has established a network of United Russia reception offices around the country, which allows Putin to be seen as a 'hands-on man of the people' and where his representatives are 'authorised to telephone local officials responsible for red tape, and, by dropping the name of the prime minister [now president], pulling strings on behalf of the citizen' (Arutunyan 2014: 45). This link between the masses and presidential power has an ordering effect: the president reifies his power and authority while implicitly acknowledging the inadequacy of the bureaucracy below him to serve the people, and at the same time gives the people hope that he is on their side. The ubiquity of these appeals is most obvious during Putin's annual addresses, in which he devotes hours to answering appeals from ordinary citizens. Journalist Shaun Walker has described these periods as the '"Vladimir Vladimirovich please solve this local issue caused by the outrageous behaviour of local officials" segment' (Walker 2013: online). In this light, Boris's wait to deliver Anna's precious documents seems logical and appropriate. As Arutunyan shows with the petition of her own informant, Sergei,

> The question of spending hours, days, or weeks first petitioning local authorities, then regional authorities, and then taking a day's journey all the way to Moscow ... made more sense than mobilising a few dozen people in his community to come up with £20,000 so that all their homes could have gas.
>
> (Arutunyan 2014: 47)

When I left the field, Anna was still waiting for the president to address her case, but the appeal itself improved her mood, and the correspondence gave her physical documents that made her prosecutors and persecutors pause.

In this section, I have described Anna's various activities as she has sought to respond to persecution and prosecution. In the absence of an effective legal defence, which is the direct consequence of Russia's institutional asymmetry, she has largely had to interpret her position within the crisis herself. Although she has tried to secure the support from within her circle of acquaintances, this support was relatively weak, with one or two exceptions. She has also sought advice from various sources in the know, but this has been relatively unproductive. I therefore argue that social capital is not necessarily the default or most effective resource for entrepreneurs in the absence of formal institutions. In Anna's case, when she fell into trouble with the state and fell victim to a powerful group of aggressors, her acquaintances tended to be conspicuous by their lack of support. Accordingly, self-help has been essential. In this light, the self-help tapes and support from the ekstrasens have been invaluable in Anna's search for moral support and motivation to keep up with her cause.

In her response to her persecutors, Anna has sought to placate them wherever possible. This is particularly time consuming, but she has endured because, even though she lost their money, she has been able to maintain that she has right on her side. Moreover, those clients know that, by their taking the law into their own hands, they are in the wrong too. In response to the prosecution, Anna also proceeds on the basis that she has right on her side and makes personal, frequent representations to prosecution service officials on that basis. This has also had some effect: prosecutors have been unable to make a sound case against her because they are also partially in the wrong, and she has been able to show that she is at least partially right. She has also strengthened her position by drawing on presidential declarations that offer some hope for her legitimacy and securing material documentation from the presidential administration that she can use to deter local officialdom. Thus, in response to both persecutors and prosecutors, Anna has been able to invoke and associate herself with the government's rhetorical support for the development of business conditions in order to make a case for her defence, even though it was her mistake that instigated the crisis. In doing so, she has also aligned herself effectively with the president and portrayed her accusers as illegitimate. The irony is that Anna's belief in the transition appeared rather naive just prior to the crisis, but her ability to show the government's support for the development of business conditions evidently contributed to her survival during the crisis, even though everybody knows the government does very little to support entrepreneurs at all.

Two observations stand out considering Anna's response to her persecutors and prosecutors. First, in some respects, Anna's entrepreneurship is significantly affected by the crisis. She has to devote significant time to dealing with the challenges of her persecution and prosecution which, as I discuss in the next section, has severely diminished her ability to continue doing business as before. Second, and in contrast, Anna has been able to use the cause for which she established CSBG – the development of business – as an argument in her defence. That is, by pointing to her years of work advancing business interests in the city, she has developed a response that plays on the illegitimacy of her accusers and their allies in the prosecution service. In this way, Anna is able to deflect attention from her own wrongdoing onto that of her adversaries. Moreover, Anna is able to invoke the government's formal support for business in her defence, which reinforces the original purpose of CSBG. Consequently, Anna is able to show that she has been right all along; the crisis just goes to show that Russian entrepreneurs face significant difficulties. To put it another way, just as the prosecution service simulates the legality of its case against her, so Anna simulates the legitimacy of her business to her prosecutors. In response to Russia's institutional asymmetry, Anna has found arguments with which she can survive. In this sense, CSBG may be a failed business in the formal sense, but in the practical sense, it enables Anna to resist her accusers. Without it, Anna would be very vulnerable, but her years of work to advance business gives her self-defence through CSBG a legitimate framework and cause to make her arguments against the authorities. By twisting the logic of business failure to her advantage, I suggest Anna must be judged as an effective, if not successful, entrepreneur under the circumstances.

Making Money During Her Crisis

In this section, I discuss how Anna makes money in the context of her crisis. As I have stated, the core business of CSBG – the foreign training programme, the seminars and the business advice – was not possible once the crisis began. To make enough money to 'get by' and repay her debts, Anna had to restructure the company and begin alternative activities. She continues to portray CSBG publicly as a viable and legitimate business (even though, as the beneficiary of foreign support, it has never successfully operated under hard budget constraints), but in reality, the company became a formal shell for a variety of activities undertaken between the formal and informal spheres. As a result, Anna's white-collar pretensions, intellectual background and international connections now count for very little; she faces the fact that her best days in business are behind her. As I conclude later, however, judging Anna's entrepreneurship according to her commercial success is not an effective or fair measure in the Russian context. I argue instead that the transformation of her business is better considered as a way of maintaining her independence from those against her, which, like Oleg's entrepreneurship, is better conceptualised by drawing on 'entrepreneurial governmentality'.

Today, CSBG is a formal business shell within which Anna pursues a variety of activities in the shadow economy. This means that she does not attempt to meet the legal obligations of a fully compliant business (such as they meaningfully exist). When the crisis began, Anna formed a new company called Travelling Businessman and made Boris its director. Through this, she channels most of the cash derived from activities she undertakes under the CSBG brand. This is necessary, Anna said, because when CSBG makes any money, she is obliged by law to put it towards servicing her debt, which leaves her very little to live with. It 'disappears', she complains. Thus, Travelling Businessman allows her to control her outgoings. However, Anna also thinks Boris is unreliable; he is older and quickly distracted, as well as moody when he feels underused or underappreciated. According to Anna, he associates business with problems, having had several commercial (ad)ventures of his own in the 1990s, so there is a chance he will neglect his commitments to Travelling Businessman. To hedge against this, Anna has registered a third business, Top Executive, through which she can move money if the need arises. Although this tri-business arrangement is complicated, its advantage is to keep cash available to ensure she can meet her basic needs. It also reveals clearly that the Western business practices she most wished to promote are absent from her own business. As I argued in Chapter 1, it is now extremely difficult for entrepreneurs to be fully compliant with the law, so breaking the law becomes both inevitable and necessary. More to the point, CSBG is no longer an effective commercial entity in the formal sense but a business operating mostly informally and through which she can defend her interests and resist her accusers. As a client from one of Anna's seminars told me, 'do not look at business structures but at the people. Do not look at Russia's business statistics, because they are untrue'. In this light, it is a mistake to judge CSBG according to recognisable business measures. Her 'business' is really what she personally makes of it, as I now elaborate.

What are the specific business activities Anna now undertakes? Although demand for her business training seminars has diminished and she no longer hosts elite trainers or coaches in person, Anna still has one product related to her original work: small seminars in which she plays American self-help and business competence audio courses to small groups, translating from English to Russian in real time. These are the same courses I described in an earlier section that she uses herself for motivation. The courses serve two important purposes. First, they allow her to keep up appearances, projecting the image that she is still the same legitimate businesswoman she has always been, with the same type of product. This is particularly important in her defence campaign (as described in the previous section). Second, the courses can be sold to new clients for cash, or she can offer them to her accusers as a substitute for cash repayment of her debt. In other words, the seminars can be given to clients as in-kind debt repayment. This has proven to be quite successful; during the courses I attended, Anna was indebted to a majority of the participants.

Indeed, Anna now generates most of her cash by drawing on her knowledge of English and 'the West': her second main source of cash is providing occasional translation and language support services. As I described in previously, this helped her meet the banker's demand for the translation of an article. She also offers a service helping clients complete visa applications for Western countries. This is a reasonably popular service because many applications are denied, so her long experience sending clients to the West means she has a high success rate, which draws a steady stream of clients hoping she can improve their chances. Thus, Anna's main product is, ironically, herself: she still draws on her knowledge of the West to survive, even though it is her cosmopolitanism that her accusers use against her. This is emblematic of 'entrepreneurial governmentality'; a recognition of knowing what is possible in the market drawing on one's own resources. However, despite Anna's ability to generate some cash in these ways, she does not make enough to reduce her debt quickly. As a result, she tries to avoid using cash to repay her debts. Wherever possible, she tries to pay business costs in kind, and earn income in cash. As I have indicated, the price for her products is therefore negotiable, and she frequently offers discounts or freebies in exchange for debt relief or as payment for favours received. To be clear, this means that Anna continues to work with some of her accusers, though these individuals tend to be more pragmatic than those seeking to intimidate her.

The informality of Anna's pricing belies her stringent book-keeping. She tracks how much she owes to each client carefully, giving receipts even when debt is repaid in kind. These in-kind payments also include alcohol, which she keeps stashed in her office to offer whenever there is a chance, but most take the form of products she acquires as a sales agent for two MLM (marketing) companies. Indeed, MLM has formed the significant proportion of Anna's business activities during the crisis. The first MLM company is an East European cosmetics business that I call *Opale*;[5] the second is an American company selling health enhancement consumables such as vitamin supplements or applications designed to remove discomfort or aid healing, which I call Vitality. Anna displays Opale products in her seminars and offers them to women in exchange for debt relief. Though fewer men accept the offer, some do and give them away as presents. Anna also tries to use Opale and Vitality instead of cash for business purchases, such as when she hires a venue for her seminars.

As with all MLM, Anna's role as a sales agent is to promote and sell their products to clients and develop her own business by finding new sales representatives to sell 'under' her, thereby increasing the marketing and selling capacity of the business and deriving a proportion of their profits too. In

Anna's particular case, she can 'afford' to give Opale products away in kind because she is indebted to the man who recruited her. Thus, working for Opale is a blessing and a curse. On the one hand, she is able to pay down debts using Opale products, which improves her situation with the group as a whole; on the other hand, the value of her debt to her boss increases, because she still owes him the value of the products she has given away (in addition to her original debt). In this sense, Anna is tied to him. He benefits by knowing that she is working in his interests by increasing the dissemination of his products and that she will, in time, repay her debt to him. However, relations between them are cordial, and Anna is not dissatisfied with MLM because she benefits from the flexibility it gives her.

Although Anna is content to work in MLM during her crisis, she does not consider it to be proper business and disassociates herself from it even as she benefits from it. She creates this distance because, as I have indicated, her accusers are known to one another through their work for an MLM company. Anna told me that MLM attracts 'simple people' and regrets her decision to take her internships onto the 'mass market' because it meant dealing with such people:

> Earlier, our clients were only business owners with whom we had a good relationship, while here is another category of people. Multilevel marketing has a different ideology, a different psychology. These people think only in the short term. They think, 'If I don't receive the money today, I am going to press you, and you will give me everything'. And they have their own system too: these people do not work alone but do whatever their leader tells them. In my case there are several of these leaders in different MLM, and they each have 15 or 20 people that wrote to the authorities.

Thus, in Anna's view, the type of people accusing her favour a hierarchical leadership structure in which subordinates unconditionally support their superiors. This is not unlike the system I encountered in *Sibtekhnika*, Oleg's business (see Chapter 3). Moreover, Anna believes these people consider ordinary business to be inherently suspicious, requiring vigilance and control by the state. Clearly, what Anna means is that these people retain a socialist attitude to business. For her, such people are unsuited to and disinclined to start or work in Western-style businesses of the sort she admires, preferring instead the defined structure and fixed role that MLM ostensibly offers. Anna therefore believes MLM is acceptable to her accusers because of the way they think and seeks to distance herself from MLM even though it is enabling her to survive the crisis: it does not fit well with the narrative she seeks to sell or use in her defence.

Anna is right that her accusers hold a different view of what legitimate business is: just as she considered MLM as a deficient form of business, so they implied that she is a pyramid schemer. Both parties seek to portray the other as illegitimate entrepreneurs. As such, it is ironic that Anna and her accusers *both* work for MLM companies now, even if she does it out of necessity and they do it willingly. I therefore argue that Russia's institutional asymmetry leaves the meaning of legitimate business undefined. In consequence, I observe that entrepreneurs must justify their business activities publicly in order to project their legitimacy. This is exactly what Oleg and Irina sought to achieve by asserting and portraying control in their everyday entrepreneurship (see Chapter 3).

It is revealing that both Anna and her accusers perceive MLM to be an effective business model, albeit for different reasons. This is ironic because pyramid schemes, direct marketing companies and MLM companies are deeply suspicious to ethnographers of the developing world. Detlev Krige, for example, perceives in them the pervasiveness of the market and the exploitation of vulnerable new actors, propelled by a policy discourse that reinforces economic empowerment, entrepreneurship and celebrates risk taking and individual self-help (Krige 2012: 87). Similarly, David Stoll asserts that MLM is merely 'the legal version' of a pyramid scheme (Stoll 2013: 278). In his view, MLM companies represent a method through which individuals in the developing world believe they can 'escape' their limited material reality and 'unlock the key to more desirable, higher-status commodities' (Stoll 2013: 280). However, Anna's conflict with her accusers over what counts as legitimate post-socialist business leads me to refute this argument as too simplistic. After all, Anna's accusers make a clear distinction between the pyramid scheme as illegitimate and MLM as legitimate. Anna herself considers MLM to be a weak form of business, attracting the 'wrong' type of people, but nevertheless derives considerable material benefit from it in the context of her crisis.

This argument might appear to be about pyramids and MLM, but it is really about what legitimate business is in Russia. To be more specific, the meaning of legitimate business continues to change in Russia. Pyramid schemes are known to be criminal and illegitimate forms of enterprise today, but they were ubiquitous in the early 1990s and had a significant impact on changing perceptions of capitalism. In her study of the giant *Caritas* pyramid in Romania, for example, Katherine Verdery argues that the scheme represented a challenge to the socialist ideas that only productive work could produce money legitimately, and that money from 'commerce and speculation was polluting, unacceptable and tainted with capitalism' (Verdery 1996a 642). In this way, for a time, Caritas represented a legitimate understanding of what capitalism was. That is not to say that investors fully understood what Caritas was, rather that the scheme offered the chance for great capital accumulation without the need for political connections and required 'only the nerve to risk one's money' (Verdery 1996a: 642–3). In the case of MMM, Russia's most infamous pyramid, the possibilities of capitalism were embodied in the scheme's advertising campaign, which drew on the soap opera genre and blurred the boundaries of socialist values and capitalist values such that 'investors' (dangerous capitalists) were reconstituted as 'partners' (productive socialists) (Borenstein 1999a: 50). As Patico has written, in this type of reconfiguration, 'investment is spun away from the Soviet-era meanings of "speculation" and is cast as active and cooperative' (Patico 2009: 216–17). Of course, when they collapsed, these schemes reinforced the very stereotypes about capitalist business that they had temporarily challenged, and, as the accusations against Anna show, pyramid scheming came to signify the worst kind of business – an allegation one could use to delegitimise business enemies.

My point is that the way in which pyramids were popular when they emerged but then perceived as dangerous when they collapsed reveals how attitudes towards business remain in flux in contemporary Russia: the present popularity of the MLM model is clearly not considered illegitimate in the way that pyramids are. As Hass has written, Russia's post-Soviet experience of business has been characterised by learning as a result of Soviet legacies that resisted the haphazard arrival of market practices. According to him, the law, the media and Western consultants all had an impact on their emergence, and actors:

> … both inadvertently and consciously transposed them onto Soviet-era principles of production, sales, and values. The end result was a troubled process of interpreting environmental signals and reacting to them – against the backdrop of privatisation, organisational restructuring, and political instability – that bred practices of sales and valuation neither entirely Soviet nor Western.
>
> (Hass 2005: 39)

Thus, Anna's move into MLM shows that a given type of business may be rationalised in different ways: she has been able to legitimate the necessity and practicality of MLM in the context of her current circumstances, even though she would prefer to be running CSBG as before. Hass demonstrates that the tacit knowledge and practice of business did not necessarily accompany the rhetoric of business (Hass 2005: 39) and that culture interferes with the adaptation of new laws and policies (Hass 2005: 40). Anna's entrepreneurship is a case in point: her rhetoric of business is not an indication of her actual business practices. Nor, as I have repeated, is the state's rhetoric of support for business an indication of its actual support. Consequently, I argue that in contemporary Russia, there are multiple interpretations of legitimate business.

Accordingly, I find that MLM offers a useful way of working in Russia's contemporary market that cannot be considered illegitimate or necessarily harmful. Besides, MLM is not illegal, and MLM brands are ubiquitous in Siberia. Indeed, their current popularity may stem, as Anna suggested, from their ability to appear satisfactory in terms of both socialist values and market principles. MLM companies offer sales agents a predetermined, recognisable role, the possibility of self and material improvement, a tangible product to sell and a role in which the agent can work within their personal network. In these respects, MLM gives members the means with which to trade, without the complication, vulnerability or financial burden of starting their own business, in a socially comprehensible way. Among many Russians of Anna's generation, those without the experience and market ideology she absorbed in the West, and for whom the appearance of the market was rapid and shocking, MLM offers meaning, status and an aid to survival in the contemporary market. Consequently, I concur with Patico, who argued that the post-socialist market must not be considered in terms of 'a local world of social embeddedness and moral obligation' that seeks 'to resist seemingly exterior, supercultural, individualistic markets' (2009: 207), but 'as a set of questions and moments of interpretation – junctures when people consider the multiple implications and valences of the specific practices in which they might engage' (Patico 2009: 208).

Patico's own informant, a regional manager for Tupperware, a well-known MLM company, had re-categorised her own commercial role over time, adopting 'a different kind of moral stance – one of approval and pride rather than shame or hesitation' (Patico 2009: 214). MLM wields a similar kind of moral legitimacy that means it cannot be conflated with pyramids in the contemporary Russian context. Thus, while I do not condone Anna's persecutors (who work for MLM), it is a fact that, while she faces a crisis partly of her making and partly of theirs, working within MLM offers her both a practical lifeline to endure the crisis while reducing her debts and a business activity that offers security because it is morally acceptable to those accusers.

Overall, Anna's crisis has made it necessary to take her business partially into the informal sphere. In order to meet her objective of surviving in business formally, which means proving the legitimacy of CSBG and her innocence from wrongdoing, Anna must work in part in the shadow economy, where she can hide money, conduct business without money, and generate enough to survive and pay her debts. In the formal sphere, Anna continues to undertake some limited activities that resemble her pre-crisis business, namely occasional business training seminars. However, because these are decreasingly popular, they mainly serve as a public relations exercise, upholding and promoting her image as a legitimate entrepreneur whose vision for business matches that of the government. The seminars generate little cash but are offered for in kind debt relief to her persecutors. Instead, Anna's main for-cash activities draw on her knowledge of English, although these are also quite insubstantial. This income is channelled as necessary through one of three companies in order to obscure its whereabouts and keep enough free to 'get by'. Wherever possible, therefore, Anna works through two MLM companies to reduce her debt through sales or in kind. MLM is not informal work per se, but Anna uses it in an informal way: it provides her with the possibility of earning some cash income and a sales network of her own but also offers her material resources that she can offer in kind in exchange for debt reduction (wherever possible). Most importantly, even though Anna dislikes MLM, it offers a type of business that is acceptable to her accusers, which mitigates their aggression.

Summary

In this chapter, I have described Anna's experience in business, which began successfully and then entered a period of crisis that is still ongoing. I began with a description of how she developed CSBG, showing that her early success profited from her ability to secure support from foreign benefactors. However, this support eventually became her downfall because it deterred her from creating a business that could survive under hard budget constraints. This meant that Anna failed to live up to the Western business model she advocated. Nevertheless, I do not consider Anna's failure to be indicative of her ability as an 'entrepreneur', but rather a failure to appreciate that the market was not changing in the way she expected. Sadly, her experience only mirrors that of Bridger et al.'s informant Irina Razumnova, who established the Guildia Small Business Development Centre in Moscow in 1991. Razumnova found developing a self-sufficient business 'a constant headache', and she was required to accept foreign funding from Avon Cosmetics in order to provide her training courses (Bridger et al. 1996: 126). Later, as rents rose and Avon reduced its sponsorship, Guildia could no longer support its trainees' businesses (Bridger et al. 1996: 144). In an uncanny precursor to Anna's experience, Guildia found that 'as their overheads increased, they were obliged to charge more for their course and materials, yet, at a time of falling living standards, fewer people could afford the fees' (Bridger et al. 1996: 144). At the time, 'a widespread sense of hopelessness about business' emerged, leading Bridger et al. to ask, 'Why bother going on a business start-up course if starting a business in the formal sense was virtually impossible?' (Bridger et al. 1996: 145). Razumnova's experience occurred 20 years before Anna experienced exactly the same thing.

However, because I have already explained that business conditions are difficult, the events that followed the withdrawal of Anna's funding are of more importance. Critically, as I described next, since Anna lost her clients' money, she has faced persecution, including physical and psychological intimidation, slurs on her character, public humiliation and racism, and a prosecution process that has failed to deliver a charge but leaves her under investigation and the threat of prison. Clearly, Anna is distinctly vulnerable to factors largely outside her control, and she is undoubtedly trapped by her circumstances. She is unable to gather any tangible support, make sufficient money, or even be sure of her position in the eyes of the law. Moreover, she spends a great deal of time responding to the whims of her accusers in order to placate them. However, despite this enormous pressure, Anna has been unwilling to yield. Instead, she has responded with a time-consuming and exhausting but effective defence, in which she portrays herself as a victim, invoking the government's formal support for the development of business on her side. As such, the crisis is now characterised by legal uncertainty despite both sides having committed wrongdoing along the way. I therefore find that the crisis has taken the form of an argument in which both sides try to portray their case as more righteous than the other. At the time of writing,

Anna's ability to secure the attention of the presidential administration and her ability to cut informal repayment deals with some of her accusers appeared to have stabilised her situation but not improve it substantially. Nevertheless, I argue that Anna's response to this crisis, which is based on her ability to make a normative case for her legitimacy that prevents those against her from getting their way, must be seen as effective entrepreneurship. That is, because Anna has been forced to react to the challenges of the business sphere as they are rather than as she wishes them to be, she has behaved very effectively.

The other element of Anna's entrepreneurship during the crisis is the transformation of her business to ensure that she can survive and repay her debts. Her priority is to maintain as much control over her finances as possible, which she achieves by channelling cash between her three company shells, and which allows her to free the money she needs while placating the demands of the authorities. To be clear, this allows Anna to minimise her formal outgoings, and obscures her accounts from the authorities. At the same time, Anna aims to maintain some of CSBG's traditional services where possible, such as the seminar programme, in order to portray the continuing legitimacy of the business and her ongoing commitment to advancing business interests, which in turn helps her in her representations to the authorities. The seminars and a variety of other services, such as translation and visa support, also generate a small but regular cash flow, and may be used in kind for debt repayment. Finally, Anna has become involved in two MLM schemes that generate some cash sales but also offer tangible products that may be offered in kind for debt repayment too. In contrast to those ethnographers who see in MLM the pervasiveness and worst of the market in developing countries, I counter that it offers Anna tangible material goods that she can trade for a value she determines and a type of business that is understandable and acceptable to her accusers. In this respect, it offers a sensible and flexible response to her needs.

What can be said about the way Anna has responded to her crisis overall? Clearly her entrepreneurship has never been determined by profit alone. She is of course in favour of making a profit, but her vision as an entrepreneur both before and since the crisis began has remained primarily to assist the development of Western business practices in Russia. I therefore find that Anna's entrepreneurship is, like Oleg's (Chapter 3) most usefully considered in normative rather than commercial terms. Having said that, when Anna's funding was withdrawn, her business was unsustainable, so she undoubtedly failed to achieve the entrepreneurial standards she advocated. Moreover, in attempting to rebuild her business, she defrauded her clients, showing her capability as a model entrepreneur to be negligible. Nevertheless, when the crisis struck, her entrepreneurial approach underwent significant adaptation. She recognised that, in order to defend herself in the face of acute pressure, which was based on destroying her personally and in business, she must continue to make the case for the development of business. This decision, I argue, can be effectively understood by drawing again on the concept of 'entrepreneurial governmentality', which considers entrepreneurship as an activity undertaken to achieve some independence and a degree of civilised reality in spite of the state. In other words, Anna deployed a normative argument for her independence as an entrepreneur in order to survive. She recognised that she could use the government's own rhetoric, which she had long supported, as the basis for her defence. She knew what could be acted upon entrepreneurially in order to secure her survival and independence: even though the government does little to support entrepreneurs in reality, she could still draw on its formal support as the basis for her defence. This served to stabilise her situation by turning the crisis from a vindictive campaign against her into a legitimate argument in which she had some claim to innocence. In this way, her 'entrepreneurial governmentality' improved. I therefore contend that Anna became a far more competent entrepreneur during the period of her crisis than she had been before. Most of all, during the crisis, Anna focused on *resisting* the state, which I have found is an integral element in contemporary entrepreneurialism.

The second key aspect of Anna's 'entrepreneurial governmentality' was to move her business in part from the formal sphere into the shadow economy. This enabled her to secure the resources necessary to survive and negotiate informal deals for the reduction of her debt. Here, Anna ceased working as an entrepreneur who profited from foreign sponsorship (which had given her accusers an excuse to punish her when she lost their money) to become an entrepreneur working in the real economy as it actually exists. In doing so, she again became a more effective entrepreneur than she had been prior to the crisis. By conducting her business between what Yurchak calls the personalised (i.e., informal) and officialised (i.e., formal) public spheres (and mainly in the former), Anna became a more effective entrepreneur. I therefore conclude that Anna's entrepreneurship has become significantly more effective *since* her crisis began. More importantly, this effectiveness has not been at the cost of her original objectives: she still seeks to bring about political economic change in favour of business, so resistance represents a critical and necessary part of her entrepreneurship. If she can save CSBG by deploying the argument that business conditions must improve (which is the government's formal position too), the result would be a continuation of that work. Therefore, I suggest, with Yurchak, that Anna's entrepreneurship may be seen not as an attempt simply to survive the crisis but as an attempt to secure a personal form of independence, an ambition for a 'civilised reality' of her own. More than that, Anna's entrepreneurship became a means to resist the state. Securing the future of her business by resisting her persecutors and prosecutors is why she is in business. Like Oleg, therefore, by seeking independence, Anna also resists the state and seeks to change the status quo. I return to this point in Chapter 6.

Notes

1 The shadow economy is defined by Radaev as 'the set of economic activities that are not displayed in official reporting and/or formal contracting due to deliberate concealment or non-coverage in official statistics' (2002: 193).
2 I have withheld these online sources to uphold Anna's anonymity.
3 This has a strong historical lineage. In the Tsarist period, there was little distinction between 'folk' and official anti-Semitism (Korey 1972: 111), and in the early twentieth century, official limits were set on 'Jewish' capital in private organisations (Carstensen and Guroff 1983: 351). During the Soviet period, chauvinism and totalitarianism combined to legitimate popular anti-Semitism because Jews' international history, worldwide religion and links with the outside world made them inherently suspicious and potentially subversive (Korey 1972: 123), even though they were formally recognised as a nationality with the right to self-determination and cultural freedom (Decter 1963: 420). Shlapentokh and Arutunyan argue, in fact, that hatred of Jews and Zionism 'cemented the ideology of the party and state apparatchiks' (2013: 57).
4 Tackling corruption was a major theme in Putin's first state of the nation speech on his return to the presidency in 2012 (Gutterman and Busvine 2012: online). This translated into a major policy initiative overseen by an anti-corruption directorate in the Presidential Administration (Monaghan 2014: online). Krastev and Inozemtsev (2013: online) have, however, criticised the sincerity of the initiative on the grounds that it will 'sink the regime'. Even so, statements about improving conditions and reducing dangers for entrepreneurs continue (for example, TASS 2014b: online), and Anna is able to invoke them in her self-defence.
5 Despite its East European origins, Opale's branding is French. This appeared to have a real effect on its popularity: when clients learned that it was 'French', they were far more inclined towards it.

5 Case Study
Aleksandr and Yurii

My third case study is based on participant observation within Promploshchad, a business established by Aleksandr in the city I call Normalnyi. Promploshchad is an industrial site on the edge of the city with several units that Aleksandr lets to small enterprises, and he runs the company with his son, Yurii. Although the company is successful and the men have plans for its development, it is not Aleksandr's first business: in the late 1990s he founded *Khoroshiidom*, a construction company that became one of the region's most successful firms. However, in 2007, success turned to crisis when he was accused of large-scale fraud and tax evasion then prosecuted in a case that eventually led to his imprisonment. Although he was later acquitted, the officials managed to acquire control of his company's assets in the process. This crisis, in which Aleksandr fell victim to corporate raiding (reiderstvo) was, like Anna's, representative of the many difficulties facing businesses that I have outlined and has left its mark on him and his family. He is now deeply suspicious of the role of the state and its representatives. Yurii has also seen several entrepreneurial projects of his own fail and, having witnessed his father's experience, holds the state responsible for their respective travails. In this chapter, I describe how Aleksandr's crisis and Yurii's frustrations have shaped their entrepreneurial attitudes and behaviour. They have both concluded that the state and its representatives are, at best, obstacles to business and, more often, a menace, yet they have chosen to continue as entrepreneurs; I seek to set out why. I outline the factors that led to the fall of Khoroshiidom and the way in which this has affected how they run their businesses today.

I begin with a description of the collapse of Khoroshiidom, focusing specifically on how local bureaucrats abused their position as government partners in a joint construction scheme to illicitly acquire the company's assets for themselves. These schemes are infamous in Russia for their susceptibility to fraud, and this instance is a case in point: the ruse worked so that even when Aleksandr belatedly proved his innocence, the bureaucrats survived and kept their ill-gotten property. Like Anna, Aleksandr was widely blamed by many of his former clients who lost their money and property in that scheme, so in the course of the investigation, he became both a villain to his clients and a

DOI: 10.4324/9780429469176-5

victim of the state. He experienced irreparable damage to his reputation, lost many friendships as people deserted him and suffered a huge loss of wealth. As I conclude, this case in itself reinforces many of the negative factors associated with post-Soviet Russian business that I discussed in Chapter 1.

In the next section, I explain how Aleksandr has responded to the crisis, which was the defining event of his entrepreneurial life. His post-crisis view of the political economy, in which he once prospered, is one of disappointment and deep suspicion of the state and its representatives who, he considers, rule in their own limited interests, and whose potential for arbitrary interference in the business sphere is dangerous to entrepreneurs and harmful to the development of the country. At the same time, Aleksandr has not fully decided how to proceed and is relatively uncertain of his long-term path. Rather, since founding Promploshchad he has kept his options open, oscillating between staying and developing the company and deciding to leave the country altogether. Even though he is energetic and has enthusiasm and talent for business, he has settled for now with overseeing Promploshchad quietly, keeping his head low and prioritising the needs of his family while he contemplates his next step with little hope that conditions for business will improve.

In the following section, I focus on everyday business in Promploshchad with Aleksandr as director and Yurii managing operations, showing how their post-crisis attitudes affect their entrepreneurship in practice. It emerges that the theoretical simplicity of their business model, based on rental income from their tenants and their intention to keep a low profile, is more complicated in practice because they have unfinished affairs from the crisis to deal with and a distaste for obeying officialdom. As I show, their wariness of the state leads them to avoid it until it is absolutely necessary, which makes apparently simple tasks complex. Moreover, their tenants are also keen to avoid ties that encumber their freedom of action, which makes management more convoluted than it might otherwise be.

In describing these behavioural tendencies, I draw on Yurii's notion of a Russian business 'mentality' (*mentalitet*) to explain how, in their resistance to officialdom and determination to protect and advance their immediate interests, they are compelled to maximise their independence before seeking a profit, even if the cost of doing so is high. This leads me to invoke the concept of 'entrepreneurial governmentality' to explain my informants' entrepreneurship. Their drive for independence from external constraint and resistance to those who might endanger them entangles them within a network of favours and obligations with their contacts, making everyday business highly tactical. Thus, Aleksandr and Yurii's perception of the malign potential of officials to interfere in their affairs has a determinant effect upon their entrepreneurship, regardless of the relative simplicity and profitability of the business itself.

In the final section of the case study, I explore the drive for independence in more detail with respect to Yurii's own business, the Spine Centre. Although his company had promise, its development was constrained by bureaucracy, which reinforces Yurii's negative view of officialdom and encourages him to avoid and undermine it. In my description of his unsuccessful ventures and current frustrations, which are reinforced by his intimate knowledge of Aleksandr's crisis, Yurii's dissatisfaction with business conditions and determination to succeed in spite of officialdom is made clear. Nevertheless, his rebelliousness was also tempered by awareness of the consequences of illegality and his conviction, influenced by his admiration of the West, that a business should be managed formally (inside the law). Therefore, the development of his business follows a path both within and outside the law. This path, or that taken by Aleksandr, is not preordained, however: in this section, I also draw on the attitudes of several of Yurii's peers, who share his view of the political economy as risky, arbitrary and overbearing, but whose approaches to entrepreneurship differ significantly from one another, varying from cautiously seeking the status quo to violent aspiration to join the elite. I find that entrepreneurs are alone in choosing their approach to business: their own perception is their guide. Nevertheless, I find that their specific aim to continue in business and to avoid predatory outsiders is shared: their ambition is for continuity of independence over increased profit and to resist impediments in their way.

In conclusion, I find that Aleksandr and Yurii are determined and capable entrepreneurs whose businesses have great potential. At the same time, their respective experiences of the potential of the state to intervene and disrupt business persuades them to proceed with caution. Like Anna, Aleksandr's entrepreneurial approach changed significantly when he was confronted with a crisis and faced the fact that officials could not be relied upon to act in his interests. Ever since, his entrepreneurship has focused on maximising his independence from officialdom rather than rebuilding a large business. In his isolation from state support, Aleksandr has had to develop his own approach to business in which his independence is paramount and in which the state must be resisted rather than trusted. In this context, caution and self-interest become priorities for action. Aleksandr and Yurii proceed using their wits from day to day, resolved to continue, hoping for the best and aiming to avoid trouble. I conclude that, as in Oleg's case, Aleksandr and Yurii's entrepreneurship is experienced as a continual effort to maintain control irrespective of material success, with the state an opponent to be hoodwinked and avoided. Unlike Oleg, however, Aleksandr is cautious about working with others, assuming that they will try to undermine him if they can.

The Raiding of Aleksandr's Business

In this section, I analyse the events leading to the collapse of Khoroshiidom, which provides an empirical illustration of the challenges facing even successful businesses in Russia. This also provides an understanding of how the specific context of the crisis, which was instigated by state employees, influences his entrepreneurial attitudes and behaviours today. Aleksandr's entrepreneurial career began in the early 1990s when he left his Soviet-era employment in a heavy industrial plant and became a shuttle trader (a common job at the time; see Humphrey 2002: 73–7), buying fruit and vegetables in one place then selling them for profit in another. At the end of that decade, he founded Khoroshiidom, a construction company specialising in new residential blocks, which became one of the most significant companies of its type in the region. At that time, many construction companies had grown by relying on cheap loans from co-investors within the industry (Puzanov 2009: 36). Bank loans, in contrast, were hard to come by because the contractors had limited security to offer in return because they often rented land for construction rather than owning it outright. Furthermore, the construction industry was 'very non-transparent', which meant lending was too risky (Puzanov 2009: 36). By the middle of the 2000s, therefore, Khoroshiidom's expansion had stalled, and Aleksandr was unable to secure additional credit from local banks. In order to continue working, he chose to become involved in a series of 'equity construction schemes',[1] in which the capital for new buildings is raised by selling the apartments in advance of construction. Such schemes are common in Russia, regulated by law[2] and, in Normalnyi, overseen by a Municipal Unitary Enterprise (*Munitzipal'noe Unitarnoe Predpriyatie*, or MUP) called *Gorodstroi*.[3] Aleksandr's relations with Gorodstroi did not lead to further growth of the business, however, but may be seen as the beginning of its destruction.

The role of Gorodstroi is to coordinate the implementation of all municipal construction orders in Normalnyi, confirming the design of new projects, organising the approval required for construction, issuing permits and title deeds, managing construction in its technical and financial aspects and commissioning the completed buildings. When Gorodstroi sought building contractors for several new projects on plots it owned, Aleksandr successfully applied to become a partner. According to their agreement, Khoroshiidom would be entitled to a percentage of the value of completed apartments, while Gorodstroi recouped its investment and increased the value of the land. Notionally, Gorodstroi also committed to investing at a 'certain stage' in the development of the buildings, so both parties would have a stake in their completion. In theory, all partners stand to benefit from such schemes: the client–investor is promised a good deal on a new apartment because they invested in the cost of construction, the building contractor makes a reasonable profit, and the municipality meets its obligations for new housing.

However, the agreement was not in practice what it was in theory and turned out as follows: Khoroshiidom became responsible for fundraising and construction while Gorodstroi retained ownership of the land and acted as a customer for the work. Thus, although Gorodstroi held the legal and exclusive right to raise money from citizen–investors, it offloaded that function to Khoroshiidom. This meant that Aleksandr was charged with raising the capital required for the construction himself, which he achieved with citizen–investors and his own funds, but he did not gain any right to the land or, therefore, the apartments he was building. Indeed, Aleksandr's only stake in the properties was a meaningless 'priority right to future partnership agreements'. Therefore, he effectively entered into the agreement trusting that

Gorodstroi would grant him a stake in the completed apartments in order to break even and make a profit. This proved to be naive.

These risks were not initially clear, although several issues emerged suggesting that Gorodstroi was not a trustworthy partner. Before building began, Khoroshiidom was required to pay over 3 per cent of the investment cost to Gorodstroi just for the building designs and gather the necessary legal documentation and permits itself even though such administration fell within Gorodstroi's remit. Over time, it became clear that Khoroshiidom had to address all problems associated with the entire process while remaining dependent upon the goodwill of Gorodstroi. As costs built up, moreover, Aleksandr could not transfer them onto clients, because he did not have the right to do so without the approval of Gorodstroi. A major problem then arose when one of the first apartment blocks was found to have numerous faults. According to Aleksandr, it had been built following Gorodstroi plans, so he asked a specialist from a Moscow institute for a second opinion, who told him that the soil was inappropriate for construction and that the plans were based on guesswork. For six months, construction work was halted.

Despite these early hiccups, when the first building was completed, the two partners concluded a satisfactory agreement on the sale of the apartments that led Aleksandr into a new deal in 2007 to construct several more buildings. Some time after work on those sites had begun, however, Aleksandr discovered that Gorodstroi had already used these plots as collateral for a loan worth millions of roubles from Sberbank (a state-controlled bank; see Radziwill and Vaziakova 2015: 13–14). This meant Sberbank held a controlling stake in the sites, and the new agreement between Khoroshiidom and Gorodstroi was worthless. This caused the unravelling of the shared equity scheme. At this point, Aleksandr had already used much of the finance he had gathered from individuals but had no way of either completing the project or offering refunds to them. The construction became severely delayed as Aleksandr tried in vain to reach an arrangement with Gorodstroi. According to him, Gorodstroi told him simply to gather the money himself and complete the project. He realised he was being deceived but also that the deceiver was a state department: he was helpless.

At the same time, customers began to demand the apartments they had been promised. Aleksandr tried to delay by explaining that they should wait a little longer until he could finish them. As with Anna's case, however, while a few were patient, the majority believed they had been cheated and demanded their money back. They wrote letters to the police and prosecutor's office and then the Prosecutor General, accusing Aleksandr of fraud. Aleksandr was invited to an interview at the economic crimes department and subsequently arrested. Following the arrest, construction was frozen, and his property, materials and paperwork were confiscated. He was charged with cheating 158 people with invalid contracts in an equity construction scheme, causing damage of well over 200 million roubles,[4] as well as tax evasion worth tens of millions of roubles. Police asked others involved in the scheme to come forward and bankruptcy proceedings were introduced. Aleksandr was sent to prison, where he faced up to ten years.

In jail, Aleksandr's situation deteriorated further. The organisation of regional constructors excluded Khoroshiidom on the false basis that membership dues had not been paid. This was a sign that former allies were deserting him. Aleksandr also heard that Gorodstroi had begun to transfer some of the unfinished projects to other contractors. From prison he protested and sought to initiate arbitration proceedings, claiming that Gorodstroi had not fulfilled its obligations and to reclaim the transferred properties and recover hundreds of millions of roubles. After two months in prison, a friend from St Petersburg posted bail of one million roubles, and he was released pending the completion of the investigation.

From the perspective of the individual investors, Aleksandr was a fraudster. He had presented himself as a builder offering affordable apartments, but the apartments had not appeared, and investors' money vanished. This view should be considered in light of the fact that joint construction schemes in Russia have a bad reputation; so-called 'grey schemes' have arisen because the law on joint construction is prone to manipulation. Cost sharing makes investors vulnerable when the question of ownership arises (Puzanov 2009: 50): promissory notes are not equivalent to contracts of sale. Thus, some investors find their apartment is smaller than was promised, and others find the contractor simply disappears and leaves the building incomplete. Hence, in the investors' mind, Aleksandr was responsible for reneging on their agreement, even if he had not run away. Gorodstroi's argument was also strong. It simply accused Aleksandr of neglecting his responsibility to pay for the construction as agreed and neglecting his obligations as investor-constructor. At the same time, Gorodstroi downplayed its own role, arguing that it had not known where the finance had come from and that keeping track of both finance and construction was 'impossible'. This was remarkably brazen: its delegation of the financial aspects of the scheme to Khoroshiidom broke the law, while managing the scheme itself was its raison d'être.

Despite the plausibility of these arguments, it was, in fact, Aleksandr who had been framed. All the risk of the scheme had been placed on him by Gorodstroi, which had taken advantage of its monopoly control over joint construction schemes. It made Aleksandr take on the role of gathering investments, knowing that he was not allowed to do so. It then pulled out of the agreement when several properties were close to completion, knowing that Aleksandr would be prosecuted, leaving them with the full ownership of the buildings. This alone does not explain why an MUP would be motivated by profit. However, in the months prior to Aleksandr's arrest, the city administration had indicated their intention to privatise Gorodstroi, such that its functions remained but it became a regular company. Therefore, if Gorodstroi's directors timed the privatisation and the downfall of Aleksandr to coincide, making it look as though Khoroshiidom had defrauded investors, they stood to become enormously wealthy. Over the course of the next two and a half years, this argument formed the basis of Aleksandr's defence and his eventual acquittal: he, and in turn his investors, had been misled by Gorodstroi in a fait accompli.

Aleksandr's acquittal would take two and a half years to achieve, a period that was extraordinarily stressful because he was fighting investors who did not believe him, government bureaucrats who wanted to destroy him, and powerful financial interests that were hostile to the preservation of his business. During the trial, he instructed his lawyer to hide documentation supporting his case in a remote location such that it could not be destroyed or obtained by the state or associates of Gorodstroi. These documents eventually provided the evidence that allowed him to win the case, but not without cost. By the time he was acquitted, he had lost Khoroshiidom, which was dissolved in bankruptcy proceedings brought against his will. Gorodstroi's involvement of Sberbank in the scheme meant that the bank voted for the liquidation of Khoroshiidom when bankruptcy procedures were brought. As such, there were three parties to the agreement rather than the initial two. Unsurprisingly, Sberbank employees involved in the ploy profited personally. Indeed, the Sberbank managers involved in the case were personally associated with Gorodstroi officials: the sister of one of these managers acquired two flats very cheaply. Several others were bought and sold quickly for huge profits. It also emerged that a major beneficiary of the scheme was in charge of the Economics Department in Gorodstroi, proving that the entire ploy was initiated by senior figures inside the organisation. Gorodstroi itself inflated the cost of construction so that it could justify the increased profit margin from the sale of some apartments. One building, Aleksandr eventually proved, cost just over 400 million roubles to build, but Gorodstroi calculated construction at nearly 500 million roubles and sold some remaining apartments for 15,000 roubles extra each. Thus, Aleksandr was unable to prevent the remaining construction from being passed to rival contractors and the company's assets, including cranes, offices and a car park, from being offloaded for almost nothing.

While Aleksandr was eventually cleared of wrongdoing, Gorodstroi survived. Indeed, it could hardly fail given its official status. According to Aleksandr, when the director of Gorodstroi was confronted with evidence of the inflation of the figures and asked to account for the difference, she replied it was a 'commercial secret' and received no further scrutiny on the issue. To put it plainly, Gorodstroi, a state agency with oversight of the construction of new apartments to the city, had systematically defrauded its citizens to the benefit of its own directors and their allies. Moreover, it appears that the investigators were incentivised not to look into the matter so that, even though Aleksandr was eventually freed, the damage was already done. On the other hand, although Aleksandr was able to make a case for his innocence, his right to the buildings was never strong. Indeed, even when acquitted, many citizen-investors rejected the decision, arguing that they had not received their entitlements. They claimed that Aleksandr had been successful in his trial because he had been able to pay for a 'Moscow lawyer'. In protest, they organised a picket, but, as the media reported, officials did not visit them on the picket lines. Like Anna, they also wrote to the president and prime minister, as well as the prosecutor general, but this appeared to have little impact. However, their case was eventually acknowledged. By 2013, a full six years after the scheme was initiated, all investors were in a new apartment. A letter on the group's website thanks the local administration for their intervention in the case. It appears that funding was found to complete the remaining apartments from social funds meant for citizens in decrepit housing and young families. In this way, the investors were eventually, gratefully, 'rescued' by the state that had defrauded them, even as they continued to blame Aleksandr.

Nevertheless, while Aleksandr was framed in this case, it is highly doubtful that his business affairs had always been transparent. Driving through the city with Yurii, for example, he pointed out an apartment that Aleksandr had given to a local official, who had then sold it for $200,000. Perhaps this was the case or perhaps it was not, but such claims indicate that Aleksandr had long operated between politics and business, which was a requirement (or reality) of the construction industry in the city. Aleksandr and his family prefer to see such favours as indicative of his good nature or befitting a man who had accrued such wealth. He was always generous, they say. He gave money to charity, sponsored youth sports teams and helped family and friends. He had started as a shuttle trader then built a successful business from nothing. Indeed, Aleksandr told me that his reputation for giving to social causes meant he was protected while in prison. However, as Evgeniya (his wife) sadly explained, his generosity did not help him during the crisis, as many former friends and associates turned on him or forgot about him.

In this section, I have shown how Aleksandr's construction business was stripped of its assets and destroyed for the benefit of local officials whose formal role was to support the construction of residential accommodation in Normalnyi. This case of reiderstvo also destroyed Aleksandr's professional reputation and many of his friendships and reiterates the difficulties of doing business under conditions of institutional asymmetry. It also reifies several post-Soviet stereotypes about the powerful using their influence and legal loopholes to generate huge personal profits and reveals the way in which bureaucrats use their formal position to their advantage in the market. Likewise, the case reinforces clichés about dubious entrepreneurs and the vulnerability of ordinary citizens in the face of wily businesspeople operating unlawfully. Each stereotype has an undeniable element of truth here, but it was actually these stereotypes that made the ruse workable: as an entrepreneur, Aleksandr was the most obvious and credible fall guy, just as Anna's business made her a credible fraudster in the perception of her clients. Ironically, the widespread notion of business as inherently dubious emerges as something that can be profited from, exploiting memories formed in the 1990s: the Gorodstroi officials appealed to the residual social categorisation of business as corrupt and exploitative while they expropriated the company's assets themselves. Indeed, it is indicative of Gorodstroi's success at discrediting Aleksandr that even though he has been exonerated, many investors still hold him responsible for the failure of the scheme. In part they are justified; they were cheated, and Aleksandr was able to gather bail money and employ an effective lawyer. At the same time, those officials who made remarkable money from the scheme kept their liberty. Overall, the case exemplifies the way in which the state has been partly privatised by officials that I described in Chapter 2 with reference to Yurchak. The behaviour of the Gorodstroi officials was entrepreneurial, taking personal advantage of institutional asymmetry or, in Yurchak's terms, the division of the state into official and personalised spheres. To be clear, they used their formal position for personal gain in the market. In the next section, I describe how Aleksandr's attitudes towards business and the state have been shaped by this experience.

Starting Again

Aleksandr's crisis had a profound impact on his life and outlook. As well as destroying his business, he was ostracised from the construction industry and lost many friends. On his release from prison, he was shaken by the experience but philosophical. Describing his mood to a regional newspaper he said:

> I have a period now when it is possible to evaluate my life and those people with whom I live. Many things in our lives are superficial. And when it's not superficial, thank God. To be happy one does not need more, but a goal is needed. If it is possible to have more, then good. We live to improve, or something like that. As for my business, we wait and see.

As it turned out, Aleksandr did start another business, but the crisis remained the major reference point in his life – a critical influence on his perceptions and decisions. Today, he holds the view that the current political economic situation in the country is unacceptable to too many people and cannot last. It is inevitable, he told me, that:

> Society will reject the current system. It is only a question of when. Maybe tomorrow, maybe in ten years, but it's certain. People have to survive with so little, as you've seen, and the country is so dependent upon oil and gas, which cannot last forever.

However, as he said, at present, society must deal with conditions as they are, which is that the decisions of the country's elite are made in their own interests rather than those of the country as a whole. As I now show, this perception has had a profound impact on the way Aleksandr considers the situation in the country, but after much consideration, he has not deviated from his desire to continue as an entrepreneur.

In the period since his release from prison, Aleksandr has formed a specific view of the way the political economy functions. Above all, he said, state power is used arbitrarily in the interests of those wielding it rather than the country as a whole. He often offered his opinion or a rumour about how the country's elite made their decisions in a way that is completely irrelevant to the daily lives of the rest of the population. For example, like many commentators, he considered the release of Mikhail Khodorkovsky as a gesture to the international community in advance of the Sochi Winter Olympics (see also Ioffe 2015: online; Lokshina 2013: online; Meyer et al. 2013: online), rather than a goodwill pardon. However, he had heard that heavy rainfall prior to the opening ceremony had flooded the Olympic stadium, which then froze and threatened the venue's readiness. According to him, only a German firm owned the technology capable of removing such ice in time for the start of the games, and the German government used the release of Khodorkovsky as the condition of their support. That is why, Aleksandr told me, Khodorkovsky left Russia on a German plane bound for Germany. He said that if politicians could manipulate the judiciary so brazenly for the most successful Russian businesspeople, it was no surprise that an ordinary entrepreneur such as him could be thrown into prison so easily.

Whether or not such stories were true, Aleksandr was not alone in indulging in this type of conjecture. For example, in Normalnyi, three businesspeople told me independently that a senior Sberbank executive threatened *Novosibirsk*'s regional administration that he would relocate the Novosibirsk office (one of the tallest and newest buildings in the city) if a neon advertising board on the street outside was not removed. Although nobody could say why the sign was so annoying, by relating the story, they portrayed Russia's elite not only as petty but preoccupied with exercising power and expending huge resources on personal whims rather than the interests of their organisations or communities. Aleksandr had developed a sideline in such stories. When we drove to the remote *Altai Krai* to meet one of his business acquaintances, for example, he described the story of the newly constructed Siberian Coin casino. The casino was built after the government decided to restrict gambling to only four mega-sites on the periphery of the country (later increased to include Sochi following the Winter Olympics and Crimea following its annexation; see TASS 2014a: online). The Siberian Coin was the most inaccessible of the four casinos, but according to Aleksandr, it was justified by the regional government as a project to advance regional development (for example, Bloomberg Business 2011: online; *Siberian Times Reporter* 2014: online). He said that the site was deemed so important that it was granted a new gas pipeline from *Biysk*, over 130 kilometres to the north. This pipeline, he complained, revealed the warped priorities of the federal government. Even *Gorno-Altaisk*, he said, capital of the Altai Republic, had only received a gas supply of its own as late as 2008 (see also Gazprom 2008: online). He found the whole story infuriating.

In a sense, Aleksandr's distaste for projects such as the Siberian Coin was justified. The casino resembled Soviet projects for the 'development' of remote Siberia with single industry settlements. However, whereas then such projects were justified in the interests of the proletariat, today they are for an elite minority. The government ban effectively disallowed the population at large from gambling on vague moral grounds, just to build new casinos where only wealthy Russians can access them.[5] Indeed, the Altai Regional Administration's own promotional material openly distinguishes between regular 'visitors' and 'VIP guests': the former will be housed in buildings 'along the middle course of the river' while the latter would stay 'deep into the territory ... hidden in the wild nature environment' (Altai Krai Region Administration 2008: 19). Even so, Aleksandr also exaggerated; the Siberian Coin would not be the only recipient of gas from this pipeline because it was to be located next to a 'Tourist-Recreational Special Economic Zone' (SEZ) called Sky-Blue Katun. This resort, one of several new federally planned resorts, provides year-round holiday facilities, and while it is not affordable or accessible to all Russians, it does not cater to the elite alone (Investment Portal of Altai Region no date: online; Altai Krai Region Official Site no date: online; Fedotkin no date: online). Aleksandr was therefore right that the government had created a gambling initiative that would only benefit the country's elite and require a costly new pipeline, but the pipe would also supply an adjacent resort meant for a larger demographic.

Although Aleksandr's exasperation and cynicism at political economic conditions is revealed in these examples, he claimed that he had not fully decided how he should respond to them. Unlike Oleg, he did not have a clear approach for developing his business and limiting the interference of outsiders. However, the question of 'what to do' next was constantly on his mind, even today, several years after his release. He told me that he has three options available. The first was to focus on developing Promploshchad, his current business. The company is sited on a reasonably large plot of land (known as the *baza*) containing several industrial units let to small manufacturing and engineering enterprises. The business already provides an income sufficient to live without any financial problems but could, he calculated, be developed to provide a better income of up to one million roubles a month (which in late 2014 was about £20,000). He would invest in improving the baza's existing facilities, buy additional land and build new units. The baza is well located on the city's outskirts for light industrial businesses, and a new village is planned further along a road that passes the gate, so he could also build a shop on the site to sell groceries to passing residents and perhaps a cafeteria.

Aleksandr's second idea is to build a medical and rehabilitation centre for wealthy Russians seeking post-hospital recuperation and therapeutic treatments. During my first visit to Normalnyi, he had already constructed a property for this purpose and partnered with a doctor who would manage the business for him on completion. However, by my second trip, the economic situation had deteriorated significantly; Aleksandr said that the market for this type of business had diminished, so he had almost decided to sell the building and concentrate on the baza instead. In any case, he had put both the baza and the medical centre building on the market to test the water and consider his options further. Even so, by the time I finished my fieldwork, Aleksandr was no further with his decision making.

If Aleksandr were to sell these properties, he would take up his third option, which is to leave the country altogether. He had decided that the Dominican Republic would be his most likely destination because, he told me, it is easy to move there and offered a good lifestyle without complications. The plight of the rouble in late 2014 pushed this option to the forefront of his mind: 'Maybe in a few months the Russian border will be closed', he speculated, as Russia's relations with Europe deteriorated, and suggested that the move could be now or never. However, while Aleksandr had seriously planned how to emigrate, Evgeniya was less enthusiastic because she had no friends abroad. Indeed, Aleksandr was also doubtful: 'I don't want to leave, this is my country', he shrugged. Thus, even though he decried the fate of his country, he had not yet convinced himself to leave.

Aleksandr's decision comes down to whether he is prepared to continue as an entrepreneur in Normalnyi, given his enthusiasm and knowhow for business on the one hand, and his disdain for business conditions on the other. Unlike Oleg, however, who continued as an entrepreneur in spite of his distaste for political economic conditions in the country because he wanted to make some change to local social conditions, Aleksandr is less interested in social development or charity than he was prior to the crisis. His experiences have made him more stoical than ambitious: his primary focus is supporting his family and keeping his head down. During the day, he travels repeatedly between work and home on constant errands and is dedicated to ensuring his family's well-being. On these trips, his philanthropic nature became clear, as well as his remarkable business success despite his humble background. Some of his family was displaced during the Soviet period, and we drove considerable distances to assist his relatives in remote locations. One stepsister, for example, lived hours from Normalnyi in the countryside in a prefabricated bungalow in a dilapidated village, so Aleksandr was overseeing the renovation of her property, ensuring that she would not have to cross the garden to an outhouse any longer. Likewise, when we visited the interior, he took potatoes and other staples to other relatives and hard-up friends. Thus, although in the back of his mind Aleksandr contemplates escaping, in practice he knows he can 'get by' locally and has the capacity to support others: he is still relatively successful today in spite of his previous problems and knows that he may not be able to replicate this success elsewhere. John Round has also encountered similar justifications for staying in Russia's remote far north among would-be migrants, who cite practical and cultural reasons for wanting to stay, compared to the risk of the unknown if they leave (2005: 718–23). Overall, Aleksandr has the knowledge that he has survived before, devotes his time and energy to getting on with everyday business and family life and avoids actually dealing with larger questions about the future.

By not significantly changing his life, Aleksandr's reaction to the crisis is, ultimately, to continue as before as an entrepreneur. Nevertheless, this time he seeks to avoid engagement with the state as much as possible and keep control of his business within his family. This suits Yurii's needs because, as I explain in later in this chapter, his own entrepreneurial projects had stalled.

Aleksandr put Yurii in charge of day-to-day operations, which gave him a regular salary and responsibility for putting plans for the development of the business into effect. In practice, Aleksandr continued to instruct Yurii from a distance, but he was less often present on site. This arrangement was obviously hard for Aleksandr, who was used to having control, but it was also hard for Yurii, who wanted to develop his own interests at the same time. Nevertheless, it also served both their needs; Aleksandr could dedicate more time to supporting his family, and Yurii could focus on making a living.

In this section, I described how Aleksandr's crisis convinced him that the state not only undermines business but that the country's elite and bureaucrats are primarily interested in themselves rather than serving the country as a whole. This perception led him to the conclusion that he could either stay in Normalnyi and live with this reality, accepting that he is powerless to change it, or to leave the country altogether. However, counter to his own expectations, he has not yet decided to leave, which has meant staying put to continue with his new business. In fact, Aleksandr really prefers not to contemplate the future in detail but to concentrate on the immediate needs of his family in the knowledge that, if he is careful, he can 'get by' quite well. By focusing on everyday matters, he suppresses his disappointment with the structure of the political economy. His priorities, therefore, are to ensure that his new business can support his family and to avoid engaging with officialdom and the state as far as possible. This plan, as I now show, is not as straightforward in practice as it sounds.

Risky Business in Reality

Promploshchad has a simple business model based on rental income from tenants who demand little except a dry unit, water supply, waste disposal and electricity. Therefore, the business is uncomplicated in principle, and this suits Aleksandr's desire for a simple, trouble-free life: the main tasks are to ensure the units have tenants, maintain the facilities and initiate their plans for expanding the baza. Nevertheless, these jobs require constant attention because the site is large, much of it in disrepair and prone to problems, particularly in winter. Indeed, Aleksandr and Yuri's success depends on their ability to stay on top of a seemingly endless list of administrative and practical chores and the onerous burden of dealing with officialdom over questions of utilities and land. It emerges that resolving these apparently simple issues is far from simple in practice and requires great flexibility and knowhow. It is in their approach to overcoming these tasks, determined also by their experiences, that their entrepreneurial attitudes and behaviours, as well as their view of business conditions, can be explained.

On my first visit to the baza, the temperature was a few degrees below zero but felt far colder thanks to a strong wind. The baza is located beside one of the city's gigantic hot water plants, but in my state of coldness, I did not notice the irony until later. In any case, the hot water supply had stopped working because a valve had gone missing, then somehow turned up a day later. It seemed that the job of reattaching the valve gave work to Kirill, a handyman, and although nothing was said, it appeared that he had removed it in the first place. In fact, it became clear that the smooth operation of the baza relied on several men like Kirill. As we emerged from the boiler room, for example, Yurii shouted to Vyacheslav, a tenant who had promised to fix the baza's electric entry gate that was wobbling in the wind. As Vyacheslav strolled up with bare hands, bare wind-bitten face and a thin worker's cap, I could not believe he was alive: although I was entering my second Siberian winter, I had never felt colder. Vyacheslav confirmed he would get on with the gate soon. Yurii told me that Vyacheslav, who had a tractor repair business, was not currently paying his rent because he had just bought a house and could not afford it, so he had agreed to fix the gate in kind. Yurii laughed when I said Vyacheslav must be cold. 'Normally he wears only slippers, even in winter!' As I wondered why he didn't wear boots, Yurii told me the monthly rent for Vyacheslav's unit is 8,000 roubles a month. This threw me into deeper confusion: on the one hand, his rent is very low, and he can only afford slippers, so his business must be struggling. On the other hand, he had just bought a house, so could not be short of money. Perhaps he was rich, perhaps not, but he had managed to make an arrangement so that he did not have to pay rent. When we saw Vyacheslav a few days later in his slippers, Yurii reminded me: 'I told you, he is a monster!' I had thought his light footwear was a sign of financial difficulty, but he was, in fact, just oblivious to the cold, and he had fixed the fence. In this scene, the baza was revealed to me less as a simple business with predictable rental income, as I had assumed, and more as the site of entwined personal dependencies that require strong relations, constant vigilance, management and bargaining.

A few days later, Yurii and I met two young men interested in renting a unit for storing the distilled water and chemicals they manufactured at another site. Yurii fielded their questions about costs and water supply, and they seemed satisfied. He explained that I was interested in what it is like to do business in Siberia, which made them laugh: 'Have you heard of the police?' one asked. We tried to enter the available unit, but it was locked so we had to return to the office where the guard was watching television beside his camp bed. He could not find the key, and Yurii lost his patience. 'Why must I do this myself?' he shouted, but the old man only mumbled and sank into the corner. Yurii grumbled to himself, and we looked in on another of the units instead, which was being refurbished for a meat and fish smoking business to move in. A couple of workers reclined as they fiddled to get a signal on a radio and made no effort to return to work when we entered. Sergey, the contractor overseeing the renovation, reported that he needed some materials, so we drove into the city to purchase them. That day and others continued in this fashion as Yurii responded to the needs of the moment and attempted to keep people doing the work he paid them for.

Besides this continuous rallying, the plan to expand the baza proved to be a major headache too. This became clear when Yurii informed me he had received notice from their electricity supplier that they needed to settle a large debt, or their supply would be cut. Over the following days, this proved to be rather more complicated than simply paying the bill. It emerged that Aleksandr and Yurii had delayed paying a Land Tax bill, and the tax authority had responded by blocking their bank account.[6] Now that the electricity supply to the baza was also threatened, access to their money had become even more essential than usual, and Yurii had to scramble. In order to pay the bill, Aleksandr called on one of his tenants to borrow the necessary cash. Actually paying the bill also proved to be just as frustrating: when we visited the electricity company, they would only take payments between three and four o'clock and only individuals rather than businesses could pay there. Yurii became increasingly anxious. A manager advised him to visit a bank in the city centre where he could make a transfer, but on arrival, we discovered that this incurred a 3 per cent surcharge, which frustrated Yurii even more. In the end, the bill was paid very reluctantly in the nick of time.

It was in Yurii's nature to portray events rather more dramatically than they could be; nevertheless, in that moment, the need for electricity was urgent. I asked Yurii why he had put off paying the electricity bills in the first place. It appeared extraordinary that a company with a healthy cash flow could allow this to happen. 'It's a mentality', he replied, as if they could not help themselves from trying to get away with it. However, over a drink on a later occasion, Yurii tried to clarify how exchange works in Russia, and his meaning became clearer. With one hand he gave me his glass, representing a product, and with the other took my hypothetical money. This is a conventional exchange as you understand it, he told me. However, in Russia, he said, the two are not simultaneous if you can help it. 'The rule is to keep your money', he said. Starting again, he gestured to give me the glass while taking the money but did not let the glass go. The point is that, unless you absolutely have to part with your money, there's no reason to give it away. Thus, Aleksandr and Yurii had applied this rule with the tax authorities. That they had incurred a fine for doing so was unfortunate but beside the point; they had tried to keep as much money as they could.

Nevertheless, Yurii's difficulties did not end when they finally paid the bill. When their bank account was reopened, they discovered 160,000 roubles missing and could not identify where it had gone. During the day, Yurii spoke about it with Konstantin, their lawyer, and realised he appeared nervous. Konstantin had been Aleksandr's lawyer when Khoroshiidom was dissolved. Before liquidation an external administrator had been appointed to oversee the insolvency process, but according to Aleksandr, he was appointed in a town hundreds of miles away, never visited Khoroshiidom, examined its documents or did anything in the interests of the business. Aleksandr argued in court that the administrator had breached his obligations to serve the interests of the business. Konstantin's role was to represent this claim in court. Nevertheless, Aleksandr theorised that Konstantin had been bribed by the administrator not to do so in exchange for a proportion of his fee, which also came from the business. This, if it were the case, would be 'classic otkat', said Yurii. Again, the logic of this theory was initially unclear to me. Why would Konstantin, who had stood so loyally by Aleksandr during his crisis, now betray him and risk his job for the sake of about £1000? Yurii replied that Aleksandr would not fire Konstantin, but they would have 'a long talk'. Indeed, Konstantin was a good friend, and we had all been on a hunting trip a few weeks earlier. In this episode, it became plain that the 'mentality' Yurii had described has to be taken seriously. Konstantin apparently did not want to damage his relations with Aleksandr and Yurii, and his intervention did not make any difference to the outcome of the insolvency process (which proceeded to liquidation), but he saw an opportunity to take a cut even though he knew it meant disobeying Aleksandr and being found out.

The way in which Konstantin stole from Aleksandr, the way Kirill coopted him, the way Vyacheslav got away without paying rent or the way Aleksandr sought to withhold payments from the electricity company all appear as a sort of fatalistic individualism, in that everyone is seeking to advance their own interests no matter what the cost. However, I assert that it is better to consider their behaviour in terms of seeking independence and resisting pressure, working between the formal and informal spheres. For example, in Konstantin's case, his official work was to represent Aleksandr, but he also sought to take advantage of this situation by creating a scheme in which he could profit from the bankruptcy of his own employer. Thus, Konstantin's status as a lawyer did not prevent him from attempting to steal from his employer but endowed him with the knowledge of how to take personal profit from his position. To put this another way, Konstantin had the knowledge to know how to steal within his role and how much he could steal without losing his job. This logic also applies to Kirill: everybody knew he stole the valve, but he still got away with it because he knew he could steal it with plausible denial and then win the work to repair it. The same logic applies to Vyacheslav: he had recently bought a house but managed to claim financial difficulty and avoid paying rent in cash, but in kind instead. And when an external administrator was appointed by the court to oversee the insolvency of Khoroshiidom, he saw an opportunity not to do the job but still get paid. Aleksandr's effort to avoid paying the electricity board was not because he was against paying in principle but because he thought he might be able to get away with it. This, I argue, underpins what Yurii means by the 'mentality' of business, and it made life more complicated for Aleksandr than he wanted.

It appears remarkable that an ostensibly successful business could become embroiled in so many informal and seemingly unnecessary complications in addressing apparently simple tasks such as collecting rent, paying fines, following the law and so on, but this is to underestimate the 'mentality' of business Yurii emphasised. Clearly, Aleksandr and Yurii view officialdom in its legal and bureaucratic forms as a menace to be avoided and resisted as much as possible. This stems not only from their crisis experience, in which senior figures within the state structures were revealed to be corrupted, but also because of the way everyday legal processes and diktat are vulnerable to informal intervention due to institutional asymmetry.

To state what is now obvious, formal processes (such as legal requirements) may be circumvented, and it is in entrepreneurs' material interests to circumvent them, especially given their continuing vulnerability to the officials who wield formal power. Thus, Yurii and Aleksandr routinely resist meeting their formal obligations or even obeying the law until it is completely unavoidable; they wait as long as possible to consider their options, and they seek to circumvent obstacles when they can. I find that everyday relations between entrepreneurs and officials develop such that both know the other is deviating from their formal duties and they must yield as little as possible. This resistance, however, can inconvenience them further, such as when Aleksandr's bank account was blocked for delaying payment of his bill. Nevertheless, as I have found, resistance in my informants' entrepreneurship is as integral and as critical as their drive for independence. This cat and mouse between entrepreneurs and officials adds stress and frustration to everyday business tasks and reinforces the idea that the state is the enemy. However, if state representatives are repeatedly revealed to be corrupted and corruptible, as they were in Aleksandr's experience, it is inevitable that businesses will avoid parting with their money until it is inescapable.

The counterpoint is that if formal procedures are vulnerable to intervention, there is a temptation to take advantage. Moreover, entrepreneurs feel justified doing so because of the arbitrary injustice they are exposed to in general. This appears to explain Konstantin's behaviour; to accept the bribe rather than do the 'right thing' by his employer appeared justified because a legal process that accepted (or could not prevent) criminal behaviour from its own administrators was already corrupted. Likewise, Aleksandr's experience of a corrupted judiciary justified not paying his debt in the first place. Therefore, it appears incumbent upon entrepreneurs to circumvent and resist the state whenever they are able. That neither Aleksandr nor Konstantin got away with it does not mean their logic was wrong. Indeed, the key point is that formal processes do not turn out as they ought because others have already personally intervened in their own interests. Thus, when the commercial court imposed an external administrator on Khoroshiidom, it could not have accounted for the administrator's improvisational behaviour, nor could Aleksandr have predicted Konstantin's own interference, which was a reaction to that of the administrator. This unpredictability, or informalisation of formal processes, invokes a sense that one should prepare for the worst possible outcome and that chances have to be taken when they are presented. At the same time, the impetus to circumvent formality takes instrumental rather than personal terms. Thus, Konstantin took his chance in spite of his friendship with Aleksandr: the mantra 'it's nothing personal, just business' seems apt.

Finally, although self-interest determines these informal behaviours, this does not negate the importance or value of social capital. In their moment of need, for example, Aleksandr and Yurii found the financial resources necessary by borrowing from their own tenants on the baza. Of course, it was in the tenants' interests to help Aleksandr prevent an electricity cut. However,

Aleksandr and Yurii are also willing to help their tenants, as Vyacheslav's no-rent arrangement shows. In this sense, there is a certain solidarity, evinced at least on the baza, among entrepreneurs seeking to 'get by' and circumvent the demands of the state. Considering these points together, I find that the 'mentality' Yurii described is less an innate Russian state of mind than a determination not to be a victim of predation by others or the state and to maximise personal advantage and independence relative to them. An important conclusion here is that, even as Aleksandr operates a successful, cash-rich business, he and Yurii still work in near battle-mode, in which basic operational requirements such as electricity, cash-flow and even the legal right to exist have to be fought over. In other words, even in this successful and growing company, everyday business activities may veer perilously close to crisis or even catastrophe, requiring informal solutions that rely on improvisation and personal connections.

In this section, I have shown how Aleksandr's perception of the state as dangerous has affected his entrepreneurship. Based on Aleksandr's experience of crisis, he and Yurii consider government bureaucracy to be an unpredictable and untrustworthy menace that they avoid until there is no other option. However, their avoidance and resistance strategies can make their situation worse and apparently simple tasks complicated. At the same time, everyday relations on the baza require close attention too because they depend on characters such as Kirill, Vyacheslav and Konstantin. Although these men depend on the baza, they also constantly look for opportunities to increase their influence over Aleksandr and Yurii, maximise their own interests and save or make money. This has created strong mutual dependencies irrespective of Aleksandr and Yurii's formal seniority. Similarly, Konstantin took advantage of an opportunity for otkat because such a chance may not have been available tomorrow. Thus, while these entrepreneurs are partially dependent upon one another, they also improvise in a way that overrides loyalty for personal gain in spite of the risks to relationships or increasing their own workload. As a result of a general sense that things can go wrong, I observed a tendency towards maximising immediate gains even at the cost of losses tomorrow. In order to explain these behaviours, Yurii offered the idea of a Russian 'mentality', but I have conceptualised this in terms of a determination to uphold their freedom of action and resist the state or other aggressive outsiders. I discuss this point further in Chapter 6.

Yurii's Development as an Entrepreneur

In this section, I seek to determine more specifically what it means to say that these entrepreneurs resist and seek independence from the state by examining Yurii's entrepreneurship in more detail, as well as the approaches some of his contemporaries have taken to developing and managing their businesses. I find that independence does not mean the same thing for everybody. On the contrary, entrepreneurs must decide their own approach and ambitions based on their experiences and perceptions of their position regarding the state and other market actors.

Yurii was in his late 20s but has long sought to establish himself as an independent and successful entrepreneur. He has started a number of enterprises, beginning at university when he made money organising dances for students. After that, he struggled for several years. He worked first as a cheesemonger, which involved late nights packing cheese, transporting it to Western Siberia's larger cities and negotiating with grocers to sell it. Although he said he was successful at this, his boss stayed in Normalnyi, did not give him enough cheese to make decent money and paid him poorly. He was also using his own car to drive fellow workers and the cheese and drove it into the ground. After a while, Yurii decided to move on and put it down to experience. In any case, Aleksandr needed support as he dealt with his crisis, so they agreed to work together during that period. Later, he tried his hand at construction, then became a warehouse manager, with a view to learning the trades, but he did not take to these jobs either. Thus, while Aleksandr's pessimistic view of political economic conditions results chiefly from his crisis, Yurii's pessimism stems both from his intimate knowledge of Aleksandr's case and his initial, unsuccessful attempts at independent entrepreneurship. In fact, while Aleksandr's pessimism is tempered by his acquittal and financial security, Yurii has to contend with the daily struggles on the baza and the challenges of developing his own projects. As a result, he is even more frustrated by political economic conditions than his father is.

However, when I conducted my fieldwork, Yurii had started a new company that showed greater promise, and he was working hard to make it succeed. The idea for this business came from a conversation with Nikolai, his girlfriend's father. Nikolai, an osteopath, had long wanted to establish a medical business but had already lost one when his partner defrauded him and was tentative about trying again. However, he had been contacted by his brother in Germany, Sergey, who had become aware of a handheld imaging device manufactured and commonly used in Europe that could greatly enhance osteopathic diagnoses in Russia. Together, they decided to try to win the right to train doctors and distribute the device in the former Soviet Union (FSU). Initially, Yurii secured a verbal agreement from the manufacturer and sought to register the device in Russia. This process, however, is still ongoing after two years. The authorities did not accept the medical data provided by the manufacturer and said that it must be recertified in Russia. The cost for this began at 100,000 roubles but was later tripled when a new director was appointed to the institute responsible for certification. The huge size of these fees, Yurii explained, meant that they had to secure the support of a third-party investor, who provided the cash but took a 25 per cent stake in the business. A catalogue of further costs and delays followed.

However, the men were determined to succeed: Yurii said that the device had a cost price of 150,000 roubles and a sale price nearly five times higher, so the potential was enormous. To keep things going, he translated the 300-page instruction document into Russian himself, while Nikolai called on another brother, a public relations executive in Moscow, to help draw attention to the product there. The problem, Yurii explained, was not that nobody wanted the product, but that bureaucracy prevented them from selling it. While they waited for better news about certification, they decided to establish a small osteopathy clinic in Normalnyi, where Nikolai could work privately and Yurii could try to develop the business in Kazakhstan, where they have not encountered such bureaucratic impediments. Their clinic, the Spine Centre, is housed in three rooms within a dilapidated former industrial site that has been cursorily renovated. They have installed baths, a single-seat sauna and treatment tables, and sell alternative medicines, particularly the blood from Maral deer antlers, famed in Russia for their supposed medicinal, healing and aphrodisiac properties (*Siberian Times Reporter* 2015: online; Sputnik 2012: online), as well as other 'natural' extracts and remedies. Most importantly, they have acquired a computer with software that allows them to make diagnoses with the imaging device, which Nikolai will use to determine appropriate treatments. Although Yurii told me that Nikolai will only 'demonstrate' the device to other doctors in the Spine Centre, it was plain that they also planned to use it for treatment in parallel to their wait for certification. In this way, Nikolai can focus on developing their reputation in the local medical community while Yurii can focus on administration and business development when he is not committed to the baza. Likewise, Sergey in Germany can be called upon to negotiate with the manufacturer in Europe when needed. When I asked Yurii if he thought the certification process would end with approval, he expressed confidence not on scientific grounds, even though the level of scrutiny is lower than that in the West, but because the institute was receiving a lot of money for the work.

At this point, I note that Yurii's entrepreneurship, which took place in both the Spine Centre and Promploshchad, is a form of portfolio employment. In the post-socialist context, this refers to individuals taking on formal and informal work in order to survive (for example, Morris 2012b: 219), which distinguishes it from that in advanced economies where it connotes working for multiple clients as a way of achieving greater independence (for example, *The Economist* 2009: online). That said, in Yurii's case, it is his choice to develop the Spine Centre, because he makes enough money to survive working for Promploshchad, his father's company. Furthermore, both businesses are legitimate to the extent that they exist formally, and the men aim to develop them as such. Therefore, I find that Yurii's case raises the importance of considering portfolio employment in normative as well as practical terms in contemporary Russia: he chooses to have a second business not out of necessity but because, like all my informants, it offers the sort of life he wants to create irrespective of the challenges. This is also the case with Oleg's Cooperative, but not with Anna, whose informal businesses are essential rather than optional. Yurii's entrepreneurship reveals that the distinction between formal and informal work is not necessarily between two types of business; rather, it seems that *all* Russian business must operate between the two spheres. Williams and Round have found, based on research in Ukraine, that formal and informal work are 'inextricably intertwined and mutually constitutive' (2009: 94). I accept this, and emphasise that Yurii's informal work takes place within his formal business, rather than separately from it, as a consequence of the unpredictable conditions he encounters in the market. I also concur with Williams and Onoshchenko who, based on a study in Ukraine, found that 'the majority of those in the formal economy rely heavily on the informal economy to secure their livelihood' (2015: 29). Indeed, it is not the case that Yurii is struggling to survive, but it is still essential for him to work informally. This, I have shown, is the consequence of institutional asymmetry.

Though Yurii does not actually need to have his own business, it is useful to consider what drives him towards it. In addition to his father's influence and success in business, he often described his 'hope for globalisation' and, like Anna, that Western business practices would take root in Russia, despite his experiences to the contrary. Hence, his ambitions reflect emergent post-socialist masculinities, associated with neoliberalism, which, according to Walker, are based on ideas of self-governance, individualisation and entrepreneurship as opposed to working class occupations that were valorised in the Soviet period (Walker 2016: e-book). In this sense, Yurii's aspirations as a young middle-class man are not unusual. However, as I found in Anna's case, they are restricted by their nonavailability, namely the problems that have arisen inhibiting the development of his businesses. Hence, portfolio entrepreneurship is a logical response: if one is ambitious, then problems have to be endured and overcome alone in the hope of eventual success.

Although Yurii is obliged to work informally to secure the future of the Spine Centre, he expressed anger at having to do so. Like his father, his frustration with business conditions stems from his experience of government bureaucracy as a burden on entrepreneurs. In turn, he idealises business conditions in Europe and the United States. He was delighted, for example, that the manufacturer of the medical device would spend 90 Euros to send him documentation to assist with the certification process. 'It showed that they believe I am a serious businessman', he said. Conversely, he was furious that he faced only doubt and bureaucracy about the value of the device at home. Like Aleksandr, Yurii had given much thought to this situation and offered constant explanations and examples of the way the political economy works. Thirty per cent of the population depends on the state for their pensions, he claimed, and perhaps 60 per cent for their salaries.[7] With such a large proportion of the population dependent on the state, support for our leader stays high, he reasoned. (As I noted in Chapter 3, Oleg drew the same conclusion… Even so, he said, many people find life here hard and are trying to escape. When I accompanied him all the way to Novosibirsk to visit the EU visa centre with paperwork for an application so that he could travel for a meeting with the device manufacturer, he laughed at the scene: 'Lots of nervous Russians behaving well!' he said sardonically in the waiting room, implying that everybody wants to leave the country if they can. 'My girlfriend tried to get a holiday visa for the USA last year but was denied it. So many

Russian women leave and do not come back'. He spoke of the large Russian populations in London and Thailand too and suggested many Russians would be there if they could. I asked how he reconciled widespread support for the status quo if so many wanted to leave the country, to which he said: 'Russians are angry with their past but keep doing the same things, repeating themselves. Russia always relives its own history. Nothing is new today'.

Yurii's sense of reliving the past is useful for understanding his attitude further. He perceives that his actions are constrained by overwhelming officialdom and bureaucracy, which are historically constant in Russia. Everyday travails tended to reinforce his view that the state and its representatives are obstacles to his ambitions. For example, when we returned to our parking space outside a shopping centre, we found that the traffic police had been lurking nearby to give tickets to unwitting parkers and they handed Yurii a 1,000-rouble fine. While we waited in the cold as an officer completed the paperwork in his car, his colleague was nearby rounding up other victims rather than advising them not to park, and they formed a shivering queue behind us. Yurii described the scene as 'absolutely typical', and evidence that the state works against its own people. When, on another occasion, we drove to have winter tyres fitted to his car, he returned home to find that his windscreen sprays had been removed from the bonnet and were presumably now on the car of his mechanic. He swore repeatedly. When we drove past the city of *Akademgorodok*, I mentioned how interesting it was to build a science town, but he said nothing had changed. He argued that Russia builds many large projects that are unnecessary and began to list them. '*Skolkovo*, for what? There's no need to copy! *Rosnano* was supposed to be for technology', he said, 'But do you know what Chubais said about why so much money has been given to Rosnano? To give people jobs! You know what we call Rosnano? *Rosbanano*! And what about the new road to *Kazan*? I don't want my taxes to go there!' He continued in this fashion, shouting at the injustice of it all. He gave such views frequently and with gusto, confident that the basic corruption of the state is beyond dispute, based on his own reading and conversations with respected people. For example, he introduced me to a professor he had met at a lecture at the local state university. The professor told me Siberia is an economic colony and that Russia lives in 'a golden age of bureaucracy'. Yurii could not agree more. 'It's simply Gazpromland!', he declared.

When these frustrations occasionally got the better of him, Yurii declared the situation in the country intolerable. Once, after we were pulled over by the traffic police and asked for our documentation, he lost his sense of reality and told me there would be a revolution within six months: 'The traffic laws are deliberately unclear so that the police can extort the people!' he cried. 'They can always find something wrong with your car!' Although this sounds melodramatic, it is worth noting that our ongoing awareness of the confusing conflict in Ukraine also added to Yurii's feeling that anything seemed possible at that time (in late 2014). During less stressful moments, however, he argued that it would be elites who would change the country rather than the people. 'Power is segmented under federal control. Regional government does not have control over the police or the army. The federal government holds power because it controls taxes and resources'. According to this rationale, the police remained dependent upon and loyal to the state. Moreover, Yurii told me, 'I am not a political person', and saw no role for himself in political events. Thus, despite his clarity of thought on political economic conditions, Yurii himself relived the past and hoped for the best from Moscow, even as he bemoaned his personal circumstances. In this circular logic Yurii believed (and showed me) that political economic conditions are intolerable, while arguing that it was not his role but that of distant elites to change them. He suggested that reliving the past was the only credible option open to him. His hope for change, such as it was, came from his feeling that the next elite could only be better.

At this point, it is useful to position Yurii's frustration in light of the views of other entrepreneurs. As I have already written, his entrepreneurial activities are informed by the 'mentality' he described: that officialdom must be avoided until it is completely necessary, and because of the arbitrary potential of the state, he must protect his interests and take opportunities whenever they are available. Nevertheless, his decision making is also informed by his belief that business should be done properly; he does not want to have to break the law but has to according to the structure of the system. However, although Yurii and Aleksandr are deeply cynical about Russia's political economy, their reaction to these conditions is not inevitable. Several of Yurii's acquaintances have responded quite differently. Nikolai, his business partner, was also frustrated by the difficulty of developing their business but was calmed by historical continuity rather than enraged by it: 'Yurii does not see that the situation is normal. In Russia, if an official says something, it must happen'. Indeed, as I now set out, although Yurii's contemporaries tend to share his view that conditions for business could be better, their reaction to this perception in their everyday business varies widely from caution to adventurism.

Igor, a mechanic in his late 20s, has a small garage in an industrial sector of the city. He offered me a few words in English and explained that he had studied in Brighton for a few weeks as a teenager. Since then, however, it appeared that his ambitions had been dampened. 'In order to succeed in business', he said, 'you need to have contacts in strategic sections', meaning local government and which he implied he did not have. This did not mean he did not retain an interest in the affairs of the country, however, and (to my surprise) he recommended a book by Simon Kordonskii of the Higher School of Economics in Moscow to help me understand more. Under such conditions, I asked, what were his hopes for his business? 'Well, to continue', he replied simply. In this way, Igor imagined a modest future role for himself, based on an assessment of his place in the order of things and an acceptance of his fate. He did not aspire for more because he did not think it was realistic, even though his intellectual references and practical skills revealed him to be a very capable man. Expressing my esteem about Igor to Yurii afterwards, he scolded me: 'Russians have enormous potential, but the problem is the government: for them, there is no need for more than oil and gas'. Thus, Yurii's view that the government stood deliberately in the way of entrepreneurs was reinforced by Igor's response. As I have already indicated, however, the argument that businesses lack potential is not always borne out: Yurii's medical business and Promploshchad are promising. Thus, if Igor occupies one position, in which the political economy is understood to be oppressive and this prevents self-improvement, Yurii occupies another, in which the political economy is oppressive but business development is possible with concerted effort and initiative (even though this has proven more hope than reality at present).

Viktor, a second acquaintance of Yurii's, is another case in point. Now in his late 20s, he started his entrepreneurial career working with criminals who took homeless men from the streets, cleaned them up, gave them some papers and a back story, then sent them into banks to apply for a loan, which they then stole. After a time, he felt uncomfortable doing this but was inspired to start a credit brokering business of his own when his wife was denied a loan. He could not understand why her application had been unsuccessful, so he visited a credit broker to find out how it worked. He decided that a business assisting people with their credit applications could be very successful. At that time, he said, only three brokers worked in Normalnyi, but the sector quickly expanded to 20, then contracted again as competition drove the majority out of business. His business model is simple, he explained: he built relationships with several local banks, which provided him with an understanding of the sort of terms under which they would agree to provide credit. He then brought them a steady stream of well-prepared applicants from his clients. The most important aspect of the role, he underlined, is a high level of service. He speaks honestly to clients about their financial circumstances, advises them about which bank will be most receptive and assists them in preparing applications. Then he approaches the bank on behalf of the applicant so that they deal with him personally. If the bank agrees, then the client visits the bank and signs the agreement. In this respect, he is personally involved in the whole application process; both client and bank rely on his integrity. In return for this work, clients pay him between 5 and 15 per cent of the loan value. Regarding his ambitions, Viktor said that, in an ideal situation, the banks would pay him to bring them new clients, and he would work only with 'quality clients', though he conceded this was unlikely at present.

Thus, today Viktor has a business that can operate, in principle, without veering into the shadow economy. However, like Promploshchad, he works between the formal and informal spheres in practice. For example, he offers bank managers cash in order to secure their agreement on loan applications. As he said, 'Of course, otkat exists today, but in five years it will be much less. Standards will improve with competition'. With this conviction, Viktor gave the impression that business conditions will improve in time, even though he had already said competition in the market has decreased significantly. What grounds did he have for such optimism? In fact, as I sat with them, it appeared that their optimism was illusory and, most likely, for their own benefit as young men facing a future in difficult business conditions. They are, in fact, pessimistic about the future. Their primary concern was the economic crisis. 'There are fewer good clients now', said Viktor. 'Anyway, nobody takes responsibility in Russia. A man can take out a loan, but forget about the responsibility to pay it back'. Moving away from the difficulties facing business temporarily, he turned to bemoan the rising cost and falling standard of living. 'For example, today it is necessary to pay for medical insurance because public doctors are awful and drunk'. At this point, Yurii took the chance to grumble too: 'Actually, people leave hospital worse than before. After hospital, an acquaintance of mine became ill and now cannot work'. They proceeded through a quick-fire list of other annoyances. 'The cost of car insurance is too high as well, so people risk it with only basic insurance or go without', said Viktor. 'And the school system is the same', he said. 'Private tutors can make a lot of money, and normal teachers with their own students after school too'. Yurii nodded vigorously: 'School is just about repetition. The government wants to produce idiots!' As I stated earlier, Yurii's views about the country closely resemble Oleg's (Chapter 3).

After continuing through several similar points, Viktor brought the subject back to a general absence of responsibility. 'Although the economy is bad', he said, 'the credit market is risk-free. When you have received the credit, just change your name and they will never find you. Or simply say your conditions have changed and you cannot pay the money back'. Would this land me in prison, I asked, but he shook his head and laughed. Here, Viktor admitted that all is not lost. In fact, his business fares better when government effectiveness is weaker. Although he believes political economic conditions and social morality have been corrupted, in the credit business, there are still opportunities because it is poorly regulated, and systems are prone to circumvention: he can make money from his clients whether they abide by their contracts or not. Viktor was being slightly disingenuous when he bemoaned political economic conditions and said that society lacks responsibility; he is successful because he has identified a market in which he can take advantage of these conditions. He is an effective entrepreneur under conditions of institutional asymmetry.

Yurii's position is similar: his father's crisis and his own difficulties have convinced him that the state should be blamed for political economic problems. If the government managed the economy well, the situation would not be getting worse, he said. For example, 'I borrowed $500 three months ago from a friend. Then the value was 20,000 roubles; now it's 23,000. This is not the sanctions, but a terrible economy'.[8] This rationale leads him to the conclusion that 'entrepreneurs do not know what will happen tomorrow: we might have work, we might not', which in turn justifies the 'mentality' that governs his entrepreneurial behaviour: the government is better to be avoided than obeyed and entrepreneurs must take their chances. This logic is clearly reactive, with the government a menace whose actions drive entrepreneurs to avoid and circumvent regulation, which in turn drives cynicism and motivates self-interest. Nevertheless, like Viktor, Yurii's business interests have developed because of his appreciation that it is only through circumventing formal obstacles, such as the certification of his medical device, that his business can be developed.

Thus far I have argued that if Igor was tentative about interaction with the government and cautious in his approach to the future, emphasising only the survival of his business, Viktor and Yurii were even more frustrated with the state, but more determined to undermine it as a result. Pavel, another of Yurii's acquaintances, takes this determination a step further still. Also in his late 20s, he has already gained a senior position within a large regional construction company similar to Khoroshiidom. When we met, he spent much time on the telephone dictating orders to staff working late into a freezing night on a construction site. Indeed, he projected aggression and showed us videos on his smartphone of his bare-knuckle boxing training and organised gang fights in the city. He related a story of punishing a wealthy local man who had refused to pay a debt, dragging him from his car and beating him up in full view of the police. This story reveals the complicity of the local authorities in his violence.

Pavel, however, was intelligent and articulate too. The most financially successful of Yurii's peers, he talked not in terms of frustration but optimism at political economic conditions. He described his entrepreneurial approach:

> First it is necessary to understand the local situation and local people. The majority want to work from nine until five o'clock then go home and drink beer. They think that's all there is. They drink at the weekend, and expect the same for their children. And then there is another type, those people that want their otkat. But it is not just business that is corrupt. When a contract for a new building is offered in competition, the requirements are written in such a way that only one company can win. The officer in charge of the competition receives some 'chocolate.' It is called the carousel.

He smiled, indicating that the officer would offer all likely bidders a chance to 'win' the contract with a bribe. In Pavel's vision of a successful businessperson, therefore, hard work goes hand in hand with violence, and both are necessary. At the same time, productive work (in this case construction) goes hand in hand with fraud (otkat). To Pavel, this is simply the way things are. The smart entrepreneur, in his view, recognises the political economy as imperfect and chooses to exploit it. Thus, exploitation appears as the key requirement for business success in the opinion of the most commercially successful of this group of entrepreneurs who reached adulthood just before or during the Putin presidency. This view, I recall, partly resembles that of Dmitrii, Oleg's son (Chapter 3): he was not outwardly aggressive and focused on everyday sales rather than corruption, but he did emphasise that a Russian business should be prepared to take any steps to protect its interests. Pavel and Dmitrii are young, bright, assertive and ambitious and believe that success means dealing with circumstances as they find them, taking what they can, as opposed to Yurii and Viktor, who are discontented with the present but hope for a better future and seek to circumvent obstacles with only their wits.

It is interesting that in justifying the beating of the wealthy businessperson, Pavel spoke approvingly of Sergey Shoigu, the Russian Defence Minister, and claimed he had also beaten subordinates when he had to. This anecdote is revealing, because Shoigu, like Putin, had a reputation as a youngster for brawling, but also started out in the Siberian construction business (*The Economist* 2015: online; Nechepurenko 2015: online). That Pavel should look to Shoigu, the longest-serving member of the Russian government, as a role model is revealing not only with respect to his background. Pavel was born as something of an outsider, to a Russian mother and Jewish father in Kazakhstan, just as Shoigu was born in remote Tyva to a Tuvan father and Russian mother. Rather, in profiles, the Defence Minister is widely described as an unlikely success, loyal, competent and politically neutral (for example, *The Economist* 2015; Nechepurenko 2015: online). Indeed, Pavel sees a potential future in politics. I asked him which party interested him. He replied that 'in Russia we have clans not parties', and suggested that he would align himself in time. This determination to be involved in politics but do so apolitically, to do what is required competently and loyally, in apparent emulation of the public image of Shoigu, is striking as an example of simulation of elite behaviour at the quotidian level. In his rise in business, these behaviours appear to have held him in good stead thus far.

I have argued that Yurii and three of his entrepreneur-acquaintances of the same generation share a reasonably unambiguous perception that the political economic conditions of the country present difficulties for business. However, the manner in which the men's attitudes determine their behaviour varies widely. Igor is cautious, Viktor and Yurii are pragmatic and Pavel is cavalier. Noticeably, it is Pavel who has achieved the most economic success to date. Even so, the circumvention of the state was a necessary activity for each entrepreneur. Thus, for example, otkat appears simultaneously as a necessity and symbol of dysfunction in the 'actually existing' economy: it is a reaction to a political economy in which the future seems uncertain and the government dangerous. On the other hand, it acts as an incentive for action, a reward for the most energetic, brave and violent. Both these positions conform to Yurii's concept of 'mentality': survival and success both require acting primarily in one's own immediate interests rather than, necessarily, according to law or the interests of wider society. This does not preclude the formation of social relations, which are clearly integral to economic activity. It does appear to explain, however, why the mutual interests of groups coalesce around short-term interests and convenience rather than long term strategies. Indeed, as Pavel emphasised, the structure of the political economy is determined by 'clans', or elite alliances: this is reflected at the level of agency in the way entrepreneurs rely on and act in the interests of their limited social network. I return to this point in Chapter 6.

Overall, these entrepreneurs share a conviction that the political economy remains problematic and that opportunities for business are closed to those unconnected to officialdom. There was no consensus on whether the future offered greater opportunities, however. Igor and Pavel, who were respectively the least and most tolerant of risk, did not expect much improvement. Yurii and Viktor however, who are seeking to build legitimate businesses, believed that the improvement of conditions would come in time and that this improvement was indeed inevitable. Today, however, their priority is to work to protect and advance their interests; this is the impetus to resist the influence of outsiders on one's business that I described earlier. The question of what these interests are, nevertheless, differed for each man: whereas Igor was cautious and sought to maintain the status quo out of a sense of place far from the elite, Pavel had a swashbuckling determination to emulate the 'clans' that hold greater influence and had decided that there is a profit to be made in both business and corruption. Viktor had identified a market in which he had outgrown many competitors and stood to profit from the continued growth of a legitimate business, but he also stood to benefit from the fact that the credit market is prone to circumvention and has established local relationships with the banks to take advantage while he can. In this situation, his plan is simply to remain flexible and pragmatic as necessary. Overall, each entrepreneur considers business conditions perilous, but each has had to develop a personal assessment of the extent to which action is constrained based upon their observations and experiences. In sum, their business ambitions were not uniform, but aimed rather at a personal version of independence.

Summary

In this case study, I explained how Aleksandr's experience of crisis affected his entrepreneurial attitudes and behaviours. Aleksandr's case shows that even the most successful independent businesses in Russia face predation, not just those like Anna's. Before the crisis, he was prepared to take risks with the development of his business, played perhaps too fast and loose in Russia's booming construction industry, and gave generously to city charities. However, he eventually entwined his company's fate with a state agency that betrayed him. Having endured the loss of his business and imprisonment, he was now content to concentrate on the day-to-day oversight of Promploshchad, his new business, and reluctant to overstretch himself, choosing a path of self-reliance, drawing on family and local contacts for assistance when required. However, although Aleksandr contemplated leaving the country, he had decided to return to entrepreneurship in spite of his experiences. I argue that this decision was not primarily motivated to recover the type of wealth he had prior to his crisis, or even to make a profit, but because it represented the only means with which he could exercise most control over his affairs and live independently, extricating himself from the predatory state and its officials. He also knew that Promploshchad offered a sufficient business with reasonable potential, if he could maintain it.

The requirement to maintain Promploshchad was therefore what primarily motivated Aleksandr, just as the survival of the Spine Centre through the certification process was what motivated Yurii, whose view of business conditions is influenced by his father's experience and his difficulties getting his own business started. Indeed, the same motivation was the daily priority for Viktor and Igor too. I argue that all these entrepreneurs viewed the arbitrary potential of the state and its bureaucrats with foreboding and did what they could to resist it to maintain their independence. This was at least as important as the growth of their businesses. Ironically, this meant that they had to take an interest in political power, even though they are all disparaging about the political system and devoted to separating themselves from it. That is, they had to develop a sense of their own prospects by constantly interpreting political economic conditions around them and do what they can to stay out of trouble. Thus, their observations and experiences of officialdom informed their activities far more than compliance with formal institutions. This did not mean that they necessarily broke the law, but the law was not a good guide to how they make decisions any more than the existence of law is a reliable guide to its enforcement. In other words, under conditions of institutional asymmetry these entrepreneurs' priorities reflected those of Oleg (Chapter 3) and Anna (Chapter 4) with respect to their ongoing effort to gain and maintain their independence from the state through entrepreneurship. This reinforces Yurchak's concept of entrepreneurship as a striving for 'civilised reality'.

What did Aleksandr specifically do to achieve his own civilised reality? He was devoted to minimising his interaction with officialdom and minding his own business. Yet he had to balance this ambition with the need to interact occasionally with officials in order to simply keep his business going and address administrative requirements. As I showed, his reluctance to do so until it became unavoidable was largely due to the injustices he suffered. However, this complicated his affairs when they could have been simpler. In this respect, I identified a tension between his desire for independence and the accompanying need to resist the state. Moreover, other individuals were acting according to their own interests on the baza, which meant that they impeded one another rather than working cooperatively. Kirill, for example, sought to make himself indispensable by damaging baza equipment that only he could repair, while Konstantin developed a ruse in which he could steal from Aleksandr, even though they worked for the same company and were friends. Moreover, by trying to avoid paying a bill, Aleksandr ended up in a situation in which he had to borrow money from one of his own tenants. The result of this type of cat and mouse behaviour, which have secondary consequences and bind these men to one another in a variety of informal ties, may yet be to antagonise officials, which explains why Aleksandr and Yurii were constantly scrambling to solve such problems. In other words, the drive for independence does not make personal relations less important but gives them a more instrumental form. I do not imply that personal relations are devalued or that Russian entrepreneurs are amoral. Rather, there is an essential impetus toward self-interest in a situation in which the economy is struggling, officialdom is overbearing and unpredictable and the future is difficult to foresee. Overall, Aleksandr and Yurii simply focus on immediate issues rather than more strategic plans, even though they have realistic and promising ambitions for the development of the baza and Spine Centre, respectively. Consequently, their business activities are defined by their unpredictability, even though their actual business is straightforward in principle.

It is striking that it was Yurii rather than Aleksandr who had conceptualised his entrepreneurial approach in terms of a Russian 'mentality' (which I interpreted as an effort to maximise one's freedom of action and assert control over one's affairs). It took a crisis for Aleksandr to distance himself from authority, whereas Yurii and his contemporaries took the necessity to do so for granted. This could reflect a greater sense of the risks facing businesses among younger entrepreneurs today than Aleksandr had prior to his crisis, having started in the 1990s. However, the younger entrepreneurs also reacted to this risk differently. Most of them associated the stability and longevity of their business – meaning independence – with distance from and avoidance of the state. However, Pavel, and Aleksandr (prior to his crisis) were prepared to associate themselves with officialdom in order to gain influence, even if they lost some independence. Pavel acknowledged corruption in the political economy but also embraced it; he was willing to do whatever it took to join the political economic elite, and it was revealing that, thus far, he was the most successful businessman. Unlike the other entrepreneurs, Pavel did not accept that corruption was bad but rather inevitable, so he reasoned that he might as well work within the system. Yurii and his other contemporaries rejected this, aiming for their own 'civilised reality'. It is telling that Pavel was not, like them, a true entrepreneur because he had not started his own business, but rather was an employee of an influential company. Thus, I argue that the drive for independence is (as I also found in Chapters 3 and 4), an essential element in contemporary Russian entrepreneurship. For Pavel, safe within a large company, the structure of the political economy could be enriching if he worked within the system. His view was that only by doing business for high stakes could the most important rewards be gained. This was out of kilter with the ambitions of the other entrepreneurs. They found the structure abhorrent and abused by elites but also saw themselves as powerless to intervene. As such, their entrepreneurship was focused on creating separation between themselves and the state while they tried to go about their business.

In this chapter, I have described Aleksandr and Yurii as ambitious but newly cautious entrepreneurs. They were experienced and capable but determined not to be victimised again. Unlike Oleg (Chapter 3), who had a degree of local control in his market and some certainty, or Anna (Chapter 4), who faced an uncertain future, Aleksandr and Yurii had to 'get by' relying on their wits and experience. In some ways, however, the crisis has been liberating for Aleksandr: he was no longer bound to forces he could not control and has the freedom to decide how to concentrate his efforts with the knowledge that crisis can be endured. Similarly, the frustration of daily business has not broken Yurii's determination. They both recognised the proximity of unpredictable state power to business and hold it in disdain but have resolved to continue. They feigned optimism about an improvement in business conditions and independently described that improvement as inevitable, but they have not the will to fight it like Anna (Aleksandr already fought for his survival) or capability to influence it in the way Oleg was attempting (he does not want to draw attention to himself again, while his past charity was unappreciated). Their path for now was to maintain and enhance their businesses in order to uphold their independence without attracting much attention.

Notes

1 Aleksandr's story made the local and regional press as it proceeded over many months through the courts. In addition to the account he related to me, I draw on some of those reports here but do not cite them to protect his anonymity.
2 Federal Law 214-FZ, 2004, 'On Participation in the Cost-Sharing Construction of Multi-Family Buildings and Other Real Estate Units, and on Amending Individual Legislative Acts of the Russian Federation' (see Rossiiskaya Gazeta 2004: online).
3 To be clear, Gorodstroi is not the real name of the MUP I describe here. MUPs are commercial organisations owned by the state, with economic autonomy but an obligation to pass their profits back to the state. MUPs are not permitted to sell or dispose of their property without the permission of their municipal authority (see Martinez-Vazquez et al. 2006: 21; Maggs et al. 1997: 51; Matantsev 1998: 443; Oda 2007: 78–9). As I explain later, Gorodstroi broke this law for the personal advantage of its staff.
4 Aleksandr was charged with violation of the law on joint construction, in addition to Article 159 of the Criminal Code (fraud committed on a large scale with the infliction of considerable damage by an individual using his official position) and Article 201 (abuse by a person performing administrative functions in commercial or other organisations resulting in grave consequences).
5 The justification for the ban on gambling was vague. It was suggested in one article that many gambling halls are owned and operated by Georgians; thus, the idea for a ban arose soon after the 2008 war with Georgia (see Antonov and Bomko 2009: online). Nevertheless, the ban was justified in moral terms, as Vasiliev and Bernhard put it in their study: 'the anti-gaming rhetoric we discovered revolved around classic themes such as deviant status of gambling and its alleged ties with organised crime, addiction and the protection of youth and other vulnerable social groups, the enforcement of class boundaries that protect the poor from gambling's temptation while allowing the rich to play if they are willing to pay and travel, and the protection of a morally sound Russian national identity' (2011: 81).
6 Russian authorities are entitled to block company accounts if tax returns are not returned on time (see, for example, Schneider Group no date: 19).
7 Yurii was broadly correct regarding pensioners but overestimated the number of state employees. Around one-third of the Russian population is currently pensioners (Piper 2015: online), and their number is forecast to grow: by 2020 there will be 100 workers for every 100 pensioners (*The Economist* 2012a: online). However, overall state employment has declined since 2000 to approximately 30 per cent in 2010 (although state employment in the oil and banking industries has increased) (Smolinski 2013: online).
8 Perhaps this is indeed the case. In a discussion by Connolly et al. it was argued that Western sanctions have had a limited impact (Connolly et al. 2015: 2).

6 Theoretical Implications

Rethinking Entrepreneurship in Russia's Political Economy

How can the observations I made in the course of fieldwork be theorised? Given that I cited numerous sources in Chapter 1 claiming that business conditions are hard, which theory can account for Oleg's apparently unusual entrepreneurial success? Which can account for why, in spite of all her problems, Anna did not give up as an entrepreneur? Which provides an explanation of why, after losing his successful business and going to prison, Aleksandr returned to start another company? As I show in this chapter, predominant theories of the Russian political economy cannot wholly answer such questions because they do not sufficiently represent the role and influence of private businesses. Rather, they consider the critical feature of the political economy to be what I describe as its 'hybridity', in which the state dominates the weak, vulnerable private sector. Undoubtedly, the central idea in hybrid theories is important: it is undeniable that my informants' primary motivation is to respond to the difficulties they associate with the state. At the same time, these theories place too much emphasis on the influence of the state over business and not enough on entrepreneurs' agency as I observed it. Indeed, the most obvious conclusion emerging from the case studies is that, although entrepreneurship is clearly difficult, entrepreneurs can survive and some, like Oleg, thrive. This has not been sufficiently explained in predominant theories, so in this chapter, I attempt to fill that conceptual gap.

I begin the chapter by reviewing the key examples of hybrid theories and show that they share a key limitation, specifically an implication that business is difficult, subordinate and vulnerable, drawing on macroeconomic evidence, policy and political analyses and anecdote. To the extent that they pay attention to business–state relations, a distinction is typically made between a dominant state and a weaker, vulnerable private sector. As Connolly has stated, the relationship between the two sectors is considered 'generally one-way' (2009: 186). This means empirical and theoretical research on the Russian political economy tends be self-reinforcing, leaving minimal impetus or incentive for observational studies of business and a misunderstanding of the role of the private sector in real business–state relations. Hybrid theories cannot account for the fact that the institutional environment does not prevent entrepreneurs from acting in their own interests, as described in the case

DOI: 10.4324/9780429469176-6

studies. My informants were not submissive to the state but exhibited a drive for independence from constraint, considerable freedom to act even when under pressure, the capabilities to change and influence their material and relational circumstances and to resist potential and actual interference. Having made this point, I return to limited access order (LAO) theory, which, in contrast, can both explain the arbitrary power of Russia's 'dominant coalition' (based on the need to limit violence among competing interests) and accommodate the specific role of the private sector (based on the study of the institutional constraints on businesses, like my case studies). In addition, LAO theory was not conceived for the Russian case alone, which means that I can treat Russia not as an exception but as subject to the same constraints as other developing countries, despite the pathologies particular to the Russian case that I have described.

Finally, I draw on the concept of 'entrepreneurial governmentality' to explain my informants' agency under LAO conditions. As North would recognise, I argue that it is the personalisation of the Russian state, rather than its dominance per se, which plays the most important role in determining entrepreneurial activities and outcomes. I also suggest that entrepreneurs represent a latent bloc of opposition to the political economic status quo: they are keenly aware of the challenges facing the development of the country and have the capacity (to greater or lesser extents, depending on their circumstances) to resist a predatory state. However, I note that any prospective unity to challenge the system is weakened by the individualism at the heart of their actions: while every entrepreneur knows their counterparts also resent the status quo, they resist it individually or within minor coalitions rather than working together, which would be a risk too far.

Entrepreneurship Is Missing in Predominant Theories of the Russian Political Economy

Gaddy and Ickes's 'rent management system' (RMS) is the pre-eminent articulation of what I have called hybridity in predominant theories of the Russian political economy. They argue that 'any examination of the Russian economy ought to take oil and gas as its starting point' (2010: 284). In the RMS, oil and gas rents are distributed between state-affiliated corporation owners, oligarchs, senior officials and important regional governors. The most important regions, cities and enterprises receive the most rent, which ensures social stability, while the need to pay rents and raise a profit ensures the oligarchs keep their rent-generating enterprises efficient and remain politically loyal (Gaddy and Ickes 2015: 19). Gaddy and Ickes's assertion that the Russian economy is 'addicted' to rents, thereby inhibiting the development of business, or more generally 'modernisation', has been a theme in their long-term work on the Russian economy (2002; 2005; 2013) and is widely accepted in the literature. Oxenstierna, for example, has made a direct link between rent addiction, the non-development of the private sector and institutions (2015: 109–110). While Connolly has clarified that the RMS is meant principally to illustrate 'the key factors that shape economic development' (2015: 11), and it is undisputed that resource industries are primarily responsible for Russia's economic growth under Putin, this has not limited Gaddy and Ickes's conclusions, including that the RMS is now inherent to Russia's political economic condition, irrespective of who holds power (2015: 26). In my view, this is too bold: first, it is not possible to test a claim about the future, and, more importantly, it relegates Russia's entrepreneurial sector to indefinite conceptual and empirical irrelevance, which my case materials refute.

In his study of Russia's prospects for modernisation, Jan Winiecki also concludes that Russia is over-dependent on mineral resource revenues (2012: 309), and the economic sphere is characterised by a strong state and a vulnerable private sector. Businesses, he argues, understand they are 'private until further orders from the government', and small- and medium-sized enterprises (SMEs) 'suffer from racketeering by mafia, the bureaucracy or (often) by both working in tandem' (Winiecki 2012: 313). He concludes that 'serious institutional and policy changes … seem to be beyond reach for political reasons' (Winiecki 2012: 314). This, he argues, will frustrate Russia's further development. Thus, Winiecki considers that business has a structurally subordinate role to the state in Russia's political economy. While I agree with these points in principle, as a study of business–state relations, it does not account for the agency I have observed among private-sector actors.

Similarly, Robinson has also argued that the state is the only actor strong enough to deliver change and meet the demands of post-Soviet Russian society and describes the political economy in terms of 'state capitalism' (2013a: 5–6). He uses the term tentatively, suggesting that there is an emerging trend toward 'the state asserting its right to be the arbiter of how property is distributed and to do this in opposition to outside interests if it chooses' (2009: 443) but that there is uncertainty about whether state capitalism is a specific form of political economy or just a project for realising 'developmental goals' (2013a: 5). He is also cautious, arguing that the term 'is frequently described as having latent properties as much as actual ones that can be analysed. This enables the analyst to impute characteristics to it without their fully being there' (Robinson 2013a: 5). All the same, I include state capitalism as a hybrid theory because such a model, in which the state is considered to be both actual and latent, is empirically problematic: if only the state (in both action and inaction) is a determinant variable, then the private sector is deemed to hold no influence. Hence, this theory does not allow for the influence my informants wield relative to the state either.

Bremmer has used the term 'state capitalism' more confidently. He argues that it is not a Russian or post-Soviet phenomenon but a general trend across the developing world (Bremmer 2009: 40). This has been endorsed by *The Economist* (2012c: online), which devoted a special edition to its worldwide emergence (2012b: online). According to Bremmer, 'the state functions as the leading economic actor and uses markets primarily for political gain' (Bremmer 2009: 41). Governments are not content to regulate the market but seek to use it 'to bolster their own domestic political positions' principally through national oil corporations, state-owned enterprises, privately owned national champions and sovereign wealth funds (Bremmer 2009: 42). He makes the case that, in Russia, 'any large business must have favourable relations with the state in order to succeed' (Bremmer 2009: 43), while close personal ties between the Kremlin and the bosses of these companies mean that politicians and bureaucrats are more closely bound to economic decision making than at any time since the Cold War (Bremmer 2009: 44). Conversely, the 'free-market tide' that began with the fall of the Soviet Union has receded (Bremmer 2009: 40–1). As *The Economist* states, state-backed companies account for over 60 per cent of the value of the Russian stock market (*The Economist* 2012c: online).

Although theories of state capitalism focus on macro-trends, there is no doubt that they are persuasive. Andrei Illarionov argued in 2006 that the Russian state had become 'corporatised' (2006: online), such that state-owned companies privatise their profits and nationalise their losses, driven by a corporate ideology in which privileges, subsidies, credits, powers and authority are offered to those who are '*nashi*' or 'ours' (Illarionov 2006: online). Simeon Djankov argues that state capitalism replaced crony capitalism in 2003 when Khodorkovsky was arrested and the state nationalised his shares in Yukos, which 'soured investor sentiment on the security of private property' (Åslund in Djankov 2015: 3). Thereafter, oligarchs were 'replaced at the heart of the economy by state-sector bureaugarchs' (*The Economist* 2012d: online). Since then, the state has dominated the economy. In 2015, 55 per cent of the economy was in state hands and so was nearly 30 per cent of the workforce, a higher proportion than in 1996 (Djankov 2015: 3). Nevertheless, despite the general effectiveness of this argument, I maintain that this concept demotes private business, and particularly entrepreneurship, to weakness and irrelevance: by definition, if big business is dependent upon the state, small business must be more dependent still.

Another influential model of hybridity is patrimonialism. According to Robinson, scholars differ over whether Russia is a 'patrimonial capitalist' state, or a 'neopatrimonial' state (Robinson 2011: 437). The former, which he endorses, occurs when traditionally patrimonial forms of political and economic organisation (in which power over the economy is personalised) are forced to undertake market reforms, instigated by external lenders or agencies (Robinson 2011: 436). In Russia, this has created a situation in which Putin must balance the tension between formal and informal institutions and the imposition of market rationality imposed by global price structures and trade flows. He must therefore govern by combining the logics of each of these demands, playing one off against the other as required (Robinson 2011: 437). Under these conditions, 'modernisation' or economic transition is hard to achieve because it would require a 'political break' that destroyed the elites' hold over the economy and an 'economic break' that introduced new actors that were 'powerful enough to supplant the elite and rewrite the political rules' (Robinson 2011: 438). To date, these breaks have not occurred. Indeed, Robinson has extended his analysis to argue that patrimonial capitalism is a post-Soviet tendency, categorising the political economies of Kazakhstan, Kyrgyzstan and Ukraine as well as Russia using this term (2013b). In these countries, elite groups are economically favoured, and their public legitimacy is based on elite agreement. The public accepts this as their 'economic order', such that 'legitimacy flows from other power-holders, not from the governed'. Hence, even if economic reform were mooted, it would suffer from 'collective action problems' (Robinson 2013b: 140). Clearly, the stability of patrimonial capitalism is derived, as with the RMS, from the ability of elites to secure income as loans or energy rents from foreign sources. Therefore, Robinson argues that only when this income starts to decline will political crises arise (2013b: 144). As a result, in this conceptualisation, the private sector is considered to be marginalised and would require elite intervention to develop. While I do not contend these conclusions, my case studies show that entrepreneurs develop their businesses without elite intervention, and, in contrast, elites need the private sector in order to develop and function too. Again, I find that a more nuanced conceptualisation is required.

Neopatrimonialism, in contrast, is determined not by external forces but the tension between Russia's traditional patrimonialism and its rational-legal institutions (Robinson 2011: 437). As Vladimir Gel'man has argued, drawing on North's work on institutions, the traditional patrimonial (informal) institutions trump the formal institutions of state. He states that specifically 'neopatrimonial political institutions' have been built to 'serve the interests of ruling groups in Russia and other post-Soviet states and consolidate their political and economic dominance', as opposed to formal institutions that would allow for a programme of Western-type modernisation (2016: 457). Oleksandr Fisun has made this argument particularly eloquently, arguing that 'in the neopatrimonial system, the ruling groups regard society as their own private domain, and the fulfilment of public functions as a legitimate means to their own personal enrichment' (Fisun 2012: 90). As with patrimonial capitalism, therefore, neopatrimonialism depicts the private sector as too weak to influence the structures that determine Russia's political and economic fate. As Fisun puts it, in a neopatrimonial system,

> The individual national leader controls the political and economic life of the country, and the personal cliental relationships with the leader play a crucial role in amassing personal wealth, or in the rise and decline of members of the political elite.
>
> (Fisun 2012: 91)

Nonetheless, this emphasis on the elite does not sufficiently allow for the material influence and resistance of private interests that my case studies revealed, so it has only partial explanatory value when considering the actual capacity and activities of businesses.

In Sutela's theory of a 'dual economy', another theory of hybridity, he perceives duality in three areas. First, Russia is so large that economic competition in remote areas is impossible on account of prohibitive transport costs, while other areas are integrated into international markets. Second, the Russian financial system is divided because households and SMEs rely on domestic financial institutions while the largest businesses operate internationally. Third, Russia's law on 'strategic sectors' exhibits dualism because these businesses are 'either owned or at least controlled to a degree deemed necessary by the state ... Those deemed of less importance are left to markets and private entrepreneurship' (2013: 64). Sutela, like Robinson, argues that the specific extent of dualism in the economy is unclear because the state cannot be clearly defined; one's affairs may not interest the Kremlin, but they could interest a regional official (Sutela 2013: 64), for example. This implies that the state's power is arbitrarily applied, and the role of officials in private enterprises varies significantly (Sutela 2012: 64–5). At the same time, the overwhelming strength of the state maintains the continual weakness and dependence of the private sector. Whether the state is dominant all of the time or not, its relative strength over the subordinate private sector is the key feature of this theory, which, like the other theories I have included in this section, means it does not give sufficient attention to the specific characteristics of the relationship between state and private sector.

Phillip Hanson has also conceived of a Russian 'dual economy' (2007: 869) but applies the term in a different way. He argues that dualism exists in the sense that the state, particularly the presidential administration (as opposed to policy makers), has taken a direct interest in some sectors of the economy, particularly but not exclusively oil and gas (Hanson 2007: 877–9) since the Yukos saga began in 2003 (Hanson 2007: 875–6). In some sectors, this intervention has done significant harm while in others, entrepreneurs have adapted 'in the belief that there is a viable framework of informal rules that they understand' (Hanson 2007: 887). Richard Sakwa has taken on Hanson's concept and argues that, under this system, market forces 'operate freely in the private sector, whereas in the state-controlled sector (but not necessarily state-owned) strategic development-oriented part of the economy, more dirigiste rules ... apply' (2013: 88). For Sakwa a dual state has been created in which patrimonial and legal-rational systems of domination exist in parallel and 'operate at the same time, reproducing dualism at all levels and allowing actors to operate elements of either but undermining the inherent internal logic of both' (Sakwa 2013: 69).

The work of Hanson and Sakwa is, again, persuasive and closely relates to the argument I made in Chapter 1, in which institutional asymmetry creates risks for the private sector, forcing entrepreneurs to adapt their behaviour. Moreover, in Sakwa's analysis of two cases of reiderstvo against private companies, one was successful and the other was not, leading him to conclude, carefully, that Russia does not have a 'prerogative state', but one 'trapped in the grey area between an administrative and a genuine constitutional state' (Sakwa 2013: 70). In his theory, therefore, Sakwa argues, unusually, that businesses *can* sometimes resist the state, which is reinforced by my findings. However, Sakwa, like Hanson, focuses upon the relationship between the state and *big* business; his work does not consider the role of ordinary entrepreneurs, so no insight is given to how small businesses can resist the state from their position of weakness. Indeed, as I have stated already, the absence of attention upon ordinary entrepreneurs is characteristic of all theories of how the Russian political economy is structured.

The final theory of hybridity I highlight is the idea that the Russian political economy is neofeudal or, as Inozemtsev describes it, a 'power vertical in which power is converted into money, and vice versa' (2011: online). Within this system, power can be bought, which means that the country is governed feudally at every level, overseen by President Putin himself and controlled dutifully by his friends and colleagues: 'All big national business is associated with the federal authorities or controlled by them; local entrepreneurs still try to bargain with regional bureaucracy' (Inozemtsev 2011: online). The hybridity in this theory is distinguished by the separation between those individuals with access to the 'vertical', and those without, who are forced to fend for themselves within their respective locales. Inozemtsev argues that this system, like the RMS, will endure because it would be 'totally illogical' for the political class to change it and because joining the system is so attractive to the rest who, like participants in a Ponzi scheme, believe being involved offers more chance of advancement than remaining outside (2011: online). Similarly, Shlapentokh and Arutunyan also describe Russian society as 'feudal', arguing that bureaucrats are able to turn their offices into fiefdoms, which become a source of enrichment not only for the individual but also for networks of his or her relatives and friends' (2013: 29). Like each of these theories, the idea of Russia as a feudal country is persuasive. Uniquely, the theory of feudalism foresees the possibility that individuals excluded from the vertical of power can become included in the system if they pay. Nonetheless, the possibility that private sector actors may have their own agenda, may reject the system itself or indeed wield their own influence independent of the state is not considered.

Overall, despite some differences over the nature of the Russian regime, these theories share the view that the political economy takes a hybrid form (except Sakwa, who argues that some big businesses have been able to resist the state, although he gives no attention to the type of small businesses I studied) and overly reduce the role of the private sector. My case studies show that the private sector is indeed comparatively weak, but entrepreneurs are able to endure, achieve a genuine level of independence that belies their vulnerable position and undertake activities that resist and undermine the state, so an improved conceptualisation is required.

Russia as a Limited Access Order

In this section, I follow North et al. (2013a: 332) and Connolly (2009) to claim that Russia's political economy is better described as an LAO. Unlike hybrid theories, the LAO concept was not developed for Russia alone and can, uniquely, accommodate both the relative power of the state and its actual (rather than conceptual) relationship with business. As I set out in Chapter 2, LAOs are one of three 'orders' within a typology developed by

North et al. to understand the way political, economic and social forces in developing countries interact (North et al. 2013b: 1).[1] They define it as follows:

> [An LAO] … creates limits on access to valuable political and economic functions as a way to generate rents. Rents are created both by limits on access to resources and functions – like worship, trade, education and warfare – and by limiting access to forms of social organization that larger society will support. Powerful individuals possess privileges and rents, and since violence threatens or reduces those rents, the risk of losing the rents can make it in the interests of powerful individuals and groups to cooperate with the coalition in power rather than to fight. Privileged individuals have privileged access to social tools enabling them, and only them, to form powerful organizations. In limited access orders the political system manipulates the economy to create rents as a means of solving the problem of violence'.
>
> (North et al. 2007: 3)

LAOs are governed by a 'dominant coalition' that manipulates the country's economic interests to create rents so that the most powerful members of society are persuaded to refrain from violence (North et al. 2007: 3–5). According to Connolly, the Russian state wields less control over the economy than its Soviet predecessor but remains in control of the main sources of revenue, which enable it to 'suppress any potential sources of economic and political power' (2009: 200). Moreover, these economic sectors are accessible only by insiders through patronage networks, so the involvement of outsiders remains limited (Connolly 2009: 200). In this way, the primary objective of Russia's dominant coalition is explained by its motivation to minimise a constant threat from internal or external challengers. It follows that economic performance depends upon how these threats are handled (Díaz-Cayeros 2013: 236). Ordinarily, the solution is not efficient in terms of the organisation of economic activity, but such arrangements are required to ensure some economic accumulation. North et al. point out that removing rents would not result in a competitive market economy but 'a society in violence and disorder' (2013b: 7). This makes LAOs stable to the extent that they can minimise violence, but 'second best in terms of productivity and growth' (Díaz-Cayeros 2013: 236). It is therefore important to recognise that LAO theory does not work within the framework of modernisation, which accounts for the failure of Putin's modernisation initiatives I described in Chapter 1. Rather, 'dualism' is a typical economic feature in an LAO, described as follows:

> Many LAOs today have dualistic economies, with a domestic economy governed by domestic rules and institutions and international enclaves run by a separate set of rules and institutions, modeled on and enforced by foreign OAOs … Participation in the enclave of the global economy, with access to international capital and secure property rights, gives third

> world elites opportunities to prosper without having to alter their domestic LAO institutions that produce security and that sustain their rents.
> (North et al. 2007: 39–40)

Dualism explains the motivation of the Russian elite (dominant coalition) to maintain political and economic power and the ongoing weakness of the private sector, which is the central feature in hybrid theories. However, unlike hybrid theory, LAOs do not assume the private sector is dependent on the state. Rather, LAOs exist on a spectrum 'differentiated by the structure of their organizations' (North et al. 2013b: 10–11) so must be examined to determine the specific 'mechanisms and institutions' by which they sustain private organisations and what motivates members of the dominant coalition to respect them (2007: 44). North et al. demand that the characteristics of the relationship between the dominant coalition and the private sector is investigated, and specifically its 'institutional matrix', as I have done in the case study chapters.[2] Overall, LAO theory provides a better framework for accommodating the relative strength of the Russian state and the influence of the private sector demonstrated by my informants. It recognises the importance of understanding how institutions work at the level of individuals and the real economy.

Entrepreneurial Governmentality in Russia's Limited Access Order

I now explain my informants' agency within the LAO framework by drawing on the idea of entrepreneurial governmentality. I start by observing that in each case study, 'the state' was manifest in a personalised rather than bureaucratic form. According to Yurchak, personal rather than formal relations between the state and entrepreneurs are significant because the state itself has been partially privatised by its own officials (2002: 312). Business has developed according to the same pattern, whereby personal rather than formal relations take precedence. The hybridity of the state means that entrepreneurs are not the only actors behaving entrepreneurially: in my case studies, regional elites, officials and criminals all did so too, which means that the boundary between the state and private sector breaks down in the real economy. As I show now, predominant theories of hybridity, which divide the stronger state and weaker private sector, look less convincing compared to Yurchak's idea that the state itself operates in hybrid form. It becomes clear that the role of the state in the business sphere is rarely experienced as a faceless bureaucracy but takes a *personal* form which requires a particular, personal response.[3]

In the first case study, Oleg's entrepreneurial approach was based on the need to 'get by' drawing on his social capital, which he did with success, building a profitable business and avoiding external interference for over two decades. Three specific capabilities explain this success. First, he knew his local competitors and worked with them to achieve shared control over supplying their market by developing a minor coalition. This functions according to the logic of limited access by reducing the potential for violence and interference over members' profit sources. It differs from the logic of the dominant coalition, which is focused on securing shared control over rent sources, but the point is that in a situation in which Oleg and his competitors are all vulnerable, they have joined forces to remove one aspect of that vulnerability, which is each other. Second, Oleg has a distinctly pragmatic approach to business relations. He recognises that the business sphere is not occupied exclusively by entrepreneurs but includes officials, the mafiya and others, so he works to develop cordial relations with them all. Third, Oleg and his team are dedicated to asserting and displaying control within the business and in their external relations as a way of promoting the seriousness and credibility of the business. This serves as a deterrent to potential aggressors and shows that Sibtekhnika staff are willing and able to get their work done effectively, know what they are doing and can resist potential interference. The aim is to show that they are not pushovers. Oleg and his team aim to show every day that they mean business, in both senses of the term. These are the characteristics of his 'entrepreneurial governmentality': he is willing to create better conditions to do business. Oleg's case shows that it is not enough to say that an entrepreneur survives by using his or her social capital. Rather, his success is associated with his particular attitude towards what is possible under local conditions and how, in particular, he deployed his social capital. The basis of his relative success, I therefore argue, is his appreciation of how to behave in a situation in which the state operates in a personalised form. This was exemplified in his work in remote Tsentralnyi with Valentina and Volodya. While they were members of the local dominant coalition, they sought to establish strong personal relations with Oleg and his team, who could provide them with resources unavailable elsewhere. Thus, relations between 'the state' and 'private sector' were not 'one way', as hybrid theories assume, but required cordiality and mutual interest. Valentina and Volodya secured their retail equipment while Oleg gained important regional contacts, an opportunity to pitch for further sales to Tsentralnyi's state budget holders and a large contract to refurbish their shops free from competition.

Furthermore, it is striking that the Sibtekhnika team's first priority is not the growth of the business per se. Rather, their effort was focused on creating the conditions and nurturing the relationships to make business possible. This is reinforced by considering the time and investment Oleg gave to the Cooperative, where his purpose was normative (to change local attitudes and create independent thinkers) rather than commercial. The Cooperative represented a personal, if surreptitious, challenge to the state and the logic of limited access. It shows that Oleg resists the vulnerability that is a feature of life outside the dominant coalition. Indeed, Oleg did not seek only independence but was also dedicated through his daily activities within Sibtekhnika to resisting predation and in the Cooperative to denying the state a monopoly on education and ideas. Abu-Lughod has argued that, when ethnographers encounter 'resistance' in their informants' activities, they should ask what it indicates 'about the forms of power that they are up against' (Abu-Lughod

1990: 47). I find that the Russian political economy is less determined by structure than by the agency of individuals and groups operating according to the logic of limited access. Entrepreneurs do not have access to the rents that are distributed among the dominant coalition, so they must seek to maximise their own interests. This observation underlines the value of studying entrepreneurship ethnographically: an attitudinal study may have captured Oleg's principled opposition to a political economy in which he is structurally vulnerable, but it would not have observed the activities he undertakes to do business and live well and create his own 'civilised reality' (see Yurchak 2002: 313), which includes certain activities that take the form of resistance. This finding may also go some way towards explaining why small business entrepreneurs tend to remain unattached to state-affiliated business organisations (see Chapter 1): they see little value in lobbying and prefer to focus on their own circumstances without drawing attention to their activities.

In the second case study, Anna was inspired by her academic understanding of the problems facing entrepreneurs in Russia, which motivated her to establish CSBG. This understanding, which was determined by her perception that the Russian economy was in transition, was misplaced. She did not prove to be an effective businessperson by the Western standards she aspired to, and this precipitated her crisis. However, if we put aside the fact that she probably defrauded her clients and concentrate on her attitudes and behaviours, that crisis also led to a significant change in her entrepreneurial approach. In desperation, she began to work almost entirely in the shadow economy and hid her income within two multilevel marketing (MLM) companies. By participating in MLM, she appeased one member of the group to whom she was indebted by working for him and gained access to material resources that enabled her to reduce her debt in kind. Her piecemeal work for the banker also enabled her to re-establish personable relations with him, reduce her liabilities and limit his influence with her accusers and the prosecution service. She then coopted the state's rhetorical support for business as a material resource in her self-defence, and she focused her appeal on the individuals she judged were most influential. By continuing her seminar programme, she also maintained her profile as an advocate for reform. In this sense, her business was ideally placed for a fight against her accusers: it is, after all, rather awkward to launch a case against a company that argues for business reform. As such, Anna used herself as an exemplar of the problems in business she had long fought against. Of course, she would have rather made money from these seminars, but in the context of her crisis, she was well placed. Most impressively, when her appeal to the presidential administration received a reply, it had a significant effect by fortifying in her a sense of righteousness and acting as a deterrent against rash interventions by her accusers and prosecution service officials. In these respects, the personal rather than procedural aspects of her defence were the most effective. By devoting such effort to defending herself, furthermore, Anna demonstrated the seriousness of her appeal and refusal to accept defeat, which conventional hybrid theories assume would be inevitable in the face of a dominant state. Considered from the perspective of limited access, Anna succeeded in reducing others' capacity for violence, and she became a better entrepreneur. In other words, she became focused on handling circumstances as they were rather than as she wished them to be, which is indicative of effective entrepreneurial governmentality.

Like Oleg, much of Anna's entrepreneurial effort was not to make a profit but to create the conditions in which she could continue in business and live an independent life. Indeed, this was her original purpose in business: she founded CSBG to promote the Western business norms in Russia, which is as normative an objective as it is commercial. However, unlike Oleg, who has kept his normative agenda to himself, Anna publicly stood for the change she wanted to see, which was brave but naive, providing ammunition for her accusers. However, it was not this objective that caused her problems because, after all, the government publicly shares these objectives. Rather, her trouble stemmed from her simple inability to make the business work in commercial terms. Indeed, most entrepreneurs (like Oleg) have grasped that small businesses are vulnerable and that the government is not supporting them, so attendance dwindled at Anna's seminars and demand for her other services fell (although her occasional seminars did survive into the crisis and advanced her normative objectives). However, if Anna's formal business reveals the weakness of her 'entrepreneurial governmentality' before the crisis, her ability to survive the crisis and resist her accusers reveals how much she had improved as an entrepreneur. What had previously been a naive belief in the support of the state for the development of business suddenly became useful in her defence. Her argument that the state had said it supported business and, therefore, must support hers (even though she had proved to be a poor businesswoman) and her faith in the essential benevolence of the president (even though her business is of no concern to him) may yet, ironically, provide the means for her to exit the crisis and retain her freedom. Overall, Anna had always wanted to change the status quo for businesses as much as 'do business' herself. That she has not run away from her mistakes and sought to earn the money to repay her accusers is testimony to her integrity in this regard. In the end, her entrepreneurship resembles Oleg's to the extent that he was dedicated to achieving an independent life in spite of the difficulty and resisting the vulnerability that came with that decision.

The third case study began with a textbook example of reiderstvo, in which officials used their formal position for personal gain. Prior to that event, Aleksandr had assumed that he was working in partnership with officials. When he later realised, or admitted to himself, that they intended to strip the assets from his business, it was too late. This had a significant effect on Aleksandr's entrepreneurial approach, but it did not deter him or his son Yurii from entrepreneurship. Rather, Aleksandr emerged from prison shaken but soon started a new business even though he could have worked for someone else, returned to state employment or left the country. Therefore,

Aleksandr's case reveals again that, despite the weakness of the private sector, vulnerability in itself has not deterred my informants from entrepreneurship. Rather, entrepreneurship represents a choice to create the conditions to live as one wishes in spite of the difficulties of doing so and a choice they willingly make over any other vocation. His son, Yurii, who followed current affairs closely, also took this view. His opinion that the state cares only about oil and gas and that business is unimportant echoes predominant theories of hybridity. Yet, neither Aleksandr nor Yurii are helpless, and they took action to change their entrepreneurial approach. Aleksandr's relentless energy testifies to his determination not to make the same mistakes again. Whereas, before the crisis, he had prioritised business development, which led him into the deal with local officials, afterwards his concern was to avoid contact with them as much as possible. Although he highlighted the development of the baza as his foremost business objective, he and Yurii spent most of their time trying to avoid and resist officialdom or dealing with the consequences of doing so. In other words, Aleksandr and Yurii might say that they are victims of a state that neglects and destroys business, but they have stayed in business and refuse to yield to their vulnerable situation.

Indeed, Aleksandr and Yurii spend many hours trying to deal with minor crises associated with avoiding officials or gaining the upper hand in personal deals instead of business development. This reinforces Yurchak's point, which I have now made with respect to each informant, that their objective is to create suitable conditions (civilised reality) for their own business. This observation is enhanced further when considering life on the baza, where several entrepreneurs work together. Unlike Oleg's situation, in which a minor coalition organises resources and ensures cooperation to limit outsiders' access to the market, Aleksandr and his tenants are entwined in a complicated game of one-upmanship in which each entrepreneur seeks to maximise their own interests. Aleksandr's tenant, Kirill, damaged the hot water system only he knew how to fix in order to get the job of fixing it. Likewise, Vyacheslav claimed he could not pay rent, even though he had just bought a house, but offered to fix the fence instead. Similarly, when Aleksandr realised that he could not pay the electricity bill because his bank account had been blocked as punishment for delaying payment, he had to borrow money from another of his tenants. The tenant could hardly say no: his business needed an electricity supply. Even Konstantin, Aleksandr's lawyer, conspired to take a personal cut from the fees for the judicial process in which he was representing Aleksandr. Thus, even in this situation, in which each entrepreneur is partly reliant on the others due to their shared location on the baza, each still behaves according to the logic of 'entrepreneurial governmentality': their priority is to advance their personal interests according to opportunities they perceive in a business sphere in which access is limited. Conversely, although the crisis did not deter Aleksandr and Yurii from entrepreneurship, it did provoke in them a determination not to seek change beyond their own circumstances. Whereas Oleg and Anna sought to change the character of Russia's political economic system, Aleksandr and Yurii were resigned to defending their marginal position within it and taking their chances. Aleksandr's overwhelming priority was to support his family; he lost many friends during the crisis as they distanced themselves from him, and he has stopped supporting the local charities to which he contributed in the past. His view was that if the state and society cannot support him when he is doing well, then he was hardly going to make new efforts now. Instead, the state must be resisted. Yurii argued that political change was inevitable and 'revolution' could be months away but, revealingly, believed it was up to Russia's next dominant coalition to bring it about rather than the likes of him. Overall, both men prioritised protecting their own position to do business.

A Reconceptualisation of Entrepreneurship in Russia's Political Economy

I have argued that entrepreneurial governmentality explains the determination of my informants to pursue a civilised reality of their own in spite of significant challenges. In this section, I elaborate on my (perhaps controversial) claim that their entrepreneurship also took a form of resistance to the state. In their marginal but determined position, entrepreneurs appear to occupy a similar place to Russia's historical intelligentsia. It has been questioned whether the intelligentsia still exists in post-Soviet Russia (Kochetkova 2010: 36), but their basic role as a distinct social group with particular resistance to conformity, a drive for freedom and independence from the political elite bears comparison with my informants' outlook (see Berlin 1978: 133; Kochetkova 2010: 13). Like the intelligentsia, these entrepreneurs view state power as overbearing, bemoaning its malign influence, and seek to avoid and resist the regime as they encounter it. Likewise, they consider themselves an enlightened (or at least hardened) persecuted political minority whose views contradict those of most Russians, particularly those working for the state, who are content with the status quo. Like the intelligentsia, they also see themselves as patriots, seeking the best for Russia on behalf of wider, less progressive society. In this respect, they reserve for themselves a special status as a persecuted but conscientious and determined minority, able to diagnose the country's problems but unable to change them, although this does not prevent them from attempting to improve local conditions for those around them (Kochetkova 2010: 17). Also like the intelligentsia, they are affiliated not by formal associations but shared values and outlook; as such, they cannot be considered an organised opposition, rather a distinct social group. Finally, they occupy a unique social position in contemporary Russia: vulnerable but independent, politically conscious but isolated, aware of the country's potential and with practical knowledge but lacking organisation. (Russia's main business associations, after all, are created or coopted by the state.) In these respects, it is no surprise that Anna and Aleksandr are former academics, although entrepreneurship is not only for the elites: before starting in business, Aleksandr worked in a factory. Entrepreneurship appears less a mere vocation and more a conscious lifestyle for those seeking independence and resistance under conditions of limited access. As Berlin wrote on the intelligentsia, 'they [were] a persecuted minority who drew strength from their very persecution; they were the self-conscious bearers of a Western message' (Berlin 1978: 144).

If this analogy seems too much, however, it is still indisputable that my informants are opposed to and determined, when possible, to quietly resist the conditions they encounter. The kind of quiet resistance my informants undertake is what Scott has called 'infrapolitics', a hidden or 'subterranean world of political conflict which [has] left scarcely a trace in the public record' (Scott 2012: 113), constituted by small acts undertaken over time, which cannot change the status quo but form 'a politics which "dare not speak its name", a diagonal politics, a careful and evasive politics that [avoids] dangerous risks' (Scott 2012: 113). As he states, infrapolitics is the 'prevailing genre of day-to-day politics for most of the world's disenfranchised, for all those living in autocratic settings' (Scott 2012: 113). I find it reasonable to see my informants' efforts to counter the state as infrapolitical. Infrapolitics is persuasive because it emphasizes the hidden or underhand character of the resistance I interpreted in my informants' activities. However, it is also quite a loose political term, and a more specific theoretical explanation of their agency is required. What does it actually mean to say that resistance is part of my informants' entrepreneurship? What makes these actions specifically resistant? One effective response is to draw a comparison with employment in an OAO. In a stable institutional environment, entrepreneurs do not have to be concerned about the arbitrary intervention of state officials. To be precise, their businesses and organisations can rely upon the rule of law, and their commercial success is largely the result of their own initiative and effort. In Russia's LAO, however, entrepreneurs start their businesses knowing they could be ruined not only by their own failures but the intervention of others. This is the essence of why my informants choose, by necessity, varying paths of resistance. Clearly, some of my informants' resistance is more pronounced than others. Among the young entrepreneurs I encountered in Normalnyi, for example, each made a personal assessment of the extent to which their actions were constrained and had arrived at different conclusions about how to respond. Thus, the resistance I encountered was not uniform, and it changed over time. For instance, Aleksandr was clearly not the same risk taker after he lost his construction business but, on the other hand, was more determined not to lose out again, so he constantly resists engagement with state organs and officials today.

This explanation does not, however, fully explain why my informants chose the risk-prone entrepreneurial path. In considering this, I have found a counterfactual useful. Suppose, for instance, that I had a secure job in an OAO. Over time, I established myself in my place of work, and, even though I am not satisfied with every aspect of the job, I consider the costs of leaving detrimental to my income and career trajectory. In this respect, I consider the costs of exit to be high. In this situation, my priority, therefore, is to minimise career risk and carry on, knowing I can cope with the everyday annoyances of my work. Moreover, even the prospect of greater independence and potentially higher earnings as an entrepreneur does not convince me to deviate from the role I already have. In my informants' cases, this kind of thinking does not apply. As entrepreneurs in Russia's LAO, the costs of exit are low while the costs of staying are potentially high: as I have shown, they could have returned to their pre-business careers in research or the factory or left the country, but they chose to stay in risk-prone employment and did so for non-commercial reasons. This is not to say that resistance is declared or the same in each case. They did not become entrepreneurs to fight with officials, and they would rather not have to. It is both undeclared but necessary to secure their position. Evidently, in some cases, like those of Oleg and Anna, this activity goes further still towards trying to change the local political economic situation more to their liking.

Summary

In this chapter, I claimed that hybrid theories cannot account for my informants' agency because they emphasise the dominance of the state over the private sector. I argued that LAO theory could, in contrast, accommodate both the relative power of Russia's dominant ruling elite in the economy and, through an examination of formal and informal institutions, provide a better account of the specific role of the private sector and business–state relations. My case studies, which were an examination of how entrepreneurs 'get by' in conditions of institutional asymmetry, provided empirical material to achieve this. I found that my informants' success was defined by what they understood was possible and what they did in response to their unpredictable situations, as opposed to the 'Western' understanding of entrepreneurship, in which profit is the main objective. I drew on entrepreneurial governmentality to conceptualise this. I also argued that my informants became and stayed entrepreneurs precisely *not* to be subordinate to the state: they knew or learnt the risks and went into or stayed in business anyway, seeking independence from the state and knowing that they would have to be resistant to it along the way. In practice, my informants were effective when they put their personal interests first and made the best of their own relationships. Indeed, their success was based on their ability to deal with (and literally make deals with) all the characters operating in the private sector, which, due to the hybridity of the state, includes officials, criminals and others acting in their personal interests too. Critically, this means relations between the dominant coalition (officials, powerful local figures, etc.) and entrepreneurs are not necessarily antagonistic. Rather, cordial relations based on mutual interests can be created because many of the resources required and sought by elites can only be sourced in the private sector. In this way, the private sector is not simply weak compared to the dominant coalition but essential to it.

Notes

1 LAOs may be seen in contrast to open access orders (OAO), which, like Western societies, 'use competition and institutions to make it in the interests of political officials to observe constitutional rules, including constitutional control over all organisations with the potential for major violence' (North et al. 2007: 4).

2 Yakovlev (2015) attempted to examine the Russian private sector using the LAO framework in a study assessing the prospects for an improved business climate in the country. He postulated that Russia's dominant coalition could become more stable and bring about long-term growth following the 2008–09 crisis if it took steps to integrate new (medium-sized) business interests into the dominant coalition. He argued that the government had a genuine will to achieve this by enhancing the status of business associations, but this was not welcomed by the siloviki (in his view the leading group in the dominant coalition), who stood to lose rent and power and whose position was also strengthened as a result of their clamp down on the mass protests of 2011 (Yakovlev 2015: 62, 74). He concluded that the involvement of medium-sized business could strengthen the stability of the dominant coalition, but this had not yet happened (Yakovlev 2015: 74). I counter that this conclusion is satisfactory in principle, but his methodological approach leads him to assume that businesses within Russia's already-existing LAO are of one mind, would be willing to be coopted into state-affiliated business organisations and would be willing to join the dominant coalition. Like the majority of studies of Russian business, and indeed predominant theories of 'hybridity', his assumptions are based on the idea that the private sector is dependent on the dominant coalition without reference to empirical data. As I have claimed, a methodology based on policy analysis cannot provide an accurate understanding of what businesses are doing in Russia. It is also unclear which businesses he is describing because 'business' is analysed as a single entity. Also, like all the theorists cited in this chapter, he does not focus on small businesses or entrepreneurs. Hence, the conditions on which it/they might join a dominant coalition is unknown.

3 These observations are reinforced by the only recent empirical study of regional state–business relations I have found (Ledyaev and Chirikova 2019), which is based on extensive interview data in five small Russian towns and concluded that 'businessmen solved their problems by negotiating with the local authorities on an informal basis, believing that they could survive on their own. This is peculiar not only to those who are directly connected with local authorities and enjoy their explicit patronage but also to businessmen who seek to ensure the safety of their business in the face of systemic risks (including the risks coming from the activities of the state and municipal structures) and maintain the status quo' (2019: 20).

7 Conclusion

In this book, my objective was to find out how Russian entrepreneurs get by in conditions of institutional asymmetry. To achieve this, I chose an ethnographic case study approach, which, unlike a majority of studies of Russian business, offers a method for understanding both attitudes and behaviours. Above all, I found that the prospect of starting a business in the face of substantial prospective difficulties was not enough to deter these individuals from doing so, and they were prepared to continue despite ongoing risk or dangerous crises. Put another way, the prospect of resisting officialdom and losing everything was outweighed by the chance of gaining a more independent life. In this chapter, I first set out four key findings and then offer thoughts on their implications.

Overall Conclusions

1. *Conditions for Russian entrepreneurs remain difficult despite the government's long-running policy to support business development.*

In Chapter 1, I showed that entrepreneurs' perceptions of business conditions in contemporary Russia have been well studied, and it is widely accepted that entrepreneurs face numerous difficulties despite longstanding government initiatives to reduce them. My first and most obvious conclusion is that this research underlines the continuance of these difficulties. My informants' experiences, particularly those of Anna and Aleksandr, reveal such difficulties very clearly. Aleksandr's experience shows that even the most successful entrepreneurs are vulnerable to predation by aggressors or officials at any time. Anna's crisis shows that even though she has almost nothing worth acquiring, her accusers take advantage of her weakness to threaten and intimidate her, and a legal case against her rolls interminably on. As a woman, she was in a particularly weak position, coupled with her high regard for the West. Moreover, even though Oleg runs a successful company, his daily activities are as focused on pre-empting and overcoming problems as they are on developing the business. Ledeneva's concept of 'suspended punishment' accurately describes the situation for private businesses irrespective of one's

DOI: 10.4324/9780429469176-7

commercial success, which shows the government's long-term policy of support for business has been more rhetorical than substantial.

2. *Despite the difficulties and vulnerabilities encountered by businesses, my informants can act in their own interests. This challenges predominant theories about the structure of the political economy.*

Each of my informants recognises their vulnerability to officials and other aggressors, whether as a result of personal experience (in the cases of Anna and Aleksandr) or because of the danger they perceive in the political economy (in the case of Oleg). However, they can all act (to lesser or greater extents) to limit this vulnerability and advance their interests. Indeed, they devote the majority of their time not to commercial imperatives but to limiting violence and creating the conditions in which to do business. To conceptualise this, I drew on 'entrepreneurial governmentality', which is a way of knowing and acting in a business environment in which the state takes a personalised form. I found that entrepreneurship must be explained not as a conventional vocation in business but as an understanding of what can be achieved in one's particular circumstances, building relations with others operating in the private sector (including other entrepreneurs, criminals and state representatives) in order to limit violence and achieve commercial objectives. Their success at getting by without formal institutional support, whether surviving a crisis in the case of Anna or thriving in regional business in the case of Oleg, leads me to challenge the assumption in predominant political economic theories that entrepreneurs are necessarily subordinate to the state, even if they are relatively weaker. Their agency must be accounted for in theory.

3. *LAO theory provides a better explanation of how the political economy works in practice, accounting for relative strength of the state and allowing for the entrepreneurial agency I observed.*

I have argued that the Russian political economy resembles an LAO in which dominant elites share privileged access to strategic resources and act arbitrarily in the real economy, which is the key reason entrepreneurship remains challenging. By examining the dynamics of state–business relations from the perspective of businesses, I have developed understanding of Russia's institutional framework. I have found that relations between elites, state representatives and entrepreneurs are determined by the need to limit violence or advance individual interests in the context of a personalised official sphere. This means that relations are not necessarily antagonistic. Moreover, elites are dependent on the private sector more than entrepreneurs are on the state, so relations cannot be defined by a zero-sum game, as hybrid theories presume. I consider this finding to be an indictment of the idea of 'modernisation', which the Russian government promotes in policy and which is commonly taken seriously in academic research on the Russian political economy. As North et al. argue, 'thinking of developing countries as limited access orders with their own social dynamic rather than as flawed or incomplete open-access societies affords new insights into the impediments and paths to development' (North et al. 2013a: 328). Even though 'modernisation' has an important role in Russian history, from an ethnographic perspective I argue that the concept contains little meaning in contemporary Russia with respect to the improvement of business conditions.

4. *Because vulnerability overshadows the private sector, it follows that entrepreneurs start businesses not simply for commercial reasons but to live autonomously and, to varying degrees, resist the state.*

On his company website, Oleg has written an unusual introductory phrase: 'Sibtekhnika reflects the most significant events of the history of perestroika in Russia, since the firm was founded in 1991 when the whole country was faced with a choice: how to live?' In my view, this unusual phrase reveals the importance of distinguishing between conventional ideas about what an entrepreneur is, associated with Russian transition or modernisation policies (see Chapter 1), and what entrepreneurship actually is, as I encountered and described it. Entrepreneurship, I found, is an attitude and set of practices undertaken in spite of the difficulty of business. Thus, even though each of my informants holds the view that the structure of the political economy limits their chances in business, they still chose to become or remain entrepreneurs. This is the case even when they encountered life-changing crises (in the case of Anna and Aleksandr). Like Yurchak, I found that Russia's entrepreneurs are motivated not simply by money but by a life separate from the state.

Still, the pursuit of an independent life does not do full justice to my informants' rejection of and challenges to the political economic status quo. Entrepreneurs are the group most aware of the inequity and problems of the political economy resulting from dominant elites' influence over the rest of the country. To this extent, they are de facto opponents of the political system. My evidence for this claim is clear: Anna went into business to advance Western commercial values and came to perceive her crisis as emblematic of that requirement. More specifically, because her business is indebted and unlikely to enrich her in the future, her decision to endure the crisis (instead of filing for bankruptcy, she chose to work her way out of it and face up to her mistakes) represents a challenge to the state to honour its policies and is certainly a personal mission. Aleksandr's decision to return to business following his imprisonment is also defiant. Moreover, his determination not to be undermined again reveals his ambition to develop a career on his own terms, even if this inconveniences him from time to time. Oleg's company, Sibtekhnika, is successful because he and his staff have created a business that works with the grain of the local political economy: he is devoted to limiting violence and cooperating wherever possible with all the characters operating in the local market. On the other hand, the Cooperative, his social entrepreneurial project, is focused on providing services, opportunities and an ideology that the state does not. Overall, my informants hold the view that the political economy functions counter to their interests, and they choose to resist it quietly when the necessity or opportunity arises.

Implications

Overall, my modest hope is that this study has been of interest to readers intrigued by life in contemporary Russia. Perhaps the determination and capabilities of Oleg, Anna and Aleksandr serve to challenge the persistent stereotype that Russians are apathetic or subordinate in the facc of their officials and leaders. More ambitiously, I believe the following implications can be drawn. First, it is likely that Russian business conditions will remain as challenging as they are now for at least the duration of the Putin presidency. There is no reason to think that new intitiatives to improve business conditions will be more effective than they have been until now. Rather, the Russian government's support for business, an important element within its 'modernisation' policy agenda, is largely inconsequential and, apparently, serves as a rhetorical device rather than a substantive set of measures. Were this policy effective, the positive influence of formal institutions on my informants' activities would have been significant; however, I found the opposite to be the case. Russian policy towards business and its business associations should be treated with greater scepticism: improving business conditions is not a question of articulating the 'right' policy, as if the current policy is wrong. Rather, the point is to recognise that current policy has not improved my informants' conditions in business because it has not been implemented formally by the dominant coalition.

Second, the conclusions do provide greater impetus to study Russia's regions rather than focusing on European Russia, as is often the case. The justification is simple: my conclusions show that policy made in Moscow is not a strong indicator of actual political economic activity in practice, so while Moscow is an easy research option, it is hardly the most interesting. At the same time, even though Siberia is an inhospitable, enormous territory and its population relatively small, which together renders business particularly challenging, my informants' experiences in business are not extraordinary given what is known about Russian business in general: 'suspended punishment' is the defining feature of everyday life in Siberia too. Accordingly, I contend that, although Siberia may be considered exceptional in many respects – home to many of the country's resources and with an outdated and much-unreconstructed Soviet infrastructure and economy – the notion that it is a mere 'resource colony' or incapable of market reform is better suited to capturing the academic imagination than revealing much about what is actually happening in the market. I therefore suggest that further research be completed in Siberia in order to draw the region in closer from the analytical cold, treating it as a normal part of the Russian political economy.

Finally, I believe these conclusions offer value to multidisciplinary scholars and analysts considering a range of tangible issues facing contemporary Russia. They are especially relevant to political economists, showing, in particular, the importance of attention on the real economy. They may also interest political scientists, for whom the autonomy and resistance of my informants will be particularly interesting 20 years into Putin's rule, even though it is often assumed that the large majority of the Russian public support the Putin government and that opposition figures are weak and divided. The idea that entrepreneurs may represent a significant if hidden bloc of opposition to the state offers an intriguing research proposal and, as I proposed in Chapter 6, may be considered further in comparison to Russia's intelligentsia, through the lens of 'infrapolitics' or, indeed, alongside Russia's other better-known opposition groups. Finally, by revealing entrepreneurs as vulnerable and marginalised but with specific group characteristics (which I likened to the intelligentsia), this study will be of relevance to sociologists considering the structure of society in the Putin era. In addition, this research may be of use beyond Russian Area Studies.

Bibliography

Abu-Lughod, L. (1990) 'The Romance of Resistance: Tracing Transformations of Power through Bedouin Women', *American Ethnologist*, 17 (1) pp. 41–55.

Adleft, P. S. and Kwon, S.-W. (2002) 'Social Capital: Prospects for a New Concept', *Academy of Management Review*, 27 (1) pp. 17–40.

Aidis, R. (2015) 'Is Russia an Entrepreneurial Society? A Comparative Perspective', in Oxenstierna, S. (ed.) *The Challenges of Russia's Politicized Economic System*, London and New York: Routledge, pp. 77–95.

Aidis, R. et al. (2008a) 'Entrepreneurship in Russia', UCL SSEES Centre for the Study of Economic and Social Change in Europe, Economics Working Paper No. 88, pp. 1–20.

Aidis, R. et al. (2008b) 'Institutions and Entrepreneurship Development in Russia: A Comparative Perspective', *Journal of Business Venturing*, 23 (2008) pp. 656–72.

Alburov, G. (2015) 'Samyi Vezhivyi iz Dvortzov ili Nezakonnoe Obogashchenie na primere Sergeya Shoigu'. Available at: http://alburov.ru/2015/10/shoygy/ (Accessed 20 January 2016).

Altai Region Official Site. (n.d) 'Sky Blue Katun'. Available at: http://www.altairegion22.ru/en/tourism/katun/ (Accessed 20 November 2015).

Antonov, M. and Bomko, V. (2009) 'Russia Bans All Gambling and Shuts Casinos', *Oddly Enough*, Reuters.com, 1 July 2009, Available at: http://www.reuters.com/article/2009/07/01/us-gambling-closure-odd-idUSTRE56045Y20090701#yWSc0PTsDpPqfCSJ.97 (Accessed 27 November 2015).

Aron, L. (2013a) 'Structure and Context in US–Russian Relations at the Outset of Barack Obama's Second Term', *American Enterprise Institute*, 11 March, Available at: http://www.aei.org/publication/structure-and-context-in-us-russian-relations-at-the-outset-of-barack-obamas-second-term/ (Accessed 27 February 2016).

Aron, L. (2013b) 'The Political Economy of Russian Oil and Gas', *American Enterprise Institute*, 29 May, Available at: http://www.aei.org/publication/the-political-economy-of-russian-oil-and-gas/ (Accessed 27 February 2016).

Arutunyan, A. (2014) *The Putin Mystique*, Talton Edge, Newbold on Stour: Skyscraper Publications.

Altai Krai Regional Headquarters for Economics and Investment. (2008) 'Gambling Zone 'Siberian Coin'', Presentation, Barnaul, no date, Available at: http://www.econom22.ru/investment/gos_chast_partnerstvo/sibcoin/SibMoneta2009eng.pdf (Accessed 20 November 2015).

Bain, C. 2007. 'Entrepreneurship in Russia: Patterns and Problems of Its Development in the Post-Soviet Period'. PhD Thesis. University of Glasgow.

Baranov, A. et al. (2015) 'How Not to Measure Russian Regional Institutions', *Russian Journal of Economics*, 1 (2) pp. 154–81.

Barnes, A. (2006) *Owning Russia*, London: Cornell University Press.

Berlin, I. (1978) *Russian Thinkers*, London: Penguin Books Ltd.

Bershidski, L. (2013) 'Putin Frustration Grows as Russia's Economy Slumps', *Bloomberg Business*, 23 May 2013, Available at: http://www.bloomberg.com/news/articles/2013-05-23/imprisoned-entrepreneurs-and-russia-s-economic-slump (Accessed 1 June 2015).

Biznes Solidarnost'. (2015) 'Pod Pressom', Available at: http://www.kapitalisty.ru/tamog/page/4/ (Accessed 7 September 2015).

Bloomberg Business. (2011) 'The Russian Vegas … in Siberia', *Bloomberg.com*, 3 March, Available at: http://www.bloomberg.com/bw/magazine/content/11_11/b4219073510600.htm (Accessed 20 November 2015).

Bonnell, V. E. and Gold, T. B. (2002) 'Introduction', in Bonnell, V. E. and Gold, T. B. (eds.) *The New Entrepreneurs of Europe and Asia: Patterns of Business Development in Russia, Eastern Europe and China*, London: M. E. Sharpe, pp. xiii–xxii.

Borenstein, E. (1999a) 'Public Offerings: MMM and the Marketing of Melodrama', in Barker, A. M. (ed.) *Consuming Russia Popular Culture, Sex, and Society since Gorbachev*, London: Duke University Press, pp. 49–75.

Borenstein, E. (1999b) 'Suspending Disbelief: 'Cults' and Postmodernism in Post-Soviet Russia', in Barker, A. M. (ed.) *Consuming Russia Popular Culture, Sex, and Society since Gorbachev*, London: Duke University Press, pp. 437–62.

Bovt, G. (2015) 'Russia's Increasingly Absurd Laws Benefit Nobody (op-ed)', *The Moscow Times*, 28 May, Available at: http://www.theMoscowTimes.com/opinion/article/russias-increasingly-absurd-laws-benefit-nobody-op-ed/522566.html (Accessed 1 June 2015).

Bremmer, I. (2009) 'State Capitalism Comes of Age: The End of the Free Market?' *Foreign Affairs*, 88 (3) pp. 40–55.

Bridger, S. et al. (1996) *No More Heroines? Russia, Women and the Market*, London: Routledge.

Buckley, N. and Weaver, C. (2013) 'Vladimir Putin Unveils $14bn Plan to Revive the Russian Economy', *R.com*, 21 June, Available at: http://www.R.com/cms/s/0/5670dcf2-da78-11e2-a237-00144feab7de.html#axzz2bla5pjjq (Accessed 12 August 2013).

Burawoy, M. et al. (2000) 'Involution and Destitution in Capitalist Russia', *Ethnography*, 1 (1) pp. 43–65.

Burawoy, M. and Verdery, K. (1999) 'Introduction', in Burawoy, M. and Verdery, K. (eds.) *Uncertain Transition Ethnographies of Change in the Post-Socialist World*, Oxford: Rowman & Littlefield Publishers, Inc, pp. 1–17.

Cantorovitch, I. (2014) 'Post-Soviet Region', in Porot, D. and Katz, Z. (eds.) *Antisemitism Worldwide 2014 General Analysis Draft*, Tel Aviv: Moshe Kantor Database for the Study of Contemporary Antisemitism and Racism, The Lester and Sally Entin Faculty of Humanities, Tel Aviv University, pp. 17–21.

Carothers, T. (2002) 'The End of the Transition Paradigm', *Journal of Democracy*, 13 (1) pp. 5–21.

Carstensen, F. V. and Guroff, G. (1983) 'Economic Innovation in Imperial Russia and the Soviet Union: Observations', in Guroff, G. and Carstensen, F. V. (eds.) *Entrepreneurship in Imperial Russia and the Soviet Union*, Princeton, NJ: Princeton University Press, pp. 347–60.

Castells, M. and Kiselyova, E. (1998) '*Russia and the Network Society An Analytical Exploration*', *Russia at the end of the 20th Century Conference*, Stanford University, 5–7 November, Available from: http://www.stanford.edu/group/Russia20/volumepdf/castells.pdf (Accessed 14 March 2013).

Chadee, D. and Roxas, B. (2013) 'Institutional Environment, Innovation Capacity and Firm Performance in Russia', *Critical Perspectives on International Business*, 9 (1/2) pp. 19–39.

Chief Economy and Investment Department of Investment Department of Altai Region. (2008) 'Gambling Zone 'Siberian Coin', *Presentation, Barnaul*, no date, Available at: http://www.econom22.ru/investment/gos_chast_partnerstvo/sibcoin/SibMoneta2009eng.pdf (Accessed *20 November 2015*).

Connolly, R. (2009) 'Economic Structure and Social Order Development in Post-Socialist Europe', PhD Book. University of Birmingham. Available at: http://findit.bham.ac.uk/ (Accessed 18 June 2015).

Connolly, R. (2013) *The Economic Sources of Social Order: Development in Post-Socialist Eastern Europe*, London and New York: Routledge.

Connolly, R. (2015) 'Troubled Times: Stagnation, Sanctions and the Prospects for Economic Reform in Russia', *Research Paper, Chatham House Russia and Eurasia Programme*, London: The Royal Institute for International Affairs.

Connolly, R. (2018) *Russia's Response to Sanctions: How Western Economic Statecraft Is Reshaping Political Economy in Russia*, Cambridge: Cambridge University Press.

Connolly, R. (2020) *The Russian Economy: A Very Short Introduction*, Oxford: Oxford University Press.

Connolly, R. et al (2015) 'Sanctions on Russia: Economic Effects and Political Rationales', *Event Summary, Chatham House Russia and Eurasia Programme*, London: The Royal Institute for International Affairs.

Daniel, B. J. (2015) 'What Surrounds us Now: Cultural Animation and the Participatory Cultural Voids in Poland', in Pleyers, G. and Sava, I. N. (eds.) *Social Movements in Central and Eastern Europe a Renewal of Protests and Democracy*, Bucharest: Editura Universităţii din Bucureşti, pp. 54–67.

Dash, M. (2013) 'For 40 Years, This Russian Family Was Cut Off from All Human Contact, Unaware of World War II', *smithsonian.com*, 28 January, Available at: http://www.smithsonianmag.com/history/for-40-years-this-russian-family-was-cut-off-from-all-human-contact-unaware-of-world-war-ii-7354256/?no-ist (Accessed *7 October 2015*).

Decter, M. (1963) 'The Status of the Jews in the Soviet Union', *Foreign Affairs*, 41 (2) pp. 420–30.

de Laine, M. (2000) *Fieldwork, Participation, Practice Ethics and Dilemmas in Qualitative Research*, London, Thousand Oaks, New Delhi: SAGE Publications.

Díaz-Cayeros, A. (2013) 'Entrenched Insiders: Limited Access Order in Mexico', in North, D. C. (eds.) *In the Shadow of Violence Politics, Economics and the Problems of Development*, Cambridge: Cambridge University Press, pp. 233–60.

Djankov, S. (2015) 'Russia's Economy under Putin: From Crony Capitalism to State Capitalism', *Policy Brief Number PB15-18*, Washington, DC: Peterson Institute for International Economics.

Dunn, E., and Dunn, S. P. (1964) 'Religion as an Instrument of Culture Change: The Problem of the Sects in the Soviet Union', *Slavic Review*, 23 (3) pp. 459–78.

Economist, The. (2009) 'Dmitry Medvedev's Building Project', *economist.com*, November 26, Available at: http://www.economist.com/node/14973198 (Accessed 1 June 2015).

Economist, The. (2012a) 'An Unaffordable System', *economist.com*, 6 October, Available at: http://www.economist.com/node/21564257 (Accessed 2 December 2015).

Economist, The. (2012b) 'Special Report State Capitalism', *economist.com*, 21 January, Available at: http://www.economist.com/node/21542931 (Accessed 26 July 2016).

Economist, The. (2012c) 'The Rise of State Capitalism', *economist.com*, 21 January, Available at: http://www.economist.com/node/21543160 (Accessed 26 July 2016).

Economist, The. (2012d) 'Themes and Variations', *economist.com*, 21 January, Available at: http://www.economist.com/node/21542924 (Accessed 26 July 2016).

Economist, The. (2014) 'Planet Plutocrat', *economist.com*, 13 March, Available at: http://www.economist.com/news/international/21599041-countries-where-politically-connected-businessmen-are-most-likely-prosper-planet (Accessed 3 April 2016).

Economist, The. (2015) 'Master of Emergencies', *economist.com*, 7 November, Available at: http://www.economist.com/news/europe/21677992-trusty-defence-minister-only-person-serve-every-government-fall (Accessed 25 November 2015).

Economist, The. (2016a) 'Government in Exile', *economist.com*, 11 February, Available at: http://www.economist.com/news/europe/21692934-new-generation-migr-s-has-plans-homeland-they-never-wanted-flee-government?frsc=dg%7Ca (Accessed 15 March 2016).

Economist, The. (2016b) 'Night of the Long Scoops', *economist.com*, 18 February, Available at: http://www.economist.com/news/europe/21693253-smashing-little-capitalists-russias-capital-night-long-scoops?zid=307&ah=5e80419d1bc9821e-be173f4f0f060a07 (Accessed 15 March 2016).

Estrin, S. et al. (2007) 'Institutions and Entrepreneurship Development in Russia: A Comparative Perspective', *William Davidson Institute Working Paper Number 867*, Available at: https://deepblue.lib.umich.edu/bitstream/handle/2027.42/57247/wp867?sequence=1 (Accessed 19 June 2016).

European Investment Bank. (2013) 'Small and Medium Entrepreneurship in Russia', Available at: http://www.eib.org/infocentre/publications/all/econ-study-small-and-medium-entrepreneurship-in-russia.htm (Accessed 15 March 2016).

Fedotkin, D. (n.d). 'Creation and Development of Tourist-Recreational Special Economic Zones in Russian Federation', Available at: http://www.rotobo.or.jp/events/forum/presentation/2-3-01Fedotkin.pdf (Accessed 24 November 2015).

Fedotov, V. (2015) 'Okolo Nolya. Pochemu Kreml' ne Uluchshit Biznes-Klimat v Rossii, slon.ru, 7 September, Available at: https://slon.ru/ posts/56059 (Accessed 7 September 2015).

Filipenok, A. and Shtykina, A. (2015) 'Biznesmen Rasskazal na Forume v Moskve o "Perepilivanii ekonomiki"', *RBK.ru*, 10 December, Available at: http://www.rbc.ru/business/10/12/2015/5668b8429a7947618f7d161d (Accessed *12 December 2015*).

Fisun, O. (2012) 'Rethinking Post-Soviet Politics from a Neopatrimonial Perspective', *Demokratizatsiya*, 20 (2) pp. 87–96.

Foa, R. S. and Nemirovskaya, A. (2016) 'How State Capacity Varies within Frontier States: A Multicountry Subnational Analysis', *Governance: An International Journal of Policy, Administration, and Institutions*, 29 (3) pp. 411–32.

Fomin, D. A. (2010) 'O Vrtimeni, v kotorom my Zhivem', *EKO, Vserossiiskii ekonomicheskii zhurnal*, 2 (February) pp. 135–53.

Freeland, C. (2000) *Sale of the Century Russia's Wild Ride from Communism to Capitalism*, Doubleday Canada.

Gaddy, C. G. and Ickes, B. W. (2002) *Russia's Virtual Economy*, Washington, DC: Brookings Institution Press.

Gaddy, C. G. and Ickes, B. W. (2005) 'Resource Rents and the Russian Economy', *Eurasian Geography and Economics*, 46 (8) pp. 559–83.

Gaddy, C. G. and Ickes, B. W. (2010) 'Russia after the Global Financial Crisis, *Eurasian Geography and Economics*, 51 (3) pp. 281–311.

Gaddy, C. G. and Ickes, B. W. (2013) *Bear Traps on Russia's Road to Modernization*, London: Routledge.

Gaddy, C. G. and Ickes, B. W. (2015) 'Putin's Rent Management System and the Future of Addiction in Russia', in Oxenstierna, S. (ed.) *The Challenges of Russia's Politicized Economic System*, London and New York: Routledge, pp. 11–32.

Gans-Morse, J. (2012) 'Threats to Property Rights in Russia: From Private Coercion to State Aggression', *Post-Soviet Affairs*, 28 (3) pp. 263–95.

Gazeta.ru. (2015) 'Razgovor Korovy s Myacnikom', *gazeta.ru*, 10 December, Available at: http://www.gazeta.ru/comments/2015/12/10_e_7950101.shtml (Accessed 12 December 2015).

Gazprom. (2008) 'Gazprom Commissions Barnaul-Biysk-Gorno-Altaisk Gas Pipeline with Branch to Belokurikha', Press Release, 21 November, Available at: http://www.gazprom.com/press/news/2008/november/article64417/ (Accessed 20 November 2015).

Gel'man, V. (2016) 'The Vicious Circle of Neopatrimonialism in Russia', *Post-Soviet Affairs*, 32 (5) pp. 455–73.

Gibson, J. L. and Howard, M. M. (2007) 'Russian anti-Semitism and the Scapegoating of Jews', *British Journal of Political Science*, 37 (2) pp. 193–223.

Golikova, V. V. (2009) 'Business Associations: Incentives and Benefits from the Viewpoint of Corporate Governance', in Dolgopyatova, T., Iwasaki, I., and Yakovlev, A. A. (eds.) *Organization and Development of Russian Business: A Frm-Level Analysis*, Basingstoke: Palgrave MacMillan, pp. 258–83.

Goncharov, I. (translated by Hogarth, C. J.). (1858, reprinted 1915) *Oblomov*, New York: Allen and Unwin.

Gordon, C. (1991) 'Governmental Rationality: An Introduction', in Burchell, G., Gordon, C., and Miller, P. (eds.) *The Foucault Effect*, Chicago: The University of Chicago Press, pp. 1–52.

Goskomstat. (2010) 'Small and Medium Business in Russia: Statistics', Available at: http://www.gks.ru/publish/prezent/infograf/mal_bisnes_eng.pdf (Accessed 24 February 2017).

Goskomstat. (2015) 'Number of Small Enterprises (excluding Micro Businesses) by Economic Activity', Available at: http://www.gks.ru/bgd/regl/b16_12/Main.htm (Accessed 24 February 2017).

Green, O. S. (2009) *Entrepreneurship in Russia: Western Ideas in Russian Translation*, PhD Book, Gothenburg Studies in Sociology No. 40, Department of Sociology: University of Gothenburg.

Greene, S. A. (2018) 'Running to Stand Still: Aggressive Immobility and the Limits of Power in Russia', *Post-Soviet Affairs*, 34(5) pp. 333–47.

Guriev, S. (2019) '20 Years of Vladimir Putin: The Transformation of the Economy', *Moscow Times*, 16 August 2019, Available at: https://www.themoscowtimes.com/2019/08/16/20-years-of-vladimir-putin-the-transformation-of-the-economy-a66854 (Accessed 30 July 2021).

Gutterman, S. and Busvine, D. (2012) 'Putin Pledges to Fight Corruption, Capital Flight', *Reuters.com*, 12 December, Available at: http://www.reuters.com/article/2012/12/12/us-russia-Putin-idUSBRE8BB1CD20121212 (Accessed 1 June 2015).

Hass, J. (2005) 'Trials and Tribulations of Learning the Market: Culture and Economic Practice in Russia's Market Transition', *The Carl Beck Papers in Russian and East European Studies, Number 1706, Centre for Russian and East European Studies*, University of Pittsburgh.

Hass, J. (2012) *Rethinking the Post-Soviet Experience: Markets, Moral Economies, and Cultural Contradictions of Post-Socialist Russia*, Basingstoke: Palgrave MacMillan.

Hanson, P. (2007) 'The Russian Economic Puzzle: Going Forwards, Backwards or Sideways?' *International Affairs*, 83 (5) pp. 869–89.

Hanson, P. (2014) *Reiderstvo Asset-grabbing in Russia*, Russia and Eurasia Programme Paper 2014/03, Chatham House, the Royal Institute of International Affairs.

Harding, L. (2007) 'The Richer They Come …', *theguardian.com*, 2 July, Available at: http://www.theguardian.com/world/2007/jul/02/russia.lukeharding1 (Accessed 21 May 2015).

Harding, L. (2016) 'Mega-Rich Homes Tour Puts Spotlight on London's Oligarchs', *theguardian.com*, 4 February, Available at: http://www.theguardian.com/uk-news/2016/feb/04/mega-rich-homes-tour-london-oligarchs-russia-alexei-navalny-Putin, (Accessed 4 February 2016).

Hill, F. (2010) 'Dinner with Putin: Musings on the Politics of Modernization in Russia', Foreign Policy Trip Reports: Brookings Institution, brookings.edu, October 2014, Available at: http://www.brookings.edu/research/reports/2010/10/russia-Putin-hill (Accessed 1 June 2015).

Hill, F. and Gaddy, C. (2003) *The Siberian Curse: How Siberian Communist Planners Left Russia out in the Cold*, Washington, DC: Brookings Institution Press.

Hobson, P. (2015) 'How to Ignore a Corruption Scandal, Kremlin Style', *theMoscow-Times.com*, 10 December, Available at: http://www.theMoscowTimes.com/news/article/how-to-ignore-a-corruption-scandal-kremlin-style/552429.html (Accessed 16 March 2016).

Hoffman, D. E. (2002) *The Oligarchs: Wealth and Power in the New Russia*, Oxford: Public Affairs.

Humphrey, C. (2002) *The Unmaking of Soviet Life: Everyday Economies after Socialism*. Ithaca, NY: Cornell University Press.

Humphrey, C. (2014) 'Schism, Event, and Revolution: The Old Believers of Trans-Baikalia', *Current Anthropology*, 55 (S10) pp. S216–S225.

Humphrey, C. and Mandel, R. (2002) 'The Market in Everyday Life: Ethnographies of Post-socialism', in Humphrey, C. and Mandel, R. (eds.) *Markets and Moralities: Ethnographies of Post-socialism*, Oxford: Berg, pp. 1–16.

Illarionov, A. (2006). 'When the State Means Business', *nyTimes.com*, 25 January, Available at: http://www.nyTimes.com/2006/01/25/opinion/when-the-state-means-business.html, (Accessed 28 July 2016).

Inozemtsev, V. L. (2011) 'Neo-Feudalism Explained', *American Interest*, 6(4), 1 March, Available at: http://www.the-american-interest.com/2011/03/01/neo-feudalism-explained/, (Accessed 30 September 2015).

Inozemtsev, V. (2013) 'Colonies vs. Dependencies: An Invitation to a Discourse', *Russia in Global Affairs*, 2 (2013) Available at: http://eng.globalaffairs.ru/number/Colonies-vs-Dependencies-An-InvitaEon-to-a-Discourse-16046, (Accessed 28 September 2015).

Inozemtsev, V. (2016) 'Zashchita Putina kak Uzakonit' Bogatctvo Chinovnikov', *snob.ru*, 4 April, Available at: https://snob.ru/selected/entry/106595 (Accessed 4 April 2016).

Investment Portal of Altai Region. (n.d) 'Molodezhnuyu Gostinitzu, Letnii Kinoteatr i EKO-otel' Postoyat v "Biryuzovoi Katuni"', *Mass Media*, Available at: http://invest.alregn.ru/en/mass-media/detail.php?ID=366 (Accessed 20 November 2015).

Ioffe, J. (2015) 'Remote Control: Can an Exiled Oligarch Persuade Russia That Putin Must Go?' *newyorker.com*, 12 January, Available from: http://www.newyorker.com/magazine/2015/01/12/remote-control-2, (Accessed 1 December 2015).

Jong-Sung, Y. (2013) 'Transition from a Limited Access Order to an Open Access Order: The Case of South Korea', in North, D. C. et al (eds.) *In the Shadow of Violence: Politics, Economics and the Problems of Development*, Cambridge: Cambridge University Press, pp. 293–327.

Kafka, F. (reprinted 1998) *The Trial*, New York: Schocken Books.

Kashpur, V. V. (2009) 'Predprinimatel'stvo kak Zhiznennaya Perspektiva Sovrtimennoi Molodezhi (na prtimere Tomskoi Oblast)', *Vestnik Tomskovo Gosudarstvennovo Universiteta*, 1 (5) pp. 53–68.

Kennedy, J. (2017) *Minding Their Own Business: An Ethnographic Study of Entrepreneurship in Putin's Russia*, PhD, University of Birmingham.

Kerr, D. (1999) 'Beheading the King and Enthroning the Market: A Critique of Foucauldian Governmentality', *Science and Society*, 63 (2) pp. 173–202.

Kesby, R. (2012) 'Why Russia Locks Up So Many Entrepreneurs', *BBC World Service*, 5 July, Available at: http://www.bbc.com/news/magazine-18706597 (Accessed 5 April 2016).

Kets de Vries, M. F. R. (2001) 'The Anarchist Within: Clinical Reflections on Russian Character and Leadership Style', *Human Relations*, 54 (5) pp. 585–627.

Khotin, L. (2007) 'A Siberian Curse?' *Problems of Economic Transition*, 49 (9) pp. 35–50.

Kochetkova, I. (2010) *The Myth of the Russian Intelligentsia: Old Intellectuals in the New Russia*, London: Routledge.

Kordonskii, S. (2012) 'Norma Otkata', *Otechestvennye Zapicki Zhurnal dlya Medlenhogo Chteniya* 2 (47), Available at: http://www.strana-oz.ru/2012/2/norma-otkata (Accessed 14 October 2015).

Korey, W. (1972) 'The Origins and Development of Soviet Anti-Semitism: An Analysis', *Slavic Review*, 31 (1) pp. 111–35.

Kornblatt, J. D. (1999) '"Christianity, Antisemitism, Nationalism": Russian Orthodoxy in a Reborn Orthodox Russia', in Barker, A. M. (ed.) *Consuming Russia Popular Culture, Sex, and Society since Gorbachev*, London: Duke University Press, pp. 414–26.

Krastev, I. and Inozemtsev, V. (2013) 'Putin's Self-Destruction: Russia's New Anti-Corruption Campaign Will Sink the Regime', *foreignaffairs.com*, 9 June, Available at: https://www.foreignaffairs.com/articles/russian-federaEon/2013-06-09/Putins-self-destruction (Accessed 1 June 2015).

Kreidenko, T. F. and Mironova, M. N. (2012) 'Modern Small Business in Russia', *Regional Research of Russia*, 2 (4) pp. 347–52.

Krige, D. (2012) 'Fields of Dreams, Fields of Schemes: Ponzi Finance and Multi-level Marketing in South Africa', *Africa*, 82 (Special Issue 01) pp. 69–92.

Kubik, J. (2013) 'From Transitology to Contextual Holism: A Theoretical Trajectory of Postcommunist Studies', in Kubik, J. and Linch, A. (eds.) *Postcommunism from Within: Social Justice, Mobilization, and Hegemony*, New York and London: New York University Press, pp. 27–94.

Kubik, J. (2015a) 'Between Contextualization and Comparison: A Thorny Relationship between East European Studies and Disciplinary 'Mainstreams'', *East European Politics and Societies and Cultures*, 29 (2) pp. 352–65.

Kubik, J. (2015b) 'What to Do with Area Studies and Cross-(Multi)disciplinarity in the 21st Century, Lecture at the Conference 'Area Studies in the 21st Century'', 9 November 2015, Available at: http://www.ceelbas.ac.uk/workshops/area-studies-in-the-twenty-first-century-podcast (Accessed 5 January 2016).

Ledeneva, A. (1998) *Russia's Economy of Favours: Blat, Networking and Informal Exchange*, Cambridge: Cambridge University Press.

Ledeneva, A. (2009) 'From Russia with *Blat*: Can Informal Networks Help Modernize Russia?' *Social Research*, 76 (1) pp. 259–88.

Ledeneva, A. (2013) 'Sistema: How Putin's Russia is Governed', *UCL SSEES Research Blog*, 11 March, Available at: http://blogs.ucl.ac.uk/ssees/2013/03/11/sistema-how-Putins-russia-is-governed (Accessed 14 March 2013).

Ledyaev, V. and Chirikova, A. (2019) 'Business in the Power Structure of Small Russian Towns', *Europe-Asia Studies*, 72 (4) pp. 686–711.

Linch, A. (2013) 'Introduction: Postcommunism in a New Key: Bottom Up and Inside Out', in Kubik, J. and Linch, A. (eds.) '*Postcommunism from Within Social Justice, Mobilization, and Hegemony*, New York and London: New York University Press, pp. 1–26.

Lindquist, G. (2006) *Conjuring Hope Healing and Magic in Contemporary Russia*, Oxford: Berghahn Books.

Lipman, M. (2014) 'No Good Economic Options for Putin', *Commentary: European Council on Foreign Relations*, 10 December, Available at: http://www.ecfr.eu/article/commentary_no_good_economic_options_for_Putin377 (Accessed 1 June 2015).

Lokshina, T. (2013) 'Russia's 2013: The Year in Human Rights', *opendemocracy.net*, 24 December, Available at: https://www.opendemocracy.net/od-russia/tanya-lokshina/russias-2013-year-in-human-rights (Accessed 1 December 2015).

Lovell, S. (2006) *Destination in Doubt Russia Since 1989*, London: Zed Books.

Luzhkov, Y. M. (2005) *Parkinson's Law: An Insight into the Irrational Russian Character*, Middlesex: Middlesex University Press.

Machalek, K. (n.d) 'Factsheet: Russia's NGO LAWS', *Freedom House*, Available at: https://freedomhouse.org/sites/default/files/Fact%20Sheet_0.pdf (Accessed 1 June 2015).

Maggs, P. B. et al. (1997) *The Civil Code of the Russian Federation: Parts 1 and 2*, London: M. E. Sharpe.

Matantsev, I. (1998) 'The Civil Law Status of a Municipal Unitary Enterprise under Russian Legislation, *Review of Central and East European Law*, 1998 (5/6) pp. 443–50.

Martin, R. L. and Osberg, S. (2007) 'Social Entrepreneurship: The Case for Definition', *Stanford Social Innovation Review Spring 2007*, Available at: http://www.ngobiz.org/picture/File/Social%20Enterpeuneur-The%20Case%20of%20Definition.pdf (Accessed 14 October 2015).

Martinez-Vazquez, J., et al. (2006) *Reforming Regional-Local Finance in Russia*, Washington, DC: The International Bank for Reconstruction and Development / The World Bank.

Matantsev, I. (1999) 'The Civil Law Status of a Municipal Unitary Enterprise under Russian Legislation', *Review of Central and East European Law*, 1998 (5/6): pp. 443–50.

McMillan, J. and Woodruff, C. (2002) 'The Central Role of Entrepreneurs in Transition Economies', *The Journal of Economic Perspectives*, 16 (3) pp. 153–70.

Medvedev, D. (2009) 'Dmitry Medvedev's Article, Go Russia!', Office of the President of Russia', *kremlin.ru*, Available at: http://eng.kremlin.ru/news/298 (Accessed 16 July 2013).

Merry, W. (2011) 'The Crisis of Russian Modernisation', *Russia and Beyond: Open Democracy*, opendemocracy.net, 20 July, Available at: https://www.opendemocracy.net/od-russia/wayne-merry/crisis-of-russian-modernisation (Accessed 1 June 2015).

Meyer, H. et al. (2013) 'Putin's Pardon of Tycoon Buoys Russia before Sochi Games', *Bloomberg.com*, 20 December, Available at: http:\\www.bloomberg.com/news/articles/2013-12-20/khodorkovsky-free-after-10-years-in-prison-as-Putin-signs-pardon (Accessed 1 December 2015).

Ministry of Economic Development of the Russian Federation. (2015) 'Vladimir Putin Named the Key Conditions for the Development of Small and Medium Business', Federal Web Portal for Small and Medium Sized Enterprises, Ministry of Economic Development of the Russian Federation, 10 April, Available at: http://en.smb.gov.ru/sme/news/263.html (Accessed 1 June 2015).

Ministry of Economic Development of the Russian Federation. (2016a) 'Federal Law from July 24, 2007 No. 209-FZ', Federal Web Portal for Small and Medium Sized Enterprises, Available at: http://en.smb.gov.ru/support/regulation/209-fz/ (Accessed 2 March 2016).

Ministry of Economic Development of the Russian Federation. (2016b) 'About SME', Federal Web Portal for Small and Medium Sized Enterprises, Available at: http://en.smb.gov.ru/sme/about/ (Accessed 7 March 2017).

Monaghan, A. (2014) 'Can Russia Ever Extract Itself from Corruption?' *Valdai Discussion Club*, valdaiclub.com, 13 February 2014, Available at: http://valdaiclub.com/politics/66805.html (Accessed 1 June 2015).

Morris, J. (2012a) 'Beyond Coping? Alternatives to Consumption within a Social Network of Russian Workers', *Ethnography*, 14 (1) pp. 85–103.

Morris, J. (2012b) 'Unruly Entrepreneurs: Russian Worker Responses to Insecure Formal Employment', *Global Labour Journal*, 3 (2) pp. 217–36.

Morris, J. and Polese, A. (2014) 'Introduction: Informality – Enduring Practices, Entwined Livelihoods', in Morris, J., and Polese, A. (eds.) *The Informal Post-Socialist Economy Embedded Practices and Livelihoods*, Abingdon: Routledge, pp. 1–18.

Moscow Times, The. (2014) 'Just 3% of Small Russian Businesses Last More Than 3 Years', *theMoscowTimes.com*, 23 October, Available at: http://www.theMoscowTimes.com/article/509984.html (Accessed 15 March 2016).

Moscow Times, The. (2015) 'Putin Frees Small Businesses from Inspections for 3 Years', *theMoscowTimes.com*, 14 July, Available at: http://www.theMoscowTimes.com/article/525639.html (Accessed 15 March 2016).

Narayan, D. (1999) 'Bonds and Bridges: Social Capital and Poverty', *Policy Research Working Paper 2067*, Washington, DC: The Word Bank.

Naval'nyi, A. (2015a) '"Chaika". Fil'm fonda bor'by s korruptsiei', 1 December, Available at: https://www.youtube.com/watch?v=eXYQbgvzxdM (Accessed 16 March 2016).

Naval'nyi, A. (2015b). 'Kto v Zamke Zhivet? FBK Dokazyvaet: Elitnuyu Londonskuyu Nedvizhimost' Vitze-Prem'er Shuvalov Arenduyet sam y sebya', 23 July, Available at: https://navalny.com/p/4346/ (Accessed 20 January 2016).

Naval'nyi, A. (2015c). 'Noven'kii Dom Press-Sekretarya Peskova', Skromno – 4700 millionov rublei, 17 September, Available at: https://navalny.com/p/4455/ (Accessed 20 January 2016).

Nechepurenko, I. (2015) 'Shoigu at 60: The Man Who Would be Russia's King?' *theMoscowTimes.com*, 21 May, Available at: http://ww.theMoscowTimes.com/news/article/shoigu-at-60-the-man-who-would-be-russias-king/522018.html (Accessed 25 December 2015).

Nellis, J. (2002) 'External Advisors and Privatization in Transition Economies', *Working Paper Number 3, Centre for Global Development Working Papers*, Washington, DC: Centre for Global Development.

Nilan, P. (2002) '"Dangerous Fieldwork' Re-Examined: The Question of Researcher Subject Position', *Qualitative Research*, 2(3) pp. 363–86.

North, D. C. (1990) *Institutions, Institutional Change and Economic Performance*, Cambridge: Cambridge University Press.

North, D. C. (1993, reprinted 1996) 'Epilogue: Economic Performance through Time', in Alston, L. J. et al. (eds.) *Empirical Studies in Institutional Change*, Cambridge: Cambridge University Press, pp. 342–55.

North, D. C. (1996) 'Epilogue: Economic Performance through Time', in Alston, L. J. et al. (eds.) *Empirical Studies in Institutional Change*, Cambridge: Cambridge University Press, pp. 342–55.

North, D. C. et al. (2007) 'Limited Access Orders in the Developing World: A New Approach to the Problems of Development', *Policy Research Working Paper 4359: The World Bank*, Washington, DC: The World Bank.

North, D. C. et al. (2009) *Violence and Social Orders*, Cambridge: Cambridge University Press.

North, D. C. et al. (2013a) 'Lessons in the Shadow of Violence', in North, D. C. et al (eds.) *In the Shadow of Violence Politics, Economics and the Problems of Development*, Cambridge: Cambridge University Press, pp. 328–50.

North, D. C. et al. (2013b) 'Limited Access Orders: An Introduction to the Conceptual Framework', in North, D. C. et al. (eds.) *In the Shadow of Violence Politics, Economics and the Problems of Development*, Cambridge: Cambridge University Press, pp. 1–23.

Oda, H. (2007) *Russian Commercial Law: Second Edition*, Leiden and Boston: Martinus Nijhoff Publishers.

Ojala, A. and Isomäki, H. (2011). 'Entrepreneurship and Small Business in Russia: A Review of Empirical Research', *Journal of Small Business and Enterprise Development*, 18 (1) pp. 97–119.

Olsen, M. (1971) *The Logic of Collective Action Public Goods and the Theory of Groups*, London: Harvard University Press.

OmbudsmanBiz. (2021) 'Upolnomochennyi Priya prezidente Rossiiskoi Federatsii po zashchite prav predprinimatelei', *OmbudsmanBiz*, Available from: https://ombudsmanbiz.ru/ob-upolnomochennom/#1 (Accessed 31 July 2021).

Organisation for Economic Co-operation and Development (OECD). (2013) *Russia Modernising the Economy, OECD 'Better Policies' Series*, Available at: http://www.oecd.org/publications/russia-modernising-the-economy-9789264207998-en.htm (Accessed 15 March 2016).

Organisation for Economic Co-operation and Development (OECD). (2014) *OECD Economic Surveys Russian Federation Overview*, Available at: http://www.oecd.org/eco/surveys/economic-survey-russian-federaEon.htm, Accessed 15 March 2016).

Organisation for Economic Co-operation and Development (OECD). (2015) *Russian Federation: Key Issues and Policies, OECD Studies on SMEs and Entrepreneurship*, Paris: OECD Publishing.

Oushakine, S. A. (2009) *The Patriotism of Despair Nation, War, and Loss in Russia*, Ithaca and London: Cornell University Press.

Oxenstierna, S. (2015) 'The Role of Institutions in the Russian Economy', in Oxenstierna, S. (ed.) *The Challenges for Russia's Politicised Economic System*, London: Routledge, pp. 96–112.

Oxenstierna, S. and Olsen, P. (2015) 'The Economic Sanctions against Russia: Impact and Prospects of Success', *Report FOI-R--4097—SE*, Stockholm: FOI.

Paert, I. K. (2004) 'Memory and Survival in Stalin's Russia: Old Believers in the Urals during the 1930s–50s', in Bertaux, D. et al (eds.) *Living Through the Soviet System*, London: Transaction Publishers, pp. 195–213.

Patico, J. (2008) *Consumption and Social Change in a Post-Soviet Middle Class*, Stanford, CA: Stanford University Press.

Patico, J. (2009) 'Spinning the Market: The Moral Alchemy of Everyday Talk in Post-Socialist Russia', *Critique of Anthropology*, 29 (2) pp. 205–24.

Pine, F. and Bridger, S. (1998) 'Introduction: Transitions to Post-Socialism and Cultures of Survival', in Pine, F. and Bridger, S. (eds.) *Surviving Post-Socialism Local Strategies and Regional Responses*, London: Routledge, pp. 2–15.

Piper, E. (2015) 'In Russia, Crisis Deepens Slide in Living Standards for Pensioners', *reuters.com*, 28 January, Available at: http://www.reuters.com/article/2015/01/28/us-russia-crisis-pensioners-idUSKBN0L10D320150128#kTZ8hL6T8Aoyc7pv.97 Accessed 2 December 2015.

Pokrovsky, N, E. and Nikolaeva, U, G. (2014) 'Blizhnii Sever kak chast' Bol'shoi Kartiny Mira', in Pokrovsky, N. E. and Nikolaeva, U. G. (eds.) *Potentsial Blizhnego Severa: Economika, Ekologia, Sel'skie Poseleniya'*, Moskva: Logos, pp. 450–79.

Pomerantsev, P. (2015) *Nothing Is True and Everything Is Possible*, London: Faber and Faber Limited.

President of Russia (2020) 'Business Big and Small', *kremlin.ru*, 12 March 2020, Available at: http://en.kremlin.ru/events/president/news/62975 (Accessed 2 October 2020).

Prezident Rossii (2013) 'V Gosdumu vnesen na Rassmotrenie Proekt Postanovleniya ob Ob'yavlenii Amnistii v Svyazi c 20-letiem Prinyatiya Konstitutsii Rossii', *Sobytiya, kremlin.ru*, 9 December, Available at: http://www.kremlin.ru/events/president/news/19811 (Accessed 10 March 2014).

Private Eye. (2016) 'It's Boom Time in Putin-on-Thames', *Private Eye*, Issue 1411, Available at: http://www.private-eye.co.uk/issue-1411/in-the-back (Accessed 18 February 2016).

Promstroi Group. (2015) 'O Kompanii', *promstroi-group.ru*, Available at: http://www.promstroi-group.ru/index.php?id=about (Accessed 14 October 2015).

Puffer, S. M. et al. (2007) 'Can Russia's State-Managed, Network-Capitalism be Competitive? Institutional Pull versus Institutional Push', *Journal of World Business*, 42 (2007) pp. 1–13.

Puffer, S. M. et al. (2009) 'Entrepreneurship in Russia and China: The Impact of Formal Institutional Voids', *Entrepreneurship Theory and Practice*, 34 pp. 441–67.

Putin, V. V. (1999) 'Rossiya na Rybezhe Tycyaeletii', *Nezavisimaya Gazeta*, 30 December 1999, Available at: https://www.ng.ru/politics/1999-12-30/4_millenium.html (Accessed 22 December 2020).

Puzanov, A. (2009) 'Development of the Real Estate Rights System in Russia in 1989–2009', *Institute of Urban Economics*, Available at: http://www.urbaneconomics.ru/eng/publications.php?folder_id=19&mat_id=86 (Accessed 27 November 2015).

Radaev, V. (2002) 'Entrepreneurial Strategies and the Structure of Transaction Costs in Russian Business', in Bonnell, V. E. and Gold, T. B. (eds.) *The New Entrepreneurs of Europe and Asia Patterns of Business Development in Russia, Eastern Europe and China*, London: M. E. Sharpe, pp. 191–213.

Radziwill, A. and Vaziakova, Y. (2015) 'Improving the Business Climate in Russia', *OECD Working Paper 1192*, Available from: https://www.oecd.org/officialdocuments/publicdisplaydocumentpdf/?cote=ECO/WKP(2015)10&docLanguage=En (Accessed 30 July 2021).

Razomasova, E. A. (2010) 'Rify v Farvatere Malogo Biznesa Sfery Uslug', *E'KO. Vserossiiskii' E'konomicheskii' Zhurnal*, January 1 pp. 127–34.

Ries, N. (2002) '"Honest Bandits" and "Warped People": Russian Narratives about Money, Corruption, and Moral Decay', in Greenhouse, C. J. et al. (eds.) *Ethnography in Unstable Places*, Durham and London: Duke University Press, pp. 276–15.

Ries, N. (2009) 'Potato Ontology', *Cultural Anthropology* 24 (2) pp. 181–12.

Robinson, N. (2009) 'August 1998 and the Development of Russia's Post-Communist Political Economy', *Review of International Political Economy*, 16 (3) pp. 433–45.

Robinson, N. (2011). 'Russian Patrimonial Capitalism and the International Financial Crisis', *Journal of Communist Studies and Transition Politics*, 27 (3–4) pp. 434–55.

Robinson, N. (2013a). 'Introduction: The Political Problems of Russian Capitalism', in Robinson, N. (ed.) *The Political Economy of Russia*, Plymouth: Rowman & Littlefield Publishers, Inc, pp. 1–14.

Robinson, N. (2013b). 'Economic and Political Hybridity: Patrimonial Capitalism in the Post-Soviet Sphere', *Journal of Eurasian Studies*, 4 (2013) pp. 136–45.

Roschin, M. (1995) 'Old Belief and Work', *Religion, State and Society*, 23 (3) pp. 263–67.

Rose, R. (1994) 'Getting by Without Government: Everyday Life in Russia', *Daedalus*, 123 (3) pp. 41–62.

Rossiyskaya Gazeta. (2004) 'Federal'nyi Zakon Rossiiskoi Federatzii ot 30 Dekabrya 2004 G. N 214-F3', *rg.ru*, 31 December, Available at: http://www.rg.ru/2004/12/31/dolevoe-stroitelstvo-dok.html (Accessed 2 December 2015).

Rossiyskaya Gazeta. 2008. 'Ukaz Prezidenta Rossisskoi Federatsii ot 15 Maya 2008g. N 797 "O Neotlozhnykh merax po likvidatsii administrativnykh ogranichenii pri ocushchestvlenii predprinimatel'skoi deyatel'nosti"', *RG.ru*, 17 May 2008, Available from: https://rg.ru/2008/05/17/biznes-podderjka-dok.html (Accessed *30 July 2021*).

Round, J. (2005) 'Rescaling Russia's Geography: The Challenges of Depopulating the Northern Periphery', *Europe-Asia Studies*, 57 (5) pp. 705–27.

Round, J. and Williams, C. (2010) 'Coping with the Social Costs of "Transition": Everyday Life in Post-Soviet Russia and Ukraine', *European Urban and Regional Studies*, 17 (2) pp. 183–96.

Ruptly TV. (2015) 'Russia: Putin Outlines Goals to Boost Entrepreneurship in Russia', *youtube.com*, 7 April, Available at: https://www.youtube.com/watch?v=vr1cW0g0w8I (Accessed 1 June 2015).

Rutland, P. (2005) 'Anti-Semitism and the Russian Oligarchs', *Eurasia Daily Monitor, The Jamestown Foundation*, 1 February, Available at: http://www.jamestown.org/

programmes/edm/single/?tx_Wnews%5BW_news%5D=27472&tx_Wnews%5BbackPid%5D=176&no_cache=1#.VWxA0GAxErV (Accessed 21 May 2015).

Rutland, P. (2015) 'Petronation? Oil, Gas and National Identity in Russia', *Post-Soviet Affairs*, 31 (1) pp. 66–89.

Sakwa, R. (2013) 'Systematic Stalemate: *Reiderstvo* and the Dual State', in Robinson, N. (ed.) *The Political Economy of Russia*, Plymouth: Rowman and Littlefield Publishers, Inc, pp. 69–96.

Sakwa, R. (2014) *Putin and the Oligarch: the Khodorkovsky–Yukos affair*, London: I. B. Tauris and Co. Ltd.

Salmenniemi, S. (2013) 'Post-Soviet *Khosiain*: Class, Self and Morality in Russian Self-Help Literature', Available at: https://www.researchgate.net/publication/289456788_Post-Soviet_Khoziain_Class_self_and_morality_in_Russian_self-help_literature (Accessed 25 February 2017).

Salmenniemi, S., Karhunen, P., and Kosonen, R. (2011) 'Between Business and *Byt*': Experiences of Women Entrepreneurs in Contemporary Russia', *Europe-Asia Studies*, 63 (1) pp. 77–98.

Salmenniemi, S. and Vorona, M. (2014) 'Reading Self-Help Literature in Russia: Governmentality, Psychology, and Subjectivity', *The British Journal of Sociology*, 65 (1) pp. 43–62.

Schneider Group. (n.d). 'Accounting and Taxes in Russia', Available at: http://schneider-group.com/sites/default/files/brochures/SCHNEIDER_GROUP_Accounting_and_taxes_in_Russia_web.pdf (Accessed 18 November 2015).

Schrader, H. (2004) 'Social Capital and Social Transformation in Russia', *Journal for East European Management Studies*, 9 (4) pp. 391–410.

Schreck, C. (2015) 'Western Scholars Alarmed by Russian Deportations, Fines', *Radio Free Europe Radio Liberty*, 31 March, Available at: http://www.rferl.org/content/russia-western-scholars-alarmed-deportaEons/26929921.html (Accessed 1 April 2016).

Schreck, C. and Shakirov, M. (2015). 'Russian Businessman Lashes out at Kremlin, Becomes *Cause Celebre*', *Radio Free Europe Radio Liberty*, 11 December, Available at: http://www.rferl.mobi/a/russia-businessman-rails-against-official-extortion/27420874.html (Accessed 12 December 2015).

Schwenk, A. (2015) '*Summer Camps in Russia – the Analysis of a Cultural Form in an Authoritarian Political Figuration*', *Conference Paper, 12th Conference of the European Sociological Association 2015*, 26 August.

Scott, J. C. (2012) 'Infrapolitics and Mobilizations: A Response by James C. Scott', *Revue Française d'études Américaines*, 1 (131) pp. 112–17.

Sharafutdinova, G. and Kisunko, G. (2014) 'Governors and Governing Institutions: A Comparative Study of State-Business Relations in Russia's Regions', Policy Research Working Paper 7038, Global Governance Practice Group: World Bank Group.

Sharafutidinova, G. and Steinbuks, J. (2017) 'Governors Matter A Comparative Study of State-Business Relations in Russia's Regions', *Economics of Transition*, 25 1–23.

Shevchenko, O. (2009) *Crisis and the Everyday in Post-Socialist Moscow*, Bloomington, IN: Indiana University Press.

Shlapentokh, V. (2007) *Contemporary Russia as a Feudal Society a New Perspective on the Post-Soviet Era*, Basingstoke: Basingstoke MacMillan.

Shlapentokh, V. and Arutunyan, A. 2013. *Freedom, Repression, and Private Property in Russia*, Cambridge: Cambridge University Press.

Sluka, J. A. (2007) 'Fieldwork Conflicts, Hazards and Dangers', in Robben, A. C. G. M. and Sluka, J. A. (eds.) *Ethnographic Fieldwork: An Anthropological Reader*, Oxford: Blackwell Publishing, pp. 217–22.

Siberian Times Reporter, The. (2014) 'All in! Siberia's First Casino Opens, Complete with Golden Sinks', *siberiantimes.com*, 8 November, Available at: http://siberiantimes.com/business/casestudy/features/f0007-all-in-siberias-first-casino-opens-complete-with-gold-sinks/ (Accessed 20 November 2015).

Siberian Times Reporter, The. (2015) 'Would You Take a Blood Bath to Boost Potency, Restore Beauty or Hold Back Aging?' *siberiantimes.com*, 25 August, Available at: http://siberiantimes.com/other/others/features/f0145-would-you-take-a-blood-bath-to-boost-potency-restore-beauty-or-hold-back-ageing/ (Accessed 22 November 2015).

Smolinski, L. (2013) 'Russia: The Dwindling Employees of the Big State', *blogs.R.com*, 24 October, Available at: http://blogs.R.com/beyond-brics/2013/10/24/russia-the-dwindling-employees-of-the-big-state/ (Accessed 2 December 2015).

Smooha, S. (2008) 'The Mass Immigrations to Israel: A Comparison of the Failure of the Mizrahi Immigrants of the 1950s with the Success of the Russian Immigrants of the 1990s', *The Journal of Israeli History*, 27 (1) pp. 1–27.

Spuknik. (2012) 'Siberian Red Deer Farms in the Altai Mountains', *sputniknews.com*, 27 June, Available at: http://sputniknews.com/analysis/20120627/174271419.html (Accessed 22 November 2015).

Stoll, D. (2013) 'Three Ethnographies of Escape via Pyramid Schemes', *Anthropological Quarterly*, 86 (1) pp. 277–85.

Sutela, P. (1999) 'Russia: The State and Future of the Economy', *Bank of Finland Institute for Economies in Transition (BOFIT)*, Available at: http://www.suomenpankki.fi/pdf/92876.pdf (Accessed 15 January 2016).

Sutela, P. (2012) *The Political Economy of Putin's Russia*, London: Routledge.

TASS. (2014a) 'Putin Signs Law Authorizing Gambling Zones in Sochi and Crimea', *tass.ru*, 23 July, Available at: http://tass.ru/en/russia/741958 (Accessed 20 November 2015).

TASS. (2014b) 'Putin: Gosudarstvo dolzhno sdelat' vse, chtoby v Biznec nikto ne lez c "Kryshevaniem"', *tass.ru*, 7 April, Available at: http://tass.ru/ekonomika/1885639 (Accessed 21 May 2015).

TASS. (2020) 'Russia's GDP Decline May Be 4–5% in 2020', 5 October, Available at: https://tass.com/economy/1208639 (Accessed 15 December 2020).

Taylor, B.D. (2011). *State Building in Putin's Russia*, Cambridge: Cambridge University Press.

The International Consortium of Investigative Journalists. (2016) 'The Panama Papers Politicians, Criminals and the Rogue Industry That Hides Their Cash', *panamapapers.icij.org*, no date, Available at: https://panamapapers.icij.org (Accessed 4 April 2016).

Tomlinson, K. (2002) 'Coping as Kin: Responses to Suffering among Displaced Meskhetian Turks in Post-Soviet Krasnodar, Russian Federation', PhD Dissertation, Department of Anthropology: University College London.

Transparency International (2016) 'Table of Results: Corruption Perceptions Index 2015', Available at: http://www.transparency.org/cpi2015#results-table (Accessed 15 March 2016).

Transparency International. (2019) 'Corruption Perceptions Index: Russia'. Available at: https://www.transparency.org/en/cpi/2019/index/rus# (Accessed 23 December 2021).

Trudolyubov, M. (2014) 'Business, Power, and Property Rights in Russia after Crimea', *Kennan Institute Event*, November 17, Available at: https://www.wilson-center.org/event/business-power-and-property-rights-russia-after-crimea (Accessed 15 March 2015).

Van Maanen, J. (1995). 'An End to Innocence: The Ethnography of Ethnographyx', in Van Maanen, J. (ed.) *Representation in Ethnography*, London: SAGE Publications Ltd.

Varese, F. (1994) 'Is Sicily the Future of Russia? Private Protection and the Rise of the Russian Mafia', *European Journal of Sociology*, 35 (2) pp. 224–58.

Vasiliev, P. V. and Bernhard, B. J. (2011) 'Prohibitions and Policy in the Global Gaming Industry: A Genealogy and Media Content Analysis of Gaming Restrictions in Contemporary Russia', *UNLV Gaming Research and Review Journal*, 15 (1) pp. 71–86.

Verdery, K. (1996a) 'Faith, Hope and Caritas in the Land of the Pyramids: Romania, 1990 to 1994', *Comparative Studies in Society and History*, 37 (4) pp. 625–69.

Verdery, K. (1996b) *What Was Socialism and What Comes Next?* Chichester, West Sussex: Princeton University Press.

Vice. (2013) 'Surviving in the Siberian Wilderness for 70 years (full length)', Video, Available at: https://www.youtube.com/watch?v=W2AYafET68 (Accessed 7 October 2015).

Volkov, V. (2002) 'The Selective Use of State Capacity in Russia's Economy', PONARS Policy Memo No. 273, Available at: http://www.ponarseurasia.org/sites/default/files/policy-memos-pdf/pm_0273.pdf (Accessed 3 March 2017).

Walker, C. (2009) 'From 'Inheritance' to Individualization: Disembedding Working-Class Youth Transitions in Post-Soviet Russia', *Journal of Youth Studies*, 12 (5) pp. 531–45.

Walker, C. (2011) 'Positionality and Difference in Cross-Cultural Youth Research: Being 'Other' in the Former Soviet Union', in Heath, S., and Walker, C. (eds.) *Innovations in Youth Research*, London: Palgrave MacMillan, pp. 210–28.

Walker, C. (2015). 'Stability and Precarity in the Lives and Narratives of Working-Class Men in Putin's Russia', *Social Alternatives*, 34 (4) pp. 28–34.

Walker, C. (2016) 'In Search of "Stability": Working-Class Men, Masculinity and Wellbeing in Contemporary Russia', in Karioris, F. G. and Lindisfarne, N. (eds.) *Masculinities Under Neoliberalism*, London: Zed Books Ltd, chapter 3 (Kindle version).

Walker, S. (2013) 'We're Now in the "Vladimir Vladimirovich Please Solve this Local Issue Caused by the Outrageous Behaviour of Local Officials"', *Segment, Twitter*, 19 December, https://twitter.com/shaunwalker7/status/413626346867134464?lang=en (Accessed 19 December 2013).

Weaver, C. (2012) 'Berezovsky-Abramovich: Why the Fuss?' *R.com*, 31 August, Available at: http://blogs.R.com/beyond-brics/2012/08/31/berezovsky-abramovich-why-all-the-fuss/ (Accessed 21 May 2015).

Williams, C. C. and Onoshchenko, O. (2015) 'Evaluating the Validity of the Contrasting Theoretical Perspectives Towards the Informal Economy in Ukraine', in Morris, J. and Polese, A. (eds.) *Informal Economies in Post-Socialist Spaces Practices, Institutions and Networks*, Basingstoke: Palgrave MacMillan, pp. 25–50.

Williams, C. C. and Round, J. (2009) 'Beyond Hierarchical Representations of the Formal/Informal Employment Dualism', *European Societies*, 11 (1) pp. 77–101.

Williams, C. C. et al. (2013) *The Role of Informal Economies in the Post-Socialist World The End of Transition?* London: Routledge.

Williams, N. and Vorley, T. (2014) 'Institutional Asymmetry: How Formal and Informal Institutions Affect Entrepreneurship in Bulgaria', *International Small Business Journal*, 33 (8) pp. 840–61.

Winiecki, J. (2012) 'Russia and China Facing the "Great Wall": How to Succeed in the Second Structural Transition. *Post-Communist Economies*, 24 (3) pp. 309–25.

Woolcock, M. (2001) 'The Place of Social Capital in Understanding Social and Economic Outcomes', *info.worldbank.com*, Available at: http://info.worldbank.org/etools/docs/library/9746/woolcock_e.pdf (Accessed 14 August 2016).

World Bank. (2016) *Doing Business 2016: Measuring Regulatory Quality and Efficiency*, Washington, DC: World Bank.

World Bank. (2019) *Doing Business 2019: Training for Reform*. Washington, DC: World Bank, p. 198. Available from: https://openknowledge.worldbank.org/handle/10986/30438 (Accessed 31 July 2021).

World Justice Project. (2016) 'Rule of Law Index', Available from: http://data.worldjusticeproject.org/#table (Accessed 15 March 2016).

World Justice Project. (2019) 'Rule of Law Index Russian Federation', Available from https://worldjusticeproject.org/rule-of-law-index/country/2020/Russian%20Federation/ (Accessed 8 January 2020).

Yakovlev, A. (2014) 'Russian Modernization: Between the Need for New Players and the Fear of Losing Control of Rent Sources', *Journal of Eurasian Studies*, 5 pp. 10–20.

Yakovlev, A. (2015) 'State-Business Relations in Russia after 2011 'New Deal' or Imitation of Changes?', in Oxenstierna, S. (ed.) *The Challenges of Russia's Politicized Economic System*, London and New York: Routledge, pp. 59–76.

Yakovleva, Ya. (2012) '100 Shagov Putina – Ochen' Malen'kikh Shagov', *slon.ru*, 2 February, Available at: https://slon.ru/economics/100_shagov_Putina_zhdem_konkretnykh_predlozheniy-737001.xhtml (Accessed 7 September 2015).

Yurchak, A. (2002) 'Entrepreneurial Governmentality in Post-Socialist Russia a Cultural Investigation of Business Practices in Russian Business, in Bonnell, V. E. and Gold, T. B. (eds.) *The New Entrepreneurs of Europe and Asia Patterns of Business Development in Russia, Eastern Europe and China*, London: M. E. Sharpe, pp. 278–24.

Yurchak, A. (2005) *Everything was Forever, Until It Was No More*, Princeton, NJ: Princeton University Press.

Zubarevich. N. (2012) 'Four Russias: Rethinking the Post-Soviet Map', *Opendemocracy*, 29 March, Available at: https://www.opendemocracy.net/en/odr/four-russias-rethinking-post-soviet-map/ (Accessed 28 February 2017).

Index

Page numbers followed by "n" refers notes numbers.

For Product Safety Concerns and Information please contact our EU representative GPSR@taylorandfrancis.com
Taylor & Francis Verlag GmbH, Kaufingerstraße 24, 80331 München, Germany

www.ingramcontent.com/pod-product-compliance
Ingram Content Group UK Ltd.
Pitfield, Milton Keynes, MK11 3LW, UK
UKHW022019180926
475701UK00005B/934
9781032100784